ANGLO-AUSTR
ATTITUDES

MICHAEL DAVIE

PIMLICO

Published by Pimlico 2001

2 4 6 8 10 9 7 5 3 1

First published in Great Britain by
Martin Secker & Warburg 2000
Pimlico edition 2001

Pimlico
Random House, 20 Vauxhall Bridge Road,
London SW1V 2SA

Random House Australia (Pty) Limited
20 Alfred Street, Milsons Point, Sydney,
New South Wales 2061, Australia

Random House New Zealand Limited
18 Poland Road, Glenfield,
Auckland 10, New Zealand

Random House (Pty) Limited
Endulini, 5A Jubilee Road, Parktown 2193, South Africa

Random House Group Limited Reg. No. 954009
www.randomhouse.co.uk

A CIP catalogue record for this book
is available from the British Library

ISBN 0-7126-6727-X

Papers used by Random House Limited are natural,
recyclable products made from wood grown in sustainable forests.
The manufacturing processes conform to the environmental
regulations of the country of origin

Printed and bound in Great Britain by
Mackays of Chatham PLC

Contents

For my quarter-Australian grandchildren:
Oliver, Alice and Isabel.

Preface

This book of Anglo–Australian stories is entirely – or almost entirely – the fault of Mr Paul Keating, the former Australian Prime Minister, who initiated the most extensive change in Anglo–Australian relations since Pitt the Younger's Cabinet decided in 1786 to found a penal colony at Botany Bay.

Loyal Australians with good memories will remember the dizzy moment when, in Monte Carlo in 1993, the International Olympic Committee announced that in 2000 the Games would be held in Sydney. The decision followed years of intense lobbying and skulduggery, particularly on the part of China, which went so far as to threaten the smaller countries of Africa with the withdrawal of Chinese aid if they did not vote for Beijing. Sydney's efforts had been no less vigorous, and more subtle (it was not until early 1999 that anyone accused Sydney of actually buying votes). Reckoning that nobody in their right minds – particularly no woman in her right mind – would prefer to spend the Olympic fortnight in Beijing, or Manchester, rather than Sydney, the Australian lobbyists had invited the key foreign voters and their wives to fly out by Qantas, first-class, to test Sydney's soft luxuries (their cover story was that they were members of the Olympic Assessment Committee). They then cosseted the visitors in the best hotels, taking them on guided tours of the best shops, beaches and restaurants, and sending them to view the site of the proposed Olympic Park aboard the new River Cats, skimming along at twenty-two knots while knocking back iced Chardonnay and devilled chicken served by polite young black-tied waiters, and wearing wrap-around dark glasses provided courtesy of Sydney Ferries.

Keating, as Prime Minister, had played his part. Parliamentary decorum, the journalist Robert Haupt once wrote, was to Keating as finger-bowls are to cannibals. He treated in the same way Olympic protocol, which forbids the denigration of cities seeking the honour of staging the Games. 'Beijing,' he said in the run-up to the Monte Carlo vote, 'is not exactly a fun city.' But I knew that already. The remark of Keating's that really set me thinking came immediately after the vote, which he attended. The decision, Keating told reporters, sent a message to Australia; and the message was that 'you people can travel on your own, under your own steam'. This struck me as an extraordinary thing to say. Under whose steam did he think Australia had been travelling thus far? The only possible answer was the United Kingdom's. But surely Keating, a highly intelligent man, could not really believe that 'you people' – his fellow-Australians – had somehow been inhibited, or that their independence had been limited, their freedom circumscribed or their energy supplied by the UK – at least not within living memory? He might well, however, *feel* all these things; Anglo-Australian relations were not liable to put a spring in the step and a song in the heart of this Australian Prime Minister, the underprivileged son of an Irish Catholic boiler-maker, and a school-leaver at fourteen. But what had he, and others who felt like him, really got against the British? Something lay buried, something rarely talked about.

Keating gave the question of Anglo-Australian relations a new (some thought spurious) force and immediacy, when he delivered a firm push to the idea of an Australian republic. This endowed the end of the twentieth century with a special significance. The year 2000 was in any case going to possess a powerful symbolic importance, since it marked the centenary of the Federation of the Australian colonies. The British Parliament passed the Commonwealth of Australia Act in 1900 and the Federation came into being on 1 January 1901. Add the unexpected prize of the Olympics, and it became tempting to conjure up a glorious vision of a new beginning for Australia on the threshold of the next millennium, its face firmly turned towards Asia, with a new republican Constitution, a new President of the Federal Republic of Australia, and a new Australian flag stripped of the Union Jack bravely reflected in the glittering splendour of Sydney Harbour: all of this displayed, thanks to the National Broadcasting Company of the United States, to a live television audience of billions (always excepting the British, who would be asleep).

Unlike the childhood memories of Keating, who probably learned in his cradle about the Black and Tans, my own early experience of Anglo-Australian relations was wholly sunny. All English children in those pre-war years were brought up to believe that if you dug deep enough with your miniature spade you reached Australia; and *The Wonder Book of Empire for Boys and Girls* told you what to expect when you got there: six million people, of whom 96 per cent 'fortunately' — I have recently checked that that was the word used — came from, or whose ancestors came from, the Homeland (capital letter likewise checked). The Australians in the illustrations looked just like English people, except for the hats turned up at the side. That is what I did indeed find when I eventually got there, although I went by sea instead of by digging. By then, in the middle of the Second World War, I had enlarged my knowledge. Bushranging I had learned about from Captain Starlight. The other book that had come my way was *We of the Never-Never*, though it was the haunting title that stayed with me, not the story or characters. The impression made by the daring Captain Starlight was confirmed by visiting Australian test cricketers: snipping out, aged ten, the innumerable newspaper pictures of the terrible Bradman to fill my scrapbooks, I was unlikely (then or later) to patronise or underestimate Australians, which was the case with many ill-informed, non-cricketing British people — though not, I suppose, those who had fought anywhere near the Australians during the First World War.

I cannot remember why my ship, HMS *London*, a cruiser based in Trincomalee, went to Fremantle in late 1943; perhaps those on the lower deck were not told. Cars lined up on the jetty to take us on leave; we took pot luck, and so did they. My uphomers owned the pub in the little country town of York — a material paradise, with no shortages, as in *The Wonder Book*. It was Christmas and the pub never shut; yet it was all very decorous, as — serving my turn behind the bar — I was well placed to observe. Looking back, however, I can see that the freeloaders of HMS *London* might not have had such a warm welcome had our hosts realised that, after the fall of Singapore in 1942, Britain had in effect abandoned Australia to the Japanese — an aspect of Anglo-Australian relations first thoroughly explored by an Australian historian, David Day (born in 1949), who published his book *The Great Betrayal* — a carefully chosen title — in 1988. The story remains largely unknown, and at least in Day's eyes a cause of shame; still, the British supplied him with a 'congenial working environment' for three years at Churchill College, Cambridge (named after the chief betrayer), while he was researching the book; and his PhD supervisor was a fellow with whom I used to attend tutorials at Oxford. Everyone in the bar at the York pub would have been surprised to learn what Day learned in Cambridge; during the Second World War news travelled slowly, which was just as well. Who, outside Darwin, knew that the town had been attacked by more than 100 Japanese aircraft after the fall of Singapore, causing mass panic followed by looting? Again, I don't think we knew that fact, in the pub.

We certainly did not realise that the slow process of the breaking of the links between Australia and the UK had begun, because the UK had shown that she could not — or would not — act as Australia's protector. The strongest link of all had snapped. British promises — and Australia's foolish assumptions — had proved hollow. At that point Australia turned to the United States for protection, where she remains; nevertheless, every Australian Prime Minister since 1942 has known that, in a crisis, American promises might prove to be as empty as those of the British. Nobody in Australia these days thinks that if the Indonesians or Chinese invaded Darwin, a British submarine would steam to the rescue and threaten the invaders with its nuclear missiles; still, the thought of breaking the final link with Britain, by becoming a republic, does induce in some people a certain psychological tremor, a feeling of impending loneliness. Di Gribble, the Melbourne publisher, has applied to this frame of mind the psychotherapists' phrase 'separation anxiety' – meaning the very powerful force that makes people wish to cling on to their early crucial relationships and which must be overcome (a major task) before they can assert their independence, fend for themselves and take full responsibility for their own lives.

My leave in York was harmonious; and it was not until a decade or so later, when I paid the first of many visits to Australia as a civilian (a newspaper reporter) that I became aware of Anglo-Australian cultural difficulties. I had barely arrived when the car I was driving on a country road had a flat tyre, luckily abreast of some sort of garage. I can change a tyre, but it was hot, I was wearing a new tropical outfit and was on expenses, so I sought help; a laconic fellow in shorts and vest appeared, fixed the fault in a trice and then, calling me 'sport', mumbled his surprise that I had not been able to do the same myself. His mind was not fast-moving, and it was only then that he realised I was English, which as far as he was concerned fully explained the mystery. He pocketed his fee with indifference; in Australia, evidently, it was not the business of the wealthy man to give employment to the artisan. I knew he was thinking that only a bloody Englishman would expect someone else to change a bloody tyre for him. The Boer War, Gallipoli, Tobruk: it was not the first time that English expectations had aroused Australian resentment.

My next cultural lesson occurred in a paddock somewhere near Tamworth, New South Wales. My first wife was a Queenslander, and her stepfather, a big white-haired man who had spent most of his life in the back-blocks, specialised by this stage of his career in buying large properties, splitting them up and selling them on. I had originally met him in London, where he and his wife rented a flat in Berkeley Square. We had met, in other words, on my territory. Soon after I arrived in Australia we flew in a small hired plane to one of his properties, where it was not long before he took me out castrating bullocks. Both parties knew it was a tease, or test, or both: Australia v. England. In his flat on Bellevue Hill he poured me colossal whiskies, which he called 'rozners', although I never heard the word anywhere else: another test, I thought.

Stereotypes were still going strong in those days: the strong, self-reliant Aussies, whose natural habitat was the bush, as in *The Wonder Book of Empire for Boys and Girls*, and the effete Englishmen. Australia's leading playwright, David Williamson, was still thinking in those terms a quarter of a century later when he wrote the script for a film about Gallipoli, in which tough Australian soldiers fought and died while English officers drank tea on the beach. It was only in the (northern-hemisphere) summer of 1996 that Castlemaine beer stopped using advertisements aimed at the British market that featured sweaty he-men saying that Australians wouldn't give a xxxx for anything else; they switched to a clean suburban boy and girl enjoying a glass together, although sexual discrimination was faithfully reflected, since the boy was drinking a pint and the girl a half-pint. Explaining the switch, the advertising agency said research showed that the British no longer thought of Australians as Crocodile Dundees, but as characters from *Neighbours*. (Twenty years ago the cartoonist Arthur Horner, returning to Australia after many years in the UK, looked around him and started drawing the typical Australian with a beer-belly, thongs and a trannie.)

This book does not attempt to be a history of Anglo-Australian relations. Its premise is that the inevitable forthcoming republic, despite the 1999 referendum, is not simply the delayed revenge of the Lizard of Oz on the snobs, the Irish Keating and his ilk versus the Anglophiles, which is how it has often been reported. It does, however, mark the end of a long period of English condescension and increasing Australian irritation and resentment. Ineluctable historic forces have been at work too, it goes without saying: the forces of economics and demography – the 'system of necessity', as Professor Herbert Butterfield called it, that governs all human affairs. Some day the subject will attract the attention of an historian of the *annales* school, who will take into account social structures, long-term trends and continuities (*la longue durée*), and states of mind (*mentalités*), as well as the events and normal concerns of traditional historians, such as administrative, financial and diplomatic history. This book merely represents episodes or incidents in Anglo-Australian relationships that have struck me in the course of fifty years of moving between the two countries. Others, no doubt, would have written much more – for instance, about the obviously crucial influence of Irish–Australians on the Australian outlook – or would have described at length particular causes of friction, such as Maralinga. But this is not a survey of any kind. All I am trying to do is examine what has happened through my personal selection of key moments of political, cultural or psychological separation: a reporter's book, not an academic's.

The term 'Anglo–Australian' will annoy some people. But the only possible alternative, 'British–Australian', is both awkward and unhistorical. Britain was a Roman province that ceased to exist in the fifth century. 'Great British–Australian', or 'United Kingdom–Australian', would be correct and would avoid resentment, but it would also be intolerably discordant. I use 'Anglo–' and 'England' not as geographical terms but as words that loosely denote a shared language, history and culture. No offence is intended towards persons of Welsh, Irish or Scottish descent.

1

The Myth of Australian Classlessness

The oldest and most persistent influence on Anglo-Australian relationships is also the hardest to pin down. This is the grisly and embarrassing subject of class.

One of the things that first attracted me to Australia was that it seemed much less class-ridden than England. How could it fail to be – I assumed in my ignorance – when there was mercifully nothing to be class-ridden about? The further a family went back, the more likely its ancestors were to have arrived in Australia as felons. True, I reminded myself, one of the grandest families in England, the Cecils, were also felons, having grown rich by the theft of church property, but their felony was on a large scale and they had had four centuries in which to practise amnesia. The more I saw of Australia, however, the more I became aware that my first view of Australia, the classless society, resembled some early painter's first view of Sydney: a pretty but deceptive ideal.

It was not even true that all Australians had wanted their country to be classless. In the mid-nineteenth century a powerful Australian actually sought to create an Australian aristocracy – an extraordinary episode passed over rather lightly, to my mind (if noticed at all), in the standard histories. William Charles Wentworth (1790–1872) was not some insignificant crackpot: to contemporary opinion he was 'Australia's greatest native son'. When he died he was honoured with Australia's first state funeral, characterised by a public holiday, a massive sarcophagus and a

8

solemn procession in Sydney from St Andrew's Cathedral to a vault in Vaucluse.

Father and Son

Historians are interested in William Charles and his father because, between them, they were involved in every aspect of the early history of New South Wales, and thus in the making of Australia. They are relevant to my theme for a slightly different reason: their rackety careers span and illustrate the beginnings of tension between Australia and the Homeland. The father possessed a name out of Jane Austen: D'Arcy Wentworth; and it suited him, an upper-class doctor-adventurer. I use the term 'upper-class' since he was a kinsman of the great Fitzwilliam family, who had picked up a barony in the peerage of Ireland in 1620 and an earldom in the peerage of Great Britain in 1716. The fourth earl (1756–1833), a patron of the Wentworths, was a figure of substance in British politics, a friend of Charles James Fox and a prominent Whig, who was appointed Lord Lieutenant of Ireland in 1795. (The fifth earl assumed the additional surname of Wentworth by royal licence in 1856; the family seat near Rotherham, in Yorkshire, was Wentworth Woodhouse, a Palladian giant that is still standing, with a façade of 600 feet and a chequered history of recent ownership. The earldom is extinct.)

D'Arcy Wentworth, at least in his youth, leaned towards crime. Having studied medicine in London (a profession then regarded as scarcely fit for gentlemen), he was tried at the Old Bailey in 1787 for highway robbery on Hounslow Heath. He was acquitted, but subsequently tried three more times for similar offences; on the last occasion, the year of the storming of the Bastille, he perhaps anticipated the court's verdict by announcing that he had secured a post as Assistant Surgeon to the Second Fleet, which was about to sail for Botany Bay – his passage paid for him, in accordance with the patronage system of the time, by Lord Fitzwilliam. About a quarter of the convicts died on that terrible voyage; Wentworth took as his mistress and impregnated one of the survivors, Catherine Crowley.

On arrival he shuttled between the primitive hospital of the grim new penal settlement on Norfolk Island (named by Captain Cook 'in honour of the noble family of Howard'), where William Charles was born, and Parramatta, just west of Sydney. Governor Bligh of the *Bounty* accused Wentworth of using his patients to work on his farm, and sacked him; not surprisingly Wentworth supported the overthrow of Bligh in the Rum Rebellion. Afterwards, in 1808, he was rewarded with a land grant and given his job back. With the arrival of Governor Macquarie, Wentworth's fortunes soared: Macquarie not only made him the colony's principal surgeon, but put him in charge of the Sydney police force, with wide magisterial powers. He also cut Wentworth in on a contract to build a new Sydney hospital. This was a highly unorthodox deal: reluctant to spend government funds, Macquarie arranged for the contractors to build the hospital in exchange for a three-year monopoly on the import of spirits. When the hospital opened, Wentworth, as the colony's chief medical officer, naturally took control, but during his term of office (1816–19) chaos reigned, with overcrowding, nobody in charge between sundown and 6 a.m., and the patients cooking and doing their washing in the wards. Wentworth was still a highwayman at heart. By the time he died, in 1827, he was probably the biggest landowner and certainly one of the richest men in the colony.

Thus D'Arcy Wentworth enjoyed a typically eighteenth-century career. Macquarie was the last governor of New South Wales with autocratic powers; when challenged about cutting Wentworth in on the hospital deal, which aroused the disapproval of the Colonial Office, he said that Wentworth was 'a Man on Whose Rectitude of Conduct and Zealous Attention to the due and faithful Execution of the Contract I could safely rely'. There could scarcely be a better example of the way in which the system of patronage that operated in England was transported – along with the convicts – lock, stock and barrel to New South Wales. A man like Wentworth was entirely dependent on the favour of the executive power for advancement. Even grandees in London could exercise influence in Sydney: Wentworth frequently wrote to Earl Fitzwilliam, asking him to do this or that through the Colonial Office.

D'Arcy Wentworth had three sons by Catherine Crowley. All of them he sent back to England to be educated, a practice that survived until recently among the Australian upper crust. One joined the British army, as the first Australian-born commissioned officer; he died in Tasmania. A second joined the navy and was drowned off Africa. Both of them needed the patronage of Lord Fitzwilliam to obtain commissions. The third son was William Charles.

Was he an Englishman or an Australian? In the 1950s Creighton Burns, later the editor of *The Age* of Melbourne, was given his first foreign posting and sent for by the chairman of David Syme & Co., the family firm that owned the paper. The chairman was Colonel Neill, who owed his post to his marriage into the Syme family, but he did his best; and seeing off fellows going to foreign parts he regarded as one of his duties. Neither he nor Burns could think of anything to say, until Burns found himself mentioning New Zealand and adding, politely as he thought, 'You're a New Zealander, aren't you, sir?'

'What on earth makes you think that?'

'Oh, I'd always heard you were born in New Zealand.'

'And what if I was? If I'd been born in Moscow, would that make me a Russian?'

Wentworth could, like the colonel, have argued that just because he was born on Norfolk Island that did not make him an Australian. He oscillated between being pro-English and anti-English; but a case can be made for regarding him as the first dinkum white Australian. Like his father and two brothers, he benefited from UK-based patronage. After going to school in England he returned to Australia in 1810 and at once, a mere youth of nineteen, was given a job by Macquarie as acting provost marshal – very soon, by a curious chance, after his father became the Sydney police chief. William Charles was the first native-born Australian to hold public office.

Three years later he formed part of the historic expedition, with the explorer Gregory Blaxland and the surveyor William Lawson, that set out to cross the Blue Mountains in search of fresh pastures for the colony's rapidly growing flocks. Having fought through almost impenetrable scrub at the rate of three or four miles a day, they did not in fact cross the main ridge of the Blue Mountains, but they were sufficiently impressed to report that enough good country lay westward 'to support the stock of the colony for the next thirty years'.

Both intellectually and materially the expedition changed Wentworth's life: it gave him a vision of Australia's future, and a reward from Macquarie of 1,000 acres that started him off as a landowner. The Aborigines played no part in this vision; nor did Wentworth for a moment suspect that the opening-up of Australia, which he had initiated, might one day be seen as the first act in a struggle between Aborigines and white Europeans for control of the continent.

He became a booster for the colony. His father wanted him to go into the army, and packed him off to London to secure a commission (Earl Fitzwilliam again). Wentworth persuaded Fitzwilliam to support him as an aspiring lawyer instead. In 1819, still not yet thirty, and despite having spent some time wandering round Europe (blazing another trail for young Australians to follow down the years), he wrote his booster-book published in London with the wonderful title *Statistical, Historical and Political Description of the Colony of New South Wales*. Four years later, in 1823, at the advanced age of thirty-two, he was admitted to Peterhouse, Cambridge, and came second in a poetry competition for the Chancellor's Medal on the prescribed subject of 'Australasia'.

Taken together, these two works earn Wentworth another first: the first Australian nationalist. High-flown eloquence and boundless optimism are their principal characteristics. As Robert Dixon, an Australian academic, has shown in *The Course of Empire*, Wentworth drew on two main sources of inspiration: the march westward of the United States, and the pastoral poems of particularly the Scottish poet James Thomson and Virgil. Wentworth wrote in his *Description*:

> The vast tide of emigration which is incessantly rolling along the banks of the Mississippi, and of its tributary streams, and the

numberless cities, towns, and settlements, that have sprung up as it were by the agency of magic, in what but a few years back was one boundless and uninterrupted wilderness, speak a language not to be mistaken by the most ignorant and prejudiced.

That a river of the enormous size of the Mississippi existed also in Australia he did not doubt: the Hawkesbury. Along the banks of this river:

> what a cheering prospect it would be for the philanthropist to behold what is now one vast and mournful wilderness becoming the smiling seat of industry and the social arts . . . and administering to the wants and contributing to the happiness of millions! What a proud sight would it be for the Briton to see his country pouring forth her teeming millions, who would otherwise perish from want, to procure an easy and comfortable subsistence in the most remote parts of the earth and forming monuments that would form indestructible records of her greatness and glory!

He himself had seen the future, as he says in his epic poem: having climbed the 'mighty ridge' and observed its chasms and 'stunted woods', 'we . . . gained . . . thy topmost heath' and:

> As a meteor shoots athwart the night,
> The boundless champaign burst upon our sight,
> Till nearer seen the beauteous landscape grew,
> Op'ning like Canaan on rapt Israel's view.

He goes on:

> Soon, Australasia, may thy inmost plains,
> A new Arcadia, teem with simple swains . . .

His vision of the course of empire spreading its blessings across the entire continent of Australia, in obedience to universal laws and in accordance with the benign policies of Macquarie, is matched by a prediction of the desolation and destruction of Britannia, which

13

will decline, like other empires before it. As the 'despotic Empress of old Ocean's tide' sinks, may her last-born infant then arise:

> And Australasia float, with flag unfurl'd,
> A new Britannia in another world.

Who Owns the Land?

The trouble was that Wentworth's vision of the new Britannia did not coincide with that of the Colonial Office and hence of the governors they sent to Sydney. He returned home well equipped for the battles ahead, both as a lawyer (soon with a thriving practice) and as a principal landowner. On arrival he added another weapon to his armoury, a newspaper, *The Australian*; its temper was democratic, its tone nationalistic and its attacks on the governor often libellous.

The key question in the developing colony was, as Professor Geoffrey Blainey has pointed out: who should possess the land, and on what terms? That question led to the next crux: who should control the Constitution? Wentworth returned to Sydney in 1824, two years after his patron Macquarie had gone back to London. For the next thirty years, as newspaper owner, lawyer, politician and leader of the squattocracy (the rich landowning squatters) he became anti-British. He fought the Colonial Office, the governors and any British attempt to acquire land that he himself coveted. When the Australian Agricultural Company was formed by a London syndicate in 1824, helped by the English-born pastoralist John Macarthur, with the stated aim in its charter of 'the Cultivation and Improvement of the Waste Lands in the Colony of New South Wales', Wentworth declaimed against them getting their 'filthy paws' on the best land. Their paws were and remained filthy, not through their own pioneering efforts but thanks to the way the Colonial Office backed them – the original capitalists included three MPs – whenever the Sydney administrators tried to curb their greed: ordering the governor to swap poor land at Port Stephens, selected by the company itself, for 600,000 acres of prime land on or near the Liverpool plains; handing the syndicate a monopoly of the Newcastle coal mines; and, when the legality of its properties was challenged, simply giving it, by the authority of the then Colonial Secretary, Earl Grey, the title deeds to all the properties whose ownership was in dispute. It was little wonder that Wentworth raved. 'Simple swains' the Australian Agricultural Company's directors were not. His temper was not improved when the governor, who could not stop the Londoners, did succeed in stopping Wentworth's attempt in 1840 to buy, with associates, about one-third of New Zealand. Britain – the source of patronage, land grants and wealth – had become in Wentworth's eyes an object of fierce resentment: an obstacle to press freedom, legal reform and the ambitions of the landed interests.

He abandoned the Bar, built up his already vast properties and went into politics as the squatters' candidate. He became Australian-looking, more bushman than townsman in his rough Australian homespun, lolling on the benches of the legislative council that he had helped to bring into existence; he roused himself occasionally to deliver passionate attacks in favour of self-government on the increasingly ill and exhausted Governor Gipps – an able soldier, but no match for a vengeful and dominant Wentworth.

How then did it happen that the radical nationalist who was Wentworth, leader of the Patriotic Association no less, turned into the man who made the most flagrant attempt to introduce into Australia the English class system in its traditional form? Frustration disturbed his judgement. The old question was: who controls the land? The new question was: who controls the labour supply? Wentworth wanted to import cheap labour: 'coolies'. He was blocked. In 1846 Gladstone floated the idea of reviving transportation; Wentworth supported him, but was blocked again. Public hostility was intense. Not surprisingly, the poorer classes bitterly opposed attempts to force them into competition with convict labour or Asiatics. Much of the hostility centred on Wentworth. The poet Charles Harpur wrote that the one-time champion of the people had become 'The bullying, bellowing champion of the Few'; Wentworth and the other 'landsharks' were driven by a desire 'to puff their windy shows of aristocracy'. Harpur was more prophetic than he knew.

Wentworth's epic imperial vision was going off the rails. Instead of 'The joyful notes of the shepherd, and the enlivening cries of the husbandman' spreading westward in the new Arcadia, as predicted a quarter of a century earlier, the loudest noise now became the abuse of Wentworth by urban radicals; and conspicuous among them was 'the low Irish mob', who were exploiting the opposition to Wentworth by linking it to a demand for political power for the working classes.

Alarmed for the future, Wentworth looked to the past. His historical imagination recalled the creed of the landed aristocracy – among them his Whig ancestors – which had ruled England in the eighteenth century. New South Wales, like eighteenth-century England, was an oligarchy. Wentworth and his squatter allies were not in politics to take a stand on political questions, but for their own purposes, prominent among which was defence of the property rights they had wrested from a reluctant British government during the previous two decades. Wentworth claimed that a political principle was involved. The landed interest that had built up the economic life of the colony, and sought and won for it political freedom, now had the duty to safeguard that freedom against the irresponsible element in the towns.

A Bunyip Aristocracy?

In 1853 Wentworth erected his roadblock. The select committee that he chaired, appointed by the legislative council, recommended the creation of peers with hereditary titles to form a body from which members of the Upper House under responsible government should be drawn. The committee stated in a preamble that its members 'have no wish to sow the seeds of a future democracy'; their aim was to place 'a safe, revising, deliberative and conservative element between the Lower House and Her Majesty's representatives in this colony . . .'

The proposals continued:

Your Committee are not prepared to recommend the introduction into this Colony of a right by descent to a seat in the Upper House; but are of opinion that the creation of hereditary titles, leaving it to the option of the Crown to annex to the title of the first Patentee a seat for life in such House, and conferring on the original Patentees and their descendants inheritors of their titles a power to elect a certain number of their order to form in conjunction with the original Patentees then living, the Upper House of Parliament, would be a great improvement upon any form of Legislative Council hitherto tried or recommended in any British colony. They conceive that an Upper House framed on this principle, whilst it would be free from the objections which have been urged against the House of Lords, on the ground of the hereditary right of legislation which they exercise, would lay the foundation of an aristocracy, which from their fortune, birth, leisure, and the superior education these advantages would superinduce would soon supply elements for the formation of an Upper House modelled, as far as circumstances will admit, upon the analogies of the British constitution. Such a House would be a close imitation of the elective portion of the House of Lords, which is supplied from the Irish and Scotch peerage; nor is the least of the advantages which would arise from the creation of a titled order, that it would necessarily form one of the strongest inducements not only to respectable families to remain in this Colony, but to the upper classes of the United Kingdom and other countries who are desirous to emigrate, to choose it for their future abode.

Next day Henry Parkes's newspaper went to town. Parkes, described by the *Australian Encyclopaedia* of 1926 as 'probably the greatest [statesman] Australia has known', was the exact opposite of Wentworth: born into a humble Warwickshire family, put to work aged eight and, before he emigrated, an active Chartist. He knew all about aristocratic landowners and political power. Wentworth's proposal for a colonial aristocracy with legislative functions, said the *Empire*, 'while it kept us slaves, would make us the laughing stock of every civilised nation'.

The laughter was infectious. A new word had just entered the Australian vocabulary – bunyip, meaning imposter, pretender, humbug. Daniel Denihy, the twenty-five-year-old son of Irish

Catholic parents, picked it up, making a mocking anti–Wentworth speech in which he said that his audience all knew how, in Australia, the common water mole was 'transferred into the duck-billed platypus'; now he supposed that, 'in some distant emulation of this degeneration', they were to be favoured with 'a bunyip aristocracy'. The phrase caught on. *The Oxford Dictionary of Folklore* goes so far as to say that 'a democratic attitude . . . firmed from this point on, so that in 1956 in his *Overlander Songbook* Ron Edwards could observe that "The very large stations . . . fostered the class feeling that was summed up with the title of 'Bunyip Aristocracy'."'

The mockery and hostility were too much for Wentworth. Reluctantly accepting that he was confronted by insurmountable opposition, he withdrew, accepted the nominee principle for an Upper House and retired a disappointed man to the rural consolations of the west of England. There, in Dorset, he spent the last seventeen years of his life, returning twice to Sydney: once to assist with a legislative crisis; and once, in 1872, to be buried on his estate in Vaucluse. No more was heard of Australia creating a peerage of its own; subsequent Australians, such as the Baillieus, were content merely to join the British House of Lords.

Class Resentment

Wentworth's proposal was an aberration, obviously self-interested and wildly at odds with the temper of his fellow-countrymen. Nothing remotely similar ever surfaced again. Still, there has always been a slice of Australian society – well off, usually with British connections – that has seemed to yearn after a social hierarchy along English lines that would set them apart from the Aussie 'gidday mate' rabble. The yearning reveals itself in snobbery and social rituals that pop up in, for instance, Sydney's Eastern Suburbs, the Adelaide hills, or Melbourne's South Yarra and Toorak.

Far more characteristic, and much more to do with the 'Australian identity' – that elusive quarry which Australians have stalked at least since the 1890s – was the body of brilliantly articulated feelings and ideas that came to be associated with *The Bulletin* journal a decade after Wentworth's sarcophagus had been lowered into its vault. These ideas included, for the first time in the new country, a widely disseminated hostility towards Britain and its nasty society, which has never since gone away. They provoked, naturally, a consequent wish to be different – at any rate among certain intellectuals and politicians. Australian nationalism – 'Australia for Australians' – begins with the rejection of England as a model.

The symbolic figure here of course is J.F. Archibald (1856–1919), who can claim to be Australia's greatest native-born journalist (which rules out Marcus Clarke and David Syme). Australia has always been a place where people could reinvent themselves, and Archibald was one of those who did just that. It must be significant that from his earliest days he was dissatisfied with his own identity. Perhaps it is not altogether surprising that a youth with literary ambitions, whose father was a policeman, should pretend that his Irish Catholic mother was French and Jewish; but to change his given names from John Feltham to Jules François was a very odd thing to do. It seems even odder when you consider where he was brought up, which was Warrnambool on the coast of Victoria, an agreeable spot but rather remote from Paris. Archibald never explained the switch. The writer and critic Vance Palmer ascribes it to his romanticism; France stood for the boulevard and the barricade – neither of them a feature of Warrnambool.

Having started as an apprentice printer on the *Warrnambool Standard*, in 1880 Archibald together with John Haynes, an enterprising young impresario who had learned his tricks on the *Mudgee Guardian*, founded *The Bulletin* in Sydney; and three years later he travelled to London as the infant journal's correspondent. He seems to have given himself the sort of brief that journalists like best: simply to write about anything that interested him. In the event, he was not so much interested by London as shocked. Was this the country that the citizens of Warrnambool regarded as home and sought to emulate? Archibald was appalled by the misery of the poor and the indifference of the rich. He wrote with contempt of English aristocrats: 'They lead a cruelly hard life. Noon after noon they rise from bed . . . and suffer unutterably in the effort to find something worth their weary, well-bred attention.' Almost the only aspect of London life that he approved of was the journalism of the radical *Reynolds News*, characterised by unsparing assaults on Queen Victoria. He reported: 'Says *Reynolds News*: "the people will soon come to the conclusion that it is no part of their duty to support Princes and Peers, paying more than two millions per annum in salaries, pensions, and grants."'

It was in Warrnambool, almost exactly a hundred years after Archibald, that Professor Blainey unwittingly aroused a storm of protest by warning (in an informal speech that he did not realise would be reported, as it was, in Archibald's old paper) against the social tensions that would, he thought, follow a too-generous immigration programme towards Asians — an echo of the virulently anti-Chinese policy promoted by Archibald in *The Bulletin* in the late 1880s.

According to Sylvia Lawson, Archibald's biographer, who knows more about the subject than anyone else, it was anti-English sentiment aroused by his visit to London — a desire on the part of Archibald and his talented colleagues to distance themselves from anything to do with the home country — that inspired *The Bulletin*'s subsequent radical, nationalist and republican policies under Archibald's editorship. (Not that a modern republican can adopt Archibald and his staff as precursors to be admired, given their anti-feminism and virulent racism.)

The journal found many causes for complaint. Did not the British government hand out titles to Australians in order to seduce them from loyalty to Australia? A *Bulletin* cartoon of 1888 shows Australia lamenting what three knighted politicians — Parkes, Berry and Griffith — might have done for Australia had they not been 'bought with a title'. Another has John Bull riding a donkey — Australia — and dangling titles in the shape of carrots before its nose.

A more securely grounded cause of resentment was the continuation of appeals from Australian courts to the Judicial

Committee of the Privy Council in London; how could anyone maintain that Australian judges were inferior to English judges, which was the only possible justification for maintaining the system?

Australians in general were beginning to resent criticism from England, whether of their boastfulness or of their financial system. They were no better pleased when England ignored them, especially given the belief – widespread at the time – that before long Australia would be a considerable power, with a population of some sixty million. Sir Henry Parkes wrote to Gladstone in 1874: 'The grievance under which we sometimes fret, but more frequently laugh, is that England, as represented by her eminent men, and by her literature, forms no adequate conception of our importance.' Another complaint was that English newspapers paid too little attention to Australian affairs, and when they did condescend to take an interest, reported only the bad things: droughts, floods and murders. English ministers, even Gladstone, did not always command respect. Alfred Deakin, visiting London as Chief Secretary of Victoria for the first Imperial Conference in 1887, did not think Gladstone was strong in 'character, consistency and steadiness of will'; on the same visit 'his candid criticism of the Colonial Office and the British Prime Minister, Lord Salisbury, set a much-needed example to other Australian delegates, and for the first time asserted the position of the self-governing colonies as integral parts of the Empire rather than dependencies of the mother country'. The other delegates were deferential in the presence of a British Prime Minister who was also a marquess. A delegate from New South Wales spoke with what one observer called 'whispering humbleness'. Deakin alone – perhaps his example was a turning point, especially as he was hailed as a hero for his boldness when he returned to Victoria – was not disposed to put up with any condescension from British aristocrats: 'the Dukes and Earls and their women are all given up to small-talk, giddiness or emptiness or clever coldness or mere sensible good manners at best'.

Back home, there were in the same period flickerings of cultural resentment that echo down the years. In a preface to his

Short Stories in Prose and Verse of 1894, Henry Lawson wrote: 'This is an attempt to publish, in Australia, a collection of sketches and stories at a time when everything Australian, in the shape of a book, must bear the imprint of a London publishing firm before our critics will condescend to notice it . . .' The fact that *Short Stories* contained 'The Drover's Wife', considered by good judges to be one of the finest stories in English, did not remove the prejudice.

The republican spasm was short-lived. It was briefly an excitement, producing turbulent public meetings, Lawson's *Song of the Republic* (1887), and his mother's noisy and ephemeral journal *The Republican* (July 1887–April 1888), but it attracted little public support and never reached much further than the hotels where *The Bulletin* journalists drank. *The Bulletin* and Lawson gave much wider currency to the idea of mateship, as the defining characteristic of the 'Australian identity', and promoted the bush as the source of typical Australian characteristics.

The 1880s seem to have been crucial in the development of the Australian 'legend', as Professor Russel Ward called it: the idea of the true Australian as the product of the bush, fiercely independent and a hater of officiousness and authority, loyal to his mates, the sworn enemy of the scab, beholden to no man, believing that Jack is not only as good as his master but probably a good deal better. The same decade saw the start of powerful unions, among miners and shearers, and the spread of aggressive nationalism. During the years since Ward wrote, in 1958, his thesis has been much argued over; one of the points made against it is that *The Bulletin* writers were not so much finding the bushman's ethic in the bush as imposing their own ideas on the bush – that the ethics they championed were in fact those of a dissatisfied urban intelligentsia. Still, it seems to be the case that the legend of the bush struck a deep chord at the time, that it later merged with the legend of the Anzacs, and that this notion of a true Australian lingers on in the minds of very many male (not female) urban Australians, even today. The impulse was to be different from the English, and sometimes still is. Americans in London tend to become more British; Australians in London are prone to behave as if they really belong among the coolabahs and dingoes, exaggerating their accents, growing bushranger beards and practising mateship in Earls Court.

This particular version of the Australian identity is not the only survival from the end of the nineteenth century. Republicanism and vague calls for independence faded away when the Crown was called upon to act as the fairy godmother who would link the six colonies together in Federation. But many of the irritants of those days live on.

Titles continued to be a source of left-wing discontent, until Prime Minister Whitlam pointedly declined the distinction of becoming a member of the Privy Council and abolished the federal award of imperial honours. Patrick White was echoing the old *Bulletin* when he savaged his former friend Sidney Nolan, after his move to London, for allowing himself to be corrupted by London society and for his acceptance of British honours: 'Sir Neddy Nolan of Hertfordshire, OM' he called him, with contempt.

The reporting of Australia by English newspapers continued to annoy Australians for exactly the same reasons that it had annoyed their nineteenth-century predecessors. English papers either ignored them or reported only events or habits that fitted the English stereotype. An aspiring academic could write a PhD on this large subject. In 1956 I wrote my first feature for an English newspaper from Sydney, which was about an illegal but well-patronised two-up gambling game in French's Forest. An Eastern Suburbs matron, who happened to see the article, asked me why I didn't write about the good things in Australia. What did she have in mind? Randwick, she replied. She explained, correctly, that English racecourses were slums by comparison and that English race-readers, if employed at all, were by comparison with their local counterparts slow, inaudible, uninformative and often inaccurate; but she did not explain why losing your money to your mates in the scrub was morally inferior to losing it to Sydney bookmakers.

But the most remarkable survival from colonial days was the persistence until 1986 of appeals from Australia to the Privy

23

Council. That small islands in the Caribbean should turn to London, to resolve awkward legal disputes that might produce accusations of bias or corruption if determined by local courts, was politically rational. In Australia decisions of the High Court might be disputed, but nobody was likely to impugn its collective competence or probity. In the 1980s, reporting for an English newspaper a libel case between *The Age* of Melbourne and Kerry Packer and his World Series cricketers that had found its way on appeal to London, I was struck, as anyone else would have been, by the anachronistic nature of the system; only lawyers could have kept it going for so long, in defiance of both logic and expense. The attendance of no fewer than eleven of them was required in order to hear the case; the cost was astronomical. Nor did the system strike me as wholly fair; Mr Packer's solicitors had secured, for a fee whose size astounded *The Age*'s solicitors, the services of Robert Alexander, QC (later Lord Alexander), one of the leading English barristers of the day and a member of the MCC. He handled the appeal judges with skill and confidence. *The Age*'s Australian barrister, probably no less clever than Alexander, never got the measure of the unfamiliar conditions; he was like a Sheffield Shield batsman in his first test match on a seaming English pitch. *The Age* would no doubt have lost the appeal in any event; but one wondered: was there the faintest hint of class in the courtroom air?

The Australian Taboo

Many Australians deny that class has anything to do with their own country — let alone that it affects, and always has affected, their attitude to the UK. Their misperceptions are often endorsed by overseas visitors. D.H. Lawrence, during his stopover in 1922, noted the absence of that 'distinction in the very being' between the proletariat and the ruling classes that was to be found in Britain. Casual English visitors observe the absence of the indications to which they are accustomed — the scarcity of titles, the lack of formal deference with which employees treat

24

employers, the way that graziers work alongside station hands, the fact that everyone enjoys the same kind of leisure at the beach and racetrack – and assume that the rough egalitarian myth that Australians themselves want to believe in is true. I came across a youth at the Melbourne Cricket Ground in 1992 who was, unconsciously I assume, struggling with this myth and doing his best to obey its spirit. *The Age* had invited me to their box for the World Cup final, and as I sat down the youth appeared at my elbow: a waiter, immaculate in black trousers, white shirt and black tie. 'Would you care for some champagne, mate?' he asked.

Looking back to the 1950s, when I spent some time in Sydney's Eastern Suburbs, it is clear to me that in the moneyed and most desirable heart of the city, class divisions were rampant. Elsewhere, no doubt, in the endless suburbs or the migrant ghettos, life went on without the benefit of social distinctions. But among the flowering shrubs of Bellevue Hill that was not the case. There the traces of English class distinctions – even a positive preference for a social hierarchy – survived. True, there were very few hereditary titles about the place: Sir Rupert Clarke of Melbourne, a baronet, was a rare bird. Viscount Bruce had no male heirs and lived in London. My stepfather-in-law used to claim that the Earl of Suffolk was to be sighted in Queensland; he personally had seen him, wearing white breeches. Lord Byron, the eleventh baron, lived in Dinninup, Western Australia.

John Betjeman unearthed a couple of others, although I have forgotten who they were. Snobbery or, to be more polite, the distinctive marks of behaviour that people believe to be of social significance, fascinated Betjeman. When he visited Australia in the 1960s he was particularly delighted by three things: the Victorian architecture of Brisbane Cathedral, the scarlet plush glory of the Senate Chamber in Melbourne, and the discovery of those two hereditary peers. Betjeman specialised in peers, but they had to be obscure before he became really excited; the more obscure and dottier they were, the more excited he became and the funnier he found them. Ireland, where he was press attaché during the Second World War, was for that reason his favourite foreign country: it was constantly throwing up a new example of the species. Like other English people – or perhaps one should say like other Anglo-Dutch people – Betjeman did not connect Australia with hereditary peers. He did not connect it at all, before he went there, with what he called 'That topic all-absorbing, as it was, is now, and ever shall be, to us – CLASS'. After he arrived he was far too socially alert not to spot its existence.

In the social gossip columns any visiting Britons with a title (even a knighthood) rated a prominent mention, however obscure they might be where they came from. Beaming hostesses produced them at parties with pride, emphasising the title, like pulling rabbits out of a hat. A lord and lady could expect free meals for weeks. Once a year there was an almost ritualistic display of Australian class distinctions when the graziers – a politer word than squatters – came to town *en masse* for the Show. Their headquarters was the Australia Hotel; and they were unmistakably a tribe: bursting with health, clean and happy; the men immaculate in flat pork-pie hats, white shirts, ties, moleskin trousers and gleaming brown elastic-sided boots; the women in flowered dresses; the daughters on the lookout for husbands; the smaller children disciplined and polite. Most of them had been to the same private school, the defining feature of the tribe. A few of the men, though none of the women, had gone on to Oxford or Cambridge. The graziers, it seemed to me, represented the upper class, their physically demanding year marked by picnic races, weddings, polo matches, the shearing season, the wool sales and the Show. Some of them paid an annual visit to England or Scotland. There were two special characteristics about this tribe: they were deeply Australian, and often more conscious and proud of their nationality if they had been to Oxford or Cambridge; and they were extraordinarily cut off from power, and indeed from metropolitan Australia. So far as the rest of the nation was concerned, they might have belonged to another planet. On their properties they were kings, their local dominion challenged occasionally by the organised shearers (and never by their wives). But they rarely sought public office and paid little attention to federal or even state politics, apart perhaps, from sending an annual contribution to the Country Party, which was supposed to represent their interests. They were the nearest thing in Australia (which was not very near) to English country gentlemen.

Breaking the Taboo

It seems incredible that it is only thirty-five years ago that Australian academics started taking an interest in class. In 1965 two Melbourne social scientists, A.F. Davies and S. Encel, announced that the subject had been 'intolerably neglected'. They attacked head-on 'the myth of Australian classlessness', conceding that they were adopting a position that went against the grain. 'Discussion of class and social stratification has been dominated for a century by the "dead level" interpretation of Australian history — the notion of an egalitarian paradise (or purgatory), fed alike by travellers' tales and by much historical writing.' They took a few side-swipes at other academics, including the great W.K. Hancock, for accepting and spreading 'the myth of egalitarianism'. Then they plunged into the jungle of figures produced by the few opinion polls on the subject. It cannot be said that this bold expedition produced very revolutionary findings, but it gave them an intellectual advantage over the traditionalists because they could point to the evidence of their tables and percentages. These demonstrated that Australians did not think of themselves as being on a 'dead level' socially. Asked whether they thought that classes existed, nine out of ten agreed that they did. Most of them readily accepted a class label. Many even recognised the existence of social snobbery.

Yet class is almost a secret subject, still causing slavishness towards England in some quarters, and resentment and suspicion in others. When Conrad Black, a Canadian, bought a controlling interest in Fairfax newspapers, the editor of his flagship paper in England, Max Hastings of the *Daily Telegraph*, wondered whether he should fly to Sydney to meet his new Australian colleagues, with whom in future he expected to co-operate. He was advised to stay at home. His rather emphatic English 'upper-class' voice, combined with his height and rather abrupt manner, was thought certain to arouse automatic and even ribald hostility among the disrespectful journos of Broadway. In fact any hostility, if caused by resentful perceptions of his 'class', would have been misplaced; both Hastings's parents were journalists and his father, Macdonald Hastings, one of the BBC's best-known television reporters after the Second World War, had a ferocious Scottish accent.

Another contemporary example – trivial enough, but showing that class is still doing business at the old stand – comes from Adelaide. When in 1980 Alexander Downer, the Liberal politician and son of Sir Alexander Downer (former Menzies minister and High Commissioner in London), returned to Australia having been educated in England, with an English wife, a Miss Nicola Robinson from the Midlands, one section of Adelaide 'society' seriously wondered whether she was 'good' enough for him – meaning, was he marrying beneath him? The social signs, on the face of it, were against her: her common surname, the Midlands (not a fashionable district) and, above all, the fact that her family was in trade: medical appurtenances, bandages, and such. These caused the sort of social alarm they would have set off in Mrs Bennet of *Pride and Prejudice*. Fortunately for Adelaide's peace of mind, Miss Robinson turned out to descend from a prosperous, prominent and long-established family firm, Robinson & Sons Ltd, whose founder was manufacturing pillboxes in his drawing room at exactly the same time (the late 1830s) that Colonel Light was surveying and recommending the layout of Adelaide (and the first wave of Prussian Lutherans was settling in the Adelaide hills). Downer himself is an example of Australian confusion about class. When I interviewed him in 1994 he bitterly condemned the English class system, which he had experienced at first hand at his English public school; thank God, he said, there was nothing like that in Australia. Australians, he added, did not think of other Australians in class terms. A few minutes later, recalling how Prime Minister Keating had attacked him because of his English education and allegedly English accent, Downer accused Keating of 'waging a thirties-style class war'. Indeed, the perception that Downer, as leader of the Liberal Party, was not a dinkum Aussie certainly had something to do with his rapid deposition from the party leadership; his colleagues concluded that he was too easy a target for Labor snipers; he could too readily be pilloried as virtually an English fifth-columnist.

Furbank and Lady Mary

Even to Australians who claim to live in a 'dead-level' country, class is an embarrassing subject. It becomes less embarrassing once it is realised that class does not really exist: that it is all in the mind. People who talk about other people's class are using the concept as a weapon. These are the arguments of the learned and subtle Professor P.N. Furbank, and they are particularly relevant to Anglo-Australian relations.

'Class', in its common meaning, does not exist objectively at all, Furbank argues. He traces the modern use of the word to Marx. Now Marx envisaged only two classes: exploiters and exploited, bourgeoisie and proletariat. He never attempted to define his classes. He divided society into classes as a rhetorical device: a call to arms. Nor was he scrupulous in his use of terms. He hailed the Paris Commune as the first manifestation in history of the strength of the working class, a proletarian triumph; but the members of the Commune were a mish-mash, many of whom were not in the least proletarian or even French. It was the violent revolution of the Commune that really excited Marx, not its working-class character, which it did not actually have.

Since Marx, says Furbank, nobody has been able to describe with any precision what they mean by such common terms as upper class, middle class and working class. The advertising industry has been accustomed to classify people as A1s, C3s, and so forth; but the classification is based on income, not class. Were it based on class, a bankrupt duke would be an A1 and a millionaire dustman a C3. Even the simple-sounding term 'aristocrat' is hopelessly elusive. The most common definition would probably be this: anyone with an inherited title. But consider one particular family with a strong Australian connection: members of an Anglo-Australian aristocracy, one might think, if such a thing exists: the Vesteys. The first Lord Vestey was ennobled in 1922; when it emerged that he had shifted much of his meat-packing business to Argentina during the First World War, putting English workers out of a job, George V was appalled that the honour had been awarded; but by then it was too late. Are we to regard the present Lord Vestey, the third baron, as an aristocrat? Surely not. Class is not an objective social phenomenon, like height or gender. Since it cannot be defined, it must be regarded as a chimera: an idea in people's heads. The cartoonist Tandberg used to draw Sir John Kerr in a top hat, a potent English class symbol; a subliminal reference to the notion that Sir John as Governor-General was the willing puppet of Buckingham Palace. Here is a neat example of class, in allegedly classless Australia, being used as a weapon; a flicker perhaps of the same anti-English sentiment that inspired the *Bulletin* cartoonists a century earlier for much the same reasons: that Australia was the plaything of London toffs and of the local 'snobocracy' (an Archibald coinage), who were London's allies.

In its pure English form, class, which centres broadly on titles, means nothing to the majority of citizens – though I noticed that when the English cricketer Ted Dexter played on Australian grounds he attracted special jeers when he misfielded (which he frequently did on his first visit), entirely because he had been nicknamed Lord Ted, on account of his allegedly lordly public school (Radley, like Alexander Downer) and Cambridge manner.

'Lady Mary Fairfax' is a prime example of the Furbank theory: that class is all in the mind. In 1959 Mary Wein from Poland married Sir Warwick Fairfax, chairman of the wealthy and well-established Fairfax newspaper group, becoming his third wife. She was socially ambitious, sending out 2,000 idiosyncratic Christmas cards, featuring the year's adventures of her family and herself. Her husband's flagship newspaper, the *Sydney Morning Herald*, reguarly featured accounts of her parties, but instead of calling her Lady Fairfax, it and other papers invariably called her (incorrectly) Lady Mary Fairfax. For those who take these things seriously, this form of address meant that she was not the wife of a knight, but the daughter of a duke, marquess or earl. Did she draw the attention of her husband's employees to their solecism? She did not. 'Lady Mary Fairfax', leader of Sydney society, was thus – one might say – an Australian fantasy. She did not exist.

Finally, to those who cling to the belief that Australia does not have a class system, I call in evidence Sir John Mason, British High Commissioner in Canberra from 1980 to 1984, who with his wife became an Australian citizen in 1987. In 1998 the National Library in Canberra published a book by him called *Diplomatic Despatches*, in which he described:

... frequent comment about the British class system. I myself have never encountered this phenomenon and, when questioned, my fellow-Australians tend to talk about private schools and Oxbridge as fortresses of privilege. They are surprised to be told that only about 3 per cent of British children go to fee-paying schools, where the figure in Australia is nearer 20 per cent; and that you get into Oxbridge, as into Sydney University, because you are bright. And when I say that I regard Australia as less egalitarian than Britain, people are incredulous, particularly if they are members of the Melbourne Club.

2
The Beginning of Doubts

Nineteenth-century doubts about the values of the British connection were grounded in class feelings, a desire for independence and a growing nationalism. Twentieth-century doubts about it were grounded in death. They flickered briefly during the Boer War, but as the century drew on came to be centred chiefly on Gallipoli, though that was not obvious at the time. They broke out again in the Second World War, after the fall of Singapore in 1942.

That Gallipoli lay unresolved at the heart of the Anglo-Australian relationship took me a long time to realise – partly, I think, because in the minds of my generation the Great War had faded into the background, while it remained alive and important in the imaginations of my Australian contemporaries.

I can date the moment when I saw the light. On 25 April 1980, while living in Melbourne, I attended the dawn service at the vast, clumsy war memorial that I used to drive past daily on the way to work. By then Anzac Day had lost its power to move most younger Australians. The Vietnam War had intervened; the traditional services and parades that had been taking place across the country since 1916, commemorating Gallipoli, seemed, sixty and more years on, to be in danger of celebrating war itself and to be awash with phoney religion and sentimentality. That was not how I felt, as the 'Last Post' sounded in an immense metropolitan silence and the shabby old men with rheumy eyes stared at their feet. I felt profoundly moved. Despite the geographical distance from the battlefields, the Great War seemed suddenly closer than ever before.

It was not as though the war had not been present in the lives of those Englishmen who, as I did, grew up between the wars. My father had, like many others, lied about his age (he was forty in 1914) in order to join up; he had been wounded and removed from the trenches on what, to a child, was the mysteriously named duckboard. But he never talked about his experiences, and the only tangible relic of them was a regimental badge of the Royal Norfolks kept in a leather stiff-collar box on top of his chest of drawers. A photograph of Cousin Angus, killed in the war, stood in a silver frame on a table in the drawing room; but for all we children knew of the circumstances of his death, he might have been lost at Waterloo or Agincourt – battles that we had been taught about at school. No one told us about the Somme. At prep school, on Armistice Day, we stood in silence at eleven o'clock for reasons that were never fully explained, although the school was practically within spitting distance of France.

Only Captain MacVean made the war seem real. He was a deplorable fellow – the deputy headmaster, no less – who became for me and my schoolfellows the absolute personification of the Great War. He must have been about forty, a bachelor (but, unlike one or two of the other masters, not homosexual), with receding gingery hair, and the capacity to reduce to total silence a class of chattering boys simply by entering the room. On ordinary days he wore an old sports jacket with patched elbows, tubular grey flannels that ended above his ankles and dirty brown shoes. On special occasions, such as Speech Day, he put on a tight dark-blue suit and an Old Malvernian tie, slightly stained. His room was a tip: unmade bed, empty beer bottles, dirty plates stacked in his washbasin, mouldy tins of food. When in the morning he came down to the dining hall, always late, his mouth was usually circled by a thin line of dried foam – the drink, we supposed. He would sip a cup of tea and then start to chain-smoke; his fingers were yellow with nicotine. He was the master in charge of football and cricket, and he had obviously been a good player before his breathing went.

As a teacher, his speciality was maths; his method was to walk in, scribble a problem on the blackboard, then settle down to read a western; at the end of the period he would write up the answer and go off to his next class. All the other masters – even the headmaster – were in awe of him, I think because of his uncanny control over the boys. Two or three times a term, drunk, he would rouse the senior classes from their beds and get them to stand on the forms in the hall and bellow 'Jerusalem' at the tops of their voices. We were in awe of him, partly because of his deadly use of sarcasm, which boys hate, and partly because we saw him as a survivor of the trenches. He walked with a slight limp. When we perceived him to be in a good mood, we would ask about the war and to amuse us he would carefully draw a machine gun or a Mills bomb on the blackboard, name the parts and explain their workings. I also remember enthralling lectures on poison gas. So presumably he had actually been at – or at any rate near – what was known as the Front and had not simply awarded himself the rank of captain.

My particular source of information about the war may have been eccentric, but I am sure the general point stands: namely that even English schoolboys were not brought up to regard it as a glorious or admirable chapter in the island story. Captain MacVean (like my father) would have been astonished to have been regarded in any way as heroic. Indeed, the very word 'heroes' had been fatally devalued through its use in an election-campaign promise – 'Homes Fit for Heroes' – that was never kept.

The national picture of the war came to be formed not by the politicians who wrote their war memoirs, such as Lloyd George or Churchill, but by the young writers, barely known before the war, who had experienced at first hand and at length what Edmund Blunden called 'the disgusting and terrible scenes in France'. Blunden spent two years at the Front, winning a Military Cross on the Somme; Wilfred Owen about eight months; Robert Graves a year; and Siegfried Sassoon sixteen months. None of them was exactly a cheer-leader for the military. Sassoon permanently planted in the English mind a picture of the 'arrogant isolation' of the High Command. Even the gentler Blunden, though not instinctively critical of all senior officers – he greatly admired his saintly colonel – imagined the generals in their chateaux sending men to their deaths merely because they wished to straighten out an untidy corner on their headquarters maps. Blunden was my Oxford tutor for a year early in the Second World War, a much-loved birdlike figure haunted by his experiences of war and its 'ironic cruelty'. The mood of the poets and writers was shared by academic historians. The Epilogue to C.R.M.F. Cruttwell's standard *History of the Great War* begins: 'War between great states . . . cannot now be regarded as an "instrument of policy". It becomes inevitably a struggle for existence, in which no limit can be placed on the expenditure of men and money, no objectives can be clearly defined and no peace by an agreed compromise obtained.' This was not an atmosphere in which legends are born, and the First World War, for the British, did not produce any.

Why was Australia different? No war memorial in Britain is as prominent as the colossal memorial in Canberra. No British painting is more pathetic than the Sidney Nolan painting of a Great War digger – a defenceless-looking youth in the uniform of the Light Horse. Despite the big, flowering plume in his hat, he looks doomed, a victim rather than an aggressor. But a victim of what, and of whom? One large and obvious difference is the way each country regards the role of the other. Every British schoolboy knew – or at least every British schoolboy who had read about the Australians in *The Wonder Book of Empire for Boys and Girls* knew – that 'the dauntless courage displayed by these "citizen soldiers" on Gallipoli and in France will never be forgotten'. But for the British, the Australian troops – however courageous – were (like the Canadians) a useful supplement whose presence, however welcome, was never going to make the difference between winning and losing the war. Australia was on the periphery of Britain's view of the war; whereas Britain was at the centre of Australia's.

Looking back, it seems likely that the key moment in Anglo-Australian relations in the twentieth century occurred in 1941, when John Curtin, the Australian Prime Minister, refused Churchill's demand to send Australian troops to Burma, on the grounds that the troops were needed to defend their own country. It also seems obvious, now, that this key moment, this angry rift, did not come out of the blue, but represented the culmination of an unresolved flaw at the heart of the relationship, which had been present for a long time. Why should Australians risk their lives in defence of British interests?

The question did not arise until Australia had its own armed forces; and it began to worry that it had no armed forces of its own only when it perceived a threat to its own territory. At moments, during the second half of the nineteenth century, some politicians and radicals proposed that Australia should separate itself altogether from Britain and go its own way. What need had Australia to take orders from London? Australia was garrisoned by British troops from 1788 to 1870 (they suppressed the Castle Hill Uprising, the Eureka Rebellion and the Lambing Flat Riots), but the colonies began to raise their own local forces before the British withdrew, and maintained them for the rest of the century.

Individual colonists went to fight in New Zealand during the Maori Wars. The first time that an Australian colonial government became involved in an imperial war was in 1885, when the New South Wales government offered to send troops to the Sudan after the news reached Australia of General Gordon's death at Khartoum. This contingent consisted of about 750 volunteers and 200 horses; they saw some fighting at Tamai, but were away for only three months and suffered no casualties, although nine men died from disease.

The Boer War was a much more serious affair. Nearly 600 Australians died on South African soil, helping Britain in a doubtful cause. In the late nineteenth century Australia seemed to be moving smoothly towards secession and some form of independence. It then appeared that the Germans were pursuing imperial ambitions in New Guinea and Samoa; and that the eyes of Japan – a rising power – seemed to be critically turned on the vast country to their south, which excluded Oriental immigrants as a matter of policy. A national policy, the White Australia policy, required a nation to enforce it. And a nation the size of Australia required railways. Both Canada and Australia moved in the same direction, into the arms of the mother country, at the same time. Maps of North America in the second half of the nineteenth century show the railway lines of the United States reaching north like greedy fingers and stopping at the Canadian border. Canada then, with great difficulty, built the Canadian Pacific Railway from east to west, linking in practice the provinces that had hitherto been linked only by law. The aim was self-protection from the industrial giant to the south. Henceforward the main route of Canadian trade was transatlantic. In Australia the length of the continent's railway lines shot up from 243 miles in 1861 to more than 10,000 miles in 1890. The railway made Federation possible; it was also a guarantee of imperial protection, and in 1901 the new Commonwealth Parliament legislated to exclude non-Europeans. Once the new nation was within the imperial embrace, as represented by the Royal Navy, it was axiomatic that most of its citizens would in turn respond with enthusiasm to the needs of the mother country. Come 1914, anti-German feeling was whipped up with surprising ease. An Australian historian, Professor Stuart Macintyre, suggested recently that the Australians were the white Gurkhas. Apart from the Maori Wars, the Sudan, the Boer War and the Great War, Australians fought in Russia during the civil war and on both sides in the Irish civil war – and of course in the Second World War and Vietnam. Which of these wars affected Australia's national interest is open to debate. Vietnam, Macintyre argued, took the steam out of Australian enthusiasm for foreign wars. Thenceforward, he thought, male national aggression found its expression in every known form of sport.

The Anzac Legend

It is an accident of history that the great Australian Anzac legend that came out of the Great War had nothing directly to do with Germany, and not much to do with Australia. Gallipoli was Churchill's idea, an attempt to force the Dardanelles, drive Turkey out of the war and open a safe sea route to Russia. A naval expedition launched in February and March 1915 failed. A military expedition followed, relying mainly on British, Australian, New Zealand and French troops, with naval support. The first landings on the Gallipoli peninsula and Asian mainland were made on 25 April 1915; the Anzac landing was made on a beach that quickly became known as Anzac Cove. Turkish resistance was strong. Further landings were made, but to no avail: stalemate. Allied troops were withdrawn in December 1915 and January 1916. Australian casualties were 7,595 killed and 19,367 wounded.

Those are the bare facts. What is the legend? First and foremost it says that the Australian volunteer troops, mainly innocent country boys, showed exceptional bravery in the face of overwhelming opposition and made heroic sacrifices. The mateship they had learned in the bush – a type of male friendship regarded as uniquely Australian – sustained them in battle. It was an aspect of the rough dignity with which they conducted themselves that they honoured the enemy: the Turks, of whom they had no knowledge; a form of chivalry.

This is the core of the legend. Around the core, other ideas came to be added. Gallipoli was seen as the crucible of the new Australian nation: the behaviour of the diggers there was said to have established the Australian identity. An Australian was someone who was proud of his country, brave, a true mate to his mates and sceptical of unearned authority.

The legend also acquired sourer ingredients, in the eyes of some – not all – Australians. First, Churchill's strategic concept was said to be criminally self-indulgent, doomed from the start. Second, it was alleged that at Gallipoli the British had used Anzac troops – expendable colonials – to undertake a mission that their own commanders wished to avoid. Third, it was further alleged that the very high casualty rates sustained by those troops were in part caused by the incompetence and ruthlessness of British officers of the upper class.

The core legend retains exceptional force. As recently as May 1997 Australia's most admired animal was given a posthumous award for bravery during the Gallipoli campaign. Murphy, the donkey that carried wounded soldiers on perilous journeys down the exposed rocky gullies to field hospitals, and whose statue stands in the War Memorial, was presented with a Purple Cross for Animal Bravery in War by the Deputy Prime Minister. The image of the donkey weighed down by a half-dead soldier in his bush hat, and tended by John Kirkpatrick, a twenty-two-year-old stretcher bearer, is one of the most powerful images in the nation's military past. Nobody thought the award absurd or incongruous – or, if they did, they did not say so publicly.

But where did the legend come from? Most people would assume, I think, if they took what is still the rather daring step of considering its origins at all, that it emerged gradually and piecemeal: from contemporary reports, from the stories told by survivors coming home from Gallipoli and from later histories. Even for an Englishman it is slightly shocking to learn, as I learned not long ago from a readily available source in the Mitchell Library in Sydney, that the legend was an artificial creation, deliberately and to some extent dishonestly created by one man.

C.E.W. Bean was the Official War Correspondent, Oxford-educated, who became famous both for his dispatches from Gallipoli and for his later twelve-volume history of the war (six written by him, six edited) produced during the many years after he was appointed Official War Historian. But it was neither his dispatches nor his history, published from 1921 to 1942, that created the legend, but *The Anzac Book*. This was the work he put together as a commemorative souvenir of an heroic but unsuccessful campaign, as that campaign was ending. He appealed for contributions from the men who were there, and claimed that the number that came in were 'enormous', which was not true. He gave the impression that the bulk of the Australian troops were bushmen, which again was not true; most of them came from the cities. From the contributions that did come in, he excluded anything that might detract from the image he wished to create – anything about the danger, the brutality, the suffering, the waste of life, the dehumanising effect of war. In his private diary he noted that few of the Anzacs wanted to fight, that some were forced into action at pistol point and that many of them wanted to run away (and did). There is no trace of any of this in *The Anzac Book*; nothing about fear. Part of the legend is that the Anzacs had a chivalrous respect for the enemy. Bean is solely responsible for adding this touch; it does not feature in any of the contributions that were sent in. It was Bean himself who wrote and included the verse:

We will judge you Mr Abdul
By the test by which we can –
That with your breath, in life, in death,
You've played the gentleman.

Distributed and bought across Australia, as well as throughout the Empire, *The Anzac Book* became an instant and monumental bestseller. Thus was the Anzac legend created in a few months in 1916.

All this was discovered from an examination of the Bean papers by D.A. Kent of the University of New England, and published in *Historical Studies*, not a very widely read journal, in 1985. His thesis seems to be well founded, even if it makes uncomfortable reading.

'The Vilest Libel of the War'

Having created the legend, Bean protected it. In 1992 the Australian Prime Minister, Paul Keating, made some remarks about the British 'betrayal' of Australia in the Second World War, which caused a flurry of controversy in both countries. Taking this event as his cue, Alistair Thomson of the University of Sussex came up with the remarkable story of how, in 1927, a disagreement between British and Australian historians (notably Bean) about the Anzac landing at Gallipoli had flared up into public outrage, and was then quickly suppressed and forgotten. These events, said Thomson, helped to explain the continuing sensitivity about British-Australian military relations, and why Keating's remarks had generated such strong feelings on both sides of the world.

Thomson is a thorough researcher. A good reporter makes one last telephone call or conducts one last interview that produces the story; Thomson, the researcher, sent for one last box of papers. He was in, of all places, the Isle of Wight looking through the papers of Brigadier-General Cecil Aspinall-Oglander, a British staff officer who had helped to plan the Gallipoli campaign and who subsequently wrote the British official history of the campaign.

(The name alone, I concede, is enough to arouse the suspicions of any true Australian: just the sort of person who might have been expected to plan a disaster; however, he tacked on the Oglander part, his wife's surname, in later life.) Aspinall-Oglander had lived on the Isle of Wight and left his papers to the County Record Office. The archivist produced for Thomson five boxes containing papers about the campaign and the history, but there was nothing in them that could not have been inferred from other sources in the Public Record Office in London or the War Memorial in Canberra. But one box in the sequence was missing. The archivist explained that it contained personal papers unrelated to Gallipoli, but Thomson asked him to bring it up from the storeroom, just in case. 'The box was jammed full with the material about life on the Isle of Wight listed at its front, but hidden away at the bottom was a slim, unmarked file.' This contained letters written by British officers who took part in the Anzac landing, commenting on Aspinall's chapters seven and eight about the events of that day. Among the letters was 'a scrawled and undated memo' by Aspinall about his history of the Anzac landing, which contained what Thomson calls 'one extraordinary claim':

This chapter was a difficult one to write because the truth about the Australians has never yet been told and in its absence a myth has sprung up that the Anzac troops did magnificently against amazing odds. The anniversary of the landings at Gallipoli is called Anzac Day, & very many people would be surprised to hear that any other troops but Australians took part in the earlier operations at Gallipoli. In my first draft I did my best to tell the truth about the landing without hurting any feelings, and to write a readable story that would be of military value to the student as well as of interest to the general public.

The draft, except in one quarter, met with entire approval. Sir Ian Hamilton, Sir W. Birdwood, General Sinclair McLagan [who commanded the Covering Force], the War Office, the Admiralty, the New Zealand Govt & War Office, all saw it and approved it without comment, and even General Edmonds [Aspinall's boss at the Historial Section] himself pronounced it 'excellent'. Col Daniel [of the Foreign

Office] also approved it. The one exception was the Australian Govt, who asked to have various amendments made. Some of these amendments were fair, others were at the expense of historical accuracy; but in the new draft every word that was objected to by the Australians has been expunged . . .

Aspinall was sacked as Official Historian by the British Historical Section in 1932. Thomson surmises that after the sacking he took the letters that supported his original version of the landing and hid them away among his personal papers, together with his memo.

Aspinall's original version ran as follows. The initial landing at Anzac Cove had been relatively easy and successful. But in the afternoon, when a 'well co-ordinated attack could scarcely have failed to beat down the Turkish opposition and to carry the line to its objective on the highest points of the range', there was confusion among the Australians. Reinforcements were delayed; there was nobody in overall command at the front line to effect that co-ordination. Towards the end of the afternoon the 'severe strain to young and untried troops in their first day of battle' was beginning to tell. 'For many the breaking point had now been passed, and numbers of unwounded men were filtering back to the beach' in an 'endless stream', so that the gullies in the rear were 'choked with stragglers and men who had had lost their way'.

According to Aspinall (Thomson continues), the presence of these stragglers was one of the main factors that persuaded the senior staff at Anzac Cove to recommend evacuation. This humiliating outcome, which might well have caused the Anzac legend to be stillborn, was averted because the British commander-in-chief feared that evacuation would cause even greater disaster. For Australian readers, says Thomson, such claims were heresy.

It was the practice of the British Historical Section to circulate an early draft of each volume of the official history to the relevant commanders. In Australia it was C.E.W. Bean who circulated these drafts among ex-AIF commanders for comments. Then the storm broke.

For Australia had already established its version of the landing in Bean's own official history published in 1921. Bean also reported the stragglers, but argued that the Australian brigadiers who recommended evacuation were mistaken in their belief that their men were demoralised; they did not yet understand the character of their soldiers. True, some men of 'weaker fibre' retreated into the gullies, but 'there was nearly always present some strong will, among either the officers or the men, who would question any order for retirement' and inspire the men around them to further efforts. Bean's own conclusion to his story of the landing went to the heart of the Anzac legend attached to that day: He asked: 'What motive sustained them?' He answered: 'It lay in the mettle of the men themselves. To be the sort of man who would give way when his mates were trusting in his firmness . . . that was the prospect which these men could not face. Life was dear, but life was not worth living unless they could be true to their idea of Australian manhood.'

Bean wrote to the Australian Department of Defence saying that Aspinall's account 'if printed as it stands will undoubtedly cause an outcry in Australia'. His very distinguished Tasmanian (and ex-Sandhurst) friend General John Gellibrand told Bean that his worry was that the civilian reader would be in danger of concluding that 'a large part of the glory of Anzac is mere propaganda'. The Department of Defence asked the Prime Minister's department to arrange for the Governor-General to cable the British Secretary of State saying that Aspinall did not do justice to the work of the Anzac Corps at the Gallipoli landing.

Bean wrote tactfully to Aspinall, praising his work in general but pointing out two misconceptions. First, Aspinall had over-estimated the possibility of Australian success. Second, he thought that Aspinall had exaggerated the straggling out of all proportion. His own observations, and those of Australian officers on the day, were that most of the men behind the lines and on the beach were members of work parties, or reserves, or soldiers who had been cut off from their units and had returned to the beach for further orders. Thus the stragglers were not the shirkers implied by the British history.

Aspinall replied saying that he was touched by Bean's compliments and valued the criticism of the expert. He would make sure the reader was left in no doubt about the difficulties of the Anzac terrain. Bean's cricitism of his account of the stragglers, however, raised a very difficult point:

> . . . I at first wanted to gloss over any failures and to give only the best side of the picture. But though I yield to no one in my admiration for what the Australians did on 25th April, I have found that unless one does point to the confusion in the rear, one is doing less than justice to the superlatively brave men in front who, but for that confusion, would have been strongly reinforced and must have been able to deal with the comparatively small numbers of Turks who were opposing them and who were in equal straits.

Aspinall went on to say that his evidence for the stragglers came from Bean himself and from Australian-unit war diaries; and the only criticism of his draft that he had received from British Gallipoli veterans (most of whom had been at or near the front line) was that it had underestimated Australian confusion and straggling. These were the letters he subsequently hid among his personal papers. He quoted a letter from a Colonel Temperley, who had been a brigade major in the New Zealand Division, and who recalled:

> You rightly lay stress on the straggling and the fact that the gullies were full of unwounded men who had left the firing line. It exceeded anything in my previous or subsequent experience [Temperley's underlining]. I myself turned back hundreds of Australians who were coming back to the beach across Plugge's Plateau . . . with the story 'the Australians have orders to "concentrate on the beach"'. I don't think – in most cases – they invented the order, though perhaps they were glad to obey it.

Next the story leaked to the press. VILEST LIBEL OF THE WAR, said the Sydney *Daily Guardian*'s headline, whose report claimed that the British history accused the Australians of being 'a disorganised rabble'. Generals and politicians exploded in outrage. The former

44

wartime Prime Minister, Billy Hughes, announced that 'if such infamous statements are published under the authority of the British Government, how can Australians listen patiently to talk about standing shoulder to shoulder with men who slander them in this fashion'. The truth was that Australia's 'sons acquitted themselves like heroes, and with a heroism unsurpassed in the history of the world'.

At this point Aspinall was moved aside and the director of the British Historical Section, Brigadier (later General) Edmonds, took over. Thomson says that Edmonds, though he had no love for Australians – sharing the regular soldier's contempt for citizen soldiers – had few qualms about falsifying history if it suited his purpose, which was often to protect the reputation of the British wartime high command. In this instance his aim was to maintain imperial goodwill. He told London journalists that the 'canard' about the British-Australian dispute might have been spread by 'Bolshevik propagandists': 'it would be a good score for them if they could create ill-feeling between the Mother Country and Dominion'. In February 1928 Edmonds wrote to tell Bean that they had 'removed anything to which objection was raised' and enclosed the revised manuscript as evidence of 'our anxiety not to say one word which could hurt the susceptibilities of Australia or give the impression that the magnificent behaviour of the Australian troops on Gallipoli was not fully appreciated in this country'.

The book – Brigadier-General C.F. Aspinall-Oglander, *Military Operations Gallipoli: Vol. 1, Inception of the Campaign to May 1915* – was published in 1929 and favourably reviewed in both Britain and Australia. 'The controversy was forgotten and the Anzac reputation remained unsullied and inviolable.'

Bean had won, and the legend he had created remained intact. Aspinall withdrew to the Isle of Wight to lick his wounds. The judicious and careful Alistair Thomson acquits Bean of any conscious desire to manipulate history in the national interest: 'More influential was his intense emotional investment in the Australian soldiers, which shaped his perception of their actions so that he saw positive behaviour as typifying national character and negative behaviour as aberrant.'

As both a participant and an historian, Bean knew more about the landing than anyone else. But, as Thomson says, 'the limitations of his evidence and . . . the filter of his national perspective' meant that the military records of 25 April – which noted 'the considerable number of unwounded men leaving the front line' in the late afternoon – were not, to him, evidence of 'shirking'. Yet Bean's own diary entry reads:

> . . . many came down to the beach. The stronger sort would go at once to Divisional HQ or some officer and try to find out where their battalion was . . . The weaker sort would get into dugouts on the hillside, and sleep there. It was very difficult for anyone in these early days to find out what everyone's business was – and many had no business – I saw many who were simply down on the beach for information and swapping yarns.

Thomson surmises that Aspinall may well have had a different investment in the story. Bean thought so. He told a friend, 'I can't get away from the notion that he is on the defensive, and thinks that too much has been made of the Australians, and that he will even things up somewhat if he shows that they were no great shakes after all.' However, Aspinall's original draft was critical of British generals, as well as Australian soldiers. Among the letters supporting his first draft, which he hid, was one from a Major Wallis, a British regular who had served as a captain in the Australian 2nd Brigade; he described 25 April as a 'tragic day' of 'chaos' – which, as Thomson says, was not the language usually associated with Anzac Day in Australia.

What is Thomson's final verdict on the events of that day? It is, he says, 'enormously difficult' to tease out the story of the stragglers. What is clear is that there were errors of planning and command; that there was 'great confusion'; and that by the afternoon the men at the front were suffering terrible strain:

> In this situation it was not surprising that while some soldiers held the line, other unwounded men withdrew from the front. Each of these men may have been motivated by some or all of a variety of reasons: to help a wounded mate, to find his unit or receive fresh orders or

supplies, to avoid capture or death, or from fear. To say this is not 'disrespectful' or 'libellous'; it simply recognises the complexity of war and soldiering and of the Anzac experience.

Thomson makes an interesting general point about imperial relationships between the wars. British official war histories were sometimes reluctant to give the dominions their due. Australians were angered by British condescension and understatement. But when a public row broke out, politicians and historians in both countries sought to minimise the disagreement and to assert the advantages of the imperial military alliance.

The Peter Weir Film

But resentment about Gallipoli rumbled on underground. It surfaced again in 1981, with the famous award-winning film *Gallipoli* made by Peter Weir. He had visited the terrain and had been, he told an interviewer, 'awestruck'. He wanted to make a film that explained why a military defeat 'is celebrated both as a national myth and as the birth of our nation'. The story centred round two young Australians who joined up, travelled by troopship to Egypt and then found themselves thrown into the horrors of Gallipoli.

Despite moving and impressive battle-scenes, I found the film irritating. I was prepared to take Weir's word for it – an inescapable deduction from the film – that the shambles was caused by British officers, but I did not see why a serious film-maker should feel the need to load the dice against the British officers by presenting them as caricatures. They seemed very unlike my father or Captain MacVean, and still less like Blunden or Sassoon. One of Weir's officers actually wore a monocle. Working also against Weir's serious purposes was a scene of extraordinary self-indulgence when the scriptwriter, David Williamson, suddenly popped up, instantly recognisable because of his height, in a Collingwood jersey, playing rules football in Egypt before the troops went to the Dardanelles.

Finance for the movie had been provided by Robert Stigwood

and Rupert Murdoch. Given Murdoch's recognised ambivalence towards Britain, suspicious people suggested that he must have been particularly interested in this, the first film he had ever backed, because his journalist father Keith, in a famous letter circulated to both governments in September 1915, had blamed the slaughter at Gallipoli on 'gross selfishness and complacency on the part of the staff', most of whom were British; how different these 'countless high officers and conceited young cubs' who were 'playing at war' were from the 'fine young soldiers' of the Australian army! Rupert Murdoch attended the première in Sydney, and afterwards gave a ball with Stigwood for 650 people in the Lower Sydney Town Hall, which had been transformed for the occasion into a replica of the ballroom scene in the film, set in the Nile Hotel, Cairo. Guests waltzed among palm trees and were offered a Middle Eastern buffet of whole lambs, fish, tubs of tabbouli and trays of Turkish delight, the whole dominated by a large ice sculpture of a sphinx. Reporters interviewed the Gallipoli survivors present, without much luck. One said that anyone who hadn't been lousy at Gallipoli hadn't been there. Another said that it wouldn't make a very good recruiting film – a remark that struck a true sardonic Anzac note, which seemed more in keeping with the spirit of the film than the showbiz ball.

Lauded though it was, *Gallipoli* did not escape criticism. The most substantial Australian attack that I saw appeared in *The Age* two months after the opening. Jill Kitson began by saying that most people who saw the film (which by now probably meant most Australians over the age of nine) believed they were seeing what really happened. She quoted the historian who advised on the film, Bill Gammage, as writing, 'Great care was taken in making the film as accurate as possible. The main sequence of events follows the historical narrative . . .' That narrative, she went on, was to be found in the official history by Bean. *Gallipoli*, on the other hand, 'is not history, but pure *Boy's Own*'. She compared at length Bean's account with the film, which did not come well out of the comparison.

The film's underlying theme, she said, was that 'the Anzacs' real enemy at Gallipoli was not Johnny Turk but the British'. The only other critic who made the same point was Evan Williams in

Murdoch's paper, *The Australian*, but he did not emphasise it. He wrote: 'In an unimportant sense the film's tone is anti-British; but . . . Weir's aim is not to accuse but to explain.' In the United States, the *Newsday* reviewer wrote, 'Peter Weir's film invokes anger and resentment at the futile sacrifice of Australians by their British leaders . . .' The *New York Daily News* (then America's biggest daily) noticed a 'definite hint that they [snobbish British officers] viewed the Australians as being dispensable'.

The Prince and Princess of Wales attended the 'royal première' in London. Soon afterwards, in December 1981, came a furious British assault on the film that was a mirror-image of Australian outrage over Aspinall's draft of 1927. In this case the assault was led by Robert Rhodes James, a Conservative MP with runs on the board as a respectable historian, a former fellow of All Souls College, Oxford, a former clerk of the House of Commons and author, among many other books, of the definitive work, *Gallipoli*.

The film, Rhodes James complained, was a 'monstrous travesty' and 'an obviously intentional slur on British soldiers. What it depicts did not happen and is simply fiction.' He went on:

> It is melancholy that so fine a film, which is so eerily accurate in its representation of the topography of Anzac and in the details of equipment and training, should depict the suicidal attack of the Australian Light Horse at the Nek at 4.30 on the morning of August 7, 1915, as a diversionary attack to assist the British landing at Suvla. The British are described as 'sitting on the beach and drinking tea'. The landing was hardly a glorious episode in many respects, but the fact that the Lancashire Fusiliers lost 60 per cent of their officers and 20 per cent of their men in the landing should be one correction to that particular fiction. [The landing at Suvla had nothing to do with the attack at the Nek.]
>
> I understand that this film – and particularly this episode – has had a deep impact on Australian audiences. It is difficult to avoid the conclusion that to blame the British for the sacrifice of the Australian Light Horse, in defiance of all the facts, [had a commercial motive].

Rhodes James's father was a lieutenant-colonel and winner of a

Military Cross; his uncle, Second Lieutenant Roy Lemon of the 1st 6th Gurkhas, was badly wounded at Gallipoli. So, he pointed out in an interview with the Melbourne *Herald*, was Bill Slim (Lord Slim, later Governor-General of Australia). Both of them had developed a tremendous love for the Anzacs. He was not for one moment underestimating the 'incredible contribution' of these troops, but it was cruel for the film to depict the British as wandering round with monocles in their eyes doing nothing while the Anzacs did all the work. British losses at Gallipoli were greater than those suffered by the Anzacs. Angry though he was, he thought Bean would have been even angrier; he rightly revered the Anzacs, but Bean also deeply respected the valour of the British; and his account of the Light Horse was absolutely accurate.

Another historian weighed in: Martin Gilbert, an Oxford don and Churchill's official biographer. He was (and is) a particularly formidable man to argue with. Blessed with a rich Marks & Spencer wife, which gives him the freedom and time of an old-fashioned scholar, he has a large study in the family house in north London crammed with copies or originals of virtually every piece of paper that relates to Churchill's career, including of course Gallipoli. In 1971 Gilbert published volume three of his Churchill life, which covered a mere two years, 1914–16, and was accompanied by two hefty volumes of documents. *The Times* (proprietor: Rupert Murdoch) asked him to comment on the accuracy of the film. There was, said Gilbert, 'considerable truth' in the charges of British lethargy at Suvla, though Churchill regarded them as 'malicious'. But the attack on the Nek was not intended as a diversion for the British landing; and the film, focusing on the Nek, did not show the more successful New Zealand attack on Rhododendron Spur nearby, or the battles in which several thousand British soldiers died.

Over the years I have learned to restrain my indignation about historical films that make things up. A film is a film, the makers invariably say, and not a documentary. David Williamson had already offered this defence before the film opened. 'We were faced with the problem of creating a totally accurate background and with following the lives of our two main characters,' he said.

'In the end we discovered that the narrative had its own laws. These simply had to be followed, otherwise, we would have ended up with a documentary.' When I called on him in Sydney in 1997, therefore, I decided that it would be fruitless to cross-examine him about a script he had written seventeen years earlier, even if I were a master of Dardanelles strategy (which I was not), and that it would be more enlightening merely to see if, unprompted, he was in any way repentant about what Rhodes James had called a slur on the British soldiery.

Williamson would not object to the label 'left-wing'. When I saw him, he had just sold his rambling old house in the vaguely Bohemian suburb of Balmain – 'That house is historic,' the financial journalist Max Walsh told me: 'The first house in Balmain to sell for a million dollars' – and had bought a modern apartment on the nineteenth floor of a distinctly non-left-wing skyscraper block near Circular Quay. In the early days this district housed the dregs of the city, among the grog-shops and brothels; the poor have long since been driven out by tourists and corporations, but even so the Williamson skyscraper seems to be on full alert for a proletarian uprising. I was inspected by a porter before I could even enter the building. The lobby was large, containing a big bowl of dried flowers, a shiny copy of an old portrait of Captain Cook, maps, a telescope and a parrot. It felt more like Dallas, Texas, than Australia. I stated my name and business to the porter. He telephoned Williamson. Then he pushed the buttons that would allow the lift doors to open at the nineteenth floor.

David and Kristin Williamson (the latter a journalist and novelist) were apologetic about the security arrangements, but not about the view through their wrap-around windows: straight down at the traffic going over the Harbour Bridge, and to left and right the enormous harbour itself, dotted with yachts and ferries, sparkling in the sun. At night, when the lights went on in the adjacent skyscrapers, you could probably imagine yourself in Manhattan. Williamson, a bit of a skyscraper himself, invited me to sit at a table facing this panorama, while he courteously sat opposite with his back to it. He was barefoot and wore shorts, as if at the beach. Not many English writers, I thought – however successful – were this gloriously housed; even Lord Archer, in his penthouse beside the Thames near the House of Commons, could not compete. Here was proof that it was no longer necessary, if it ever had been, for an Australian author to move to England, like Germaine Greer and Clive James, in order to make a decent living.

Williamson did not demur when I suggested that his film had done more to fix a particular version of Gallipoli in the popular imagination than anything else. How had it happened?

'Peter Weir asked me if I would script *Gallipoli* for him, and with him, which I readily agreed to do; it was a subject that interested me and certainly interested Peter. He'd been to Gallipoli and stood on the shores, which I still haven't been to, and felt awestruck. This was a very significant, sacred site for European Australian society, and he wanted to make a film about the myth. We started with a whole panorama, almost a documentary of the whole campaign, and then gradually funnelled it down – as we realised that our original aim was impossible – to the simple story of two young lads going off to fight this war.'

How about the idea that it was anti-British?

'The scene that caused the most contentious and angry reaction from the British press, not to mention some of our press here, was the scene in which an officer commands the Australian troops in the third wave to go out at the Battle of the Nek to certain death. The officer was based on a real officer, Antill; he was Australian, but Peter's research had showed that he was a Duntroon graduate and that those sort of officers spoke with what is perceived in the film as an English accent. The uniform was Australian, but there was an Australian class at that time that identified strongly with Britain, and used very British accents. So in fact the Australian who orders them out to their deaths is clearly in an Australian uniform, but because he didn't have an obvious Australian accent it was assumed by just about everyone that this was a British officer.

'There was a later line in the film that caused contention when the Mel Gibson character runs up to the commanding Australian officer and says, "Look, they're just running to their deaths", or something like that, and the officer says, "Well, the English have got ashore at Suvla and all they're doing is sitting on the beach and drinking cups of tea." That caused a lot of anger, too; here were the Australians running to their deaths, while the British had come ashore to the north at Suvla, and instead of moving inland rapidly to join up with the push, the New Zealanders and the Australians were making to break through the perimeter – well, in fact that's historically true. The whole operation was meant to be a concerted three-way operation. The New Zealanders and the Australians were to stage diversionary attacks to draw the Turkish troops down towards the Anzac lines, so that the British could get ashore safely at Suvla Bay and move rapidly to join up with the Australians. That Suvla landing was chaotic and mismanaged. It was under the charge of an English general, who was in command of the whole Gallipoli operation, called Stopford. He is now usually admitted to have been incompetent, and the Suvla landing was highly incompetent, and they did sit on the beach drinking tea instead of moving rapidly; the whole thing was a shambles and so, in this sense, the lines in the film are totally correct.

'Having said that, the fact is that England itself at that stage had lost so many men in the war that they were down to what was described as bottom-of-the-barrel conscripts, because all their best troops were fighting on the western front. The ones that were assigned to the Suvla landing were not what you would call crack troops, and they were not well led. So there were extenuating circumstances, as is made clear in the film. But the fact is that Australian and New Zealand lives were sacrificed in great numbers at that particular time for no military benefit.'

He turned to the wider question of how Australians perceived what happened to their fellow-countrymen in the First World War. He said that the Gallipoli campaign was symbolic of a wider feeling among the population that the Australians were used as cannon-fodder. 'Certainly the casualty rates of the Australians and New Zealanders and Canadians in these battles on the western front were higher proportionately than any other nation that fought in the war. The effect of the First World War on Australia was devastating; one in three men of eligible age was either wounded or killed. So *per capita* Australia actually suffered mightily from that war – as did England, and as did France and as did

Germany. But *per capita* we did statistically worse. And the historical question is whether Australians were needlessly sacrificed by the English High Command because there was a perception that Australians were colonials and lesser human beings and therefore more expendable. That's a popular Australian view, that we were thought to be sub-human and expendable. Or was it that our own commanders volunteered our troops for the difficult assignments in order to prove how heroic and brave they were? There are two schools of opinion. Now whether they were brutally used by the English, or whether the Australians volunteered them – I don't know what the evidence is on that one, but certainly the popular Australian perception is they were rather callously used as shock-troops and suffered much higher casualties than they should have.' (Martin Gilbert, in his *History of the Twentieth Century*, says that when the Allies withdrew from Gallipoli 'more than 28,000 British, 10,000 French, 7,595 Australians and 2,431 New Zealanders had been killed'. Turkish casualties were 66,000.)

'There's some evidence from the war histories that the Australian commanders may have been eager to volunteer them. There's a marvellous scene in Bean; he wrote several days after the landing at Gallipoli, when the Australians and New Zealanders had established themselves there. Reports in the British press of that landing came back to the Australian and New Zealand troops, and Bean said rather sardonically that this was probably the first and last time that the Australians were ever referred to positively by the British press. They described them as tall, sun-bronzed, Hellenic warriors storming the bastions with incredible bravery, and Bean says the hills were alive with the flapping of newspapers as the Australian troops read their own crits. Of course, it was in England's interest to boost the colonials' egos, because they were useful, and there's some suggestion that from then on the Australians tried to live up to the myth of sun-bronzed, tall Hellenic warriors that had been created for them by the British press. So who knows whether we were trying to perpetuate a myth, or whether we were callously and cruelly used as shock-troops; certainly the second perception is the one that stuck with the Australian population. And that was reinforced by the famous

Second World War incident.' (We shall come to this 'incident' later in the book.)

I left Williamson thinking that if he was right – if the Australian population really did believe that the Australians, both at Gallipoli and on the western front, were callously and cruelly used as shock-troops by the British – then the gap between the way the two countries perceived the war was unbridgeable. The British have a folk-memory of Australian bravery in that war; they are not aware of this alleged common Australian perception and, even if they were, they could never admit that it was justified. These memories are too firmly fixed to be disturbed by historians. Australians are unlikely to revise the Anzac legend. When I told Andrew Denton, the broadcasting wit and a clever man, of the awkward fact that the chaos on 25 April 1915 at Anzac Cove had very nearly caused the landing to be aborted, he said that this information was 'like a slap in the face'.

Finally, one puzzle about Gallipoli is why both British and Australians remember the campaign as not only tragic but futile. Bean himself said in his history that, if the bungled offensive had succeeded, it might have resulted 'in the falling back of the already shaken Turks from Anzac, the adherence of wavering Bulgaria, the forcing of the Dardanelles, the fall of Constantinople, the opening of the sea route to Russia, a comparatively early victory, and a complete alteration in the course and consequence of the war'. This assessment, as Jill Kitson remarked, gives some meaning to the Australian lives lost at the Nek, at Lone Pine and on Sari Bar. Yet nobody seems to want to believe it.

3

The Puzzle of the Governors

There is no greater puzzle in the story of Anglo-Australian relationships than the survival of those constitutional coelacanths, the state governors. Settling down in Melbourne as a journalist in the late 1970s, I became almost obsessed by the most striking and wonderfully sited building in the city, the turreted and white Government House, on its rise next to the Botanical Gardens. If ever there was a reminder of the old colonial days, when Australia was run from London, this was it. Everyone knew that its architecture imitated Queen Victoria's holiday residence, Osborne House, on the Isle of Wight. But what was its purpose nowadays? What was the governor for? Nobody knew. Even before Federation in 1901, governors had long since lost their original role of maintaining civil order. The historian Geoffrey Serle says that as early as the 1880s in Victoria 'governors arrived with inflated ideas of their powers and were surprised to find that by local custom they were little more than figureheads'. Yet nine decades later they were still *en poste*.

One afternoon soon after I arrived in Melbourne I was invited to tea at Government House. The youthful aide who met me at the door, an Australian, possessed the perfect good manners that characterise the sovereign's courtiers — male and female — throughout the Commonwealth; the Governor, too, Sir Henry Winneke, a lawyer, was courtesy itself. I recall the comforting smell of floor polish inside the building and the immaculate lawns and herbaceous borders beyond the windows of the drawing room in which tea was served. A formal photograph of Queen Elizabeth reminded me that I was visiting one of a chain of no fewer than six comparable oases dotted about the continent – seven, counting the Governor-General's establishment – whose existence derived ultimately from Buckingham Palace. Why I was asked to tea I never discovered; nor, I dare say, did the Governor. Our conversation was inconsequential. Afterwards, however, chatting to the aides, I gathered that the whole building hummed with action from dawn till dusk: there were speeches to be written, invitations to lay foundation stones, to give away school prizes or attend agricultural shows to be accepted or rejected, state papers to be perused, legislation to be formally approved, reports to be submitted, dinner parties to be planned and, above all, the giving of offence to be avoided. The Prince of Wales was due to visit; who should be asked to the Government House reception for him? Should Sir Bruce Larrikin, who might any day be charged with fraud, be on the list or not?

All this social activity I could understand. I could even see that it served a sort of purpose. In Washington, like anyone who has ever worked there as a reporter, I was initially surprised by the way the President, being the head of state as well as the head of government, was frequently compelled to interrupt his serious business as leader of the Western world, the master of the nuclear button, in order to greet on the White House lawn a deputation from, say, the Yellow Rose Society of Texas. At least, I reflected, an Australian governor saved the state Premier time and travel (though this argument assumed that a Premier could better serve the public weal by sitting at his desk than by opening a new school in the outback, which was perhaps not self-evidently the case). Even so, this incidental benefit (if it was a benefit) scarcely answered my question. It was not clear to me why, if the governor's only political function was to give assent on the sovereign's behalf to state legislation – in other words, to be a rubber stamp – the governors should not be done away with altogether and the cost that they incurred and the buildings they inhabited put to better use.

Nor could I understand why the Australians themselves – noted for their pragmatism, priding themselves on their egalitarianism –

were prepared to tolerate these most flagrant relics of the old colonial relationship. Constitutional lawyers would wearily point out that they were part of the Constitution. Indeed they were. Consulting Professor Colin Howard's useful commentary, *Australia's Constitution*, and reading with care the little-known document itself, I found, however, that they were mentioned once only in any substantive way. This was in Section 12, which reads: 'The Governor of any State may cause writs to be issued for elections of senators for the State.' (They also feature in Section 15, which outlines the procedure to be followed 'if the place of a senator becomes vacant before the expiration of his term of service . . . [and] if the Parliament of the State is not in session when the vacancy is notified'. But in that event their role is merely to act on the advice of the Executive Council in appointing someone to hold the place temporarily.) The reason why a state governor, and not a state government, must issue the writs for senatorial elections was explained by Professor Howard with his usual clarity: senators represent the people of the state, not state governments or parliaments. He did not explain why this responsibility should not be undertaken by some other independent person or authority who could be trusted to act in the public, not the government, interest. The issuing of writs is scarcely a frequent occurence; and if this responsibity is truly, as it seems to be, the one and only answer to the question 'What Is That Man For?', then it sheds an odd light on the ingenuity of constitutional lawyers and the apathy of politicians and voters.

The fact is that the Founding Fathers, working away in the 1890s, with the British Colonial Office looking over their shoulders and old Queen Victoria in the background, took it for granted that under the new Constitution the sovereign would continue to need a representative in each state; and the states thought the governors would help them to uphold their separate identities in the new Federation. Hence they were symbols rather than essential working parts of the political machinery; a requirement, one might think, that has faded away with the vast changes in the world since the 1890s. Nobody considered this proliferation of governors odd and extravagant in 1901, and to my knowledge nobody has seriously challenged it since. Australian governors have replaced British governors, but the show itself goes on amazingly undisturbed; in Victoria there was a brief ripple of scandal in 1982 when an admiral–appointed governor resigned, after admitting that he had misused his office in the matter of airline tickets; in New South Wales, in 1996, the Governor was required to move out of Government House in order to save money; otherwise, little has changed in a hundred years, and the governor and the governor's spouse – in the eyes of those who are interested in such matters (more than one might assume) – remain at the pinnacle of local society.

The earliest governors' main task had of course been to run the colonies, not to provide a social peak for colonists to scale; but just as in England the monarchy, in Queen Victoria's reign, shook off its raffish past and became respectable, so in Australia it became vital during the nineteenth century for the occupants of Government Houses to provide examples of socially acceptable behaviour. As Jessie Serle has pointed out, the emergence of Government House in Hobart, Tasmania, as one of Australia's most admired centres of good behaviour is particularly striking, given the state's unpropitious early days. It took a while for Tasmania (hived off from New South Wales in 1826) to shake off its wild past: the lamentable Lieutenant-Governor David Collins, the founder in 1804 of Hobart, took snuff in handfuls while watching men being flogged, and installed the wife of a convict as his mistress in Government House. His successor, another drunken and lascivious army officer, Colonel Thomas Davey, was known as Mad Tom the Governor. He drank a concoction called Blow My Skull, a mixture of brandy, rum and gin topped up with port, madeira or sherry, and was eventually dismissed from his post after he celebrated the King's birthday by standing outside the gates of Government House offering passers-by a pannikin of rum from a cask.

Until the 1850s, when transportation to Tasmania came to an end and a new, substantial and elegant Government House was built, the socially conscious visitor from England was unlikely to be uplifted. 'A very second-rate society' was the verdict of Mrs Nixon, a bishop's wife, in 1843. But the handsome and well-sited building in Hobart, with its fine gardens and extensive views, and the sober behaviour of the later incumbents worked wonders; added to that, the interiors, in the expert opinion of Jessie Serle, were 'pure transplantation of British Establishment taste'. Thus by 1872 Anthony Trollope was so impressed that he called Government House 'the best belonging to any British colony', lacking 'nothing necessary for a perfect English residence'. He was equally impressed by the people he met, whom he described in a letter to the London *Daily Telegraph* as 'beyond measure loyal and English'. He went on to give his prescription for success in the job: 'It is required of a governor in such a country that he should not say silly things, that he should be discreet, hospitable, willing to spend his salary, and above all be a gentleman.' In respectable Australian circles, the quasi-monarchical role of the governors was clear: the ultra-respectable *Age* of Melbourne took a rather more elevated view of the job than Trollope. 'A solar system without a sun would be as great an anomaly as colonial society without a well-accredited representative of royalty,' the paper wrote in 1876.

Nine decades later, in the early 1960s, when John Moorehead, the English-born and -educated son of the Australian writer Alan Moorehead, made his first visit to the land of his paternal forebears, he decided to look up one of his school friends who, on leaving Eton, had acquired a post on the staff of the governor of Queensland. Moorehead had been roughing it after leaving his cousins in Melbourne, working in the fruit orchards round Mildura; he got off the plane in Brisbane looking less than immaculate. Thanks to the old-boy network he had been invited to stay at Government House, and his friend had promised to pick him up at the airport; Moorehead was nevertheless astonished when a figure approached him in a kind of fancy dress and swept him off in an embassy car, with the explanation that duty required their immediate attendance at some gubernatorial event. Moorehead found himself observing a ceremony that struck him as a Ruritanian fantasy, with brass bands, flag-waving and cocked hats with feathers. Forty years on, he recalled that his first thought was 'What a racket!' He was witnessing the lingering aftermath of the phenomenon – at its strongest between the wars – of governors as a system of outdoor relief for the English upper classes.

Lord Beauchamp

For much of the nineteenth century the governors appointed to the colonies were men of some substance: often army officers or engineers. But by the end of the century the general calibre of the governors had slowly declined. That in the following hundred years the governors, though Australian, scarcely changed the nature of the office was an astonishing example of institutional (or Australian) lethargy. The story of the seventh Earl Beauchamp illustrates both points: the astoundingly casual method of his appointment – which might well have caused deep offence to any sensitive Australian, had the method (or lack of it) been more widely known – and the unchanging nature of a governor's preoccupations.

I came across Beauchamp's traces in the 1970s when I was editing the diaries of Evelyn Waugh. Beauchamp was governor of New South Wales as a very young man, from 1899 to 1901. After New South Wales, he became grander and grander: Knight of the Garter, Lord Steward of the Household, Lord President of the Council, Lord Warden of the Cinque Ports, leader of the Liberal Party in the House of Lords. His house was Madresfield Court, an immense moated manor house in Worcestershire. He married the sister of the Duke of Westminster, who gave him a chapel as a wedding present the year after he came back from Sydney, and fathered seven children. On the least excuse he wore the blue ribbon of the Garter, and he always referred to his children by their titles: Lord Elmley, the Lady Lettice, the Lady Mary. Then, in 1931, disaster struck. His brother-in-law the Duke of Westminster accused him of a homosexual relationship with his valet. George V heard of the accusation. Three of Beauchamp's peers were sent to tell him that he must either leave the country instantly or face prosecution. He left the country. 'Luckily,' Lady Mary (known to Waugh as Maimie) told me years later, 'he had two hundred pounds on him.' He returned secretly to England in 1936, to attend the funeral of his second son, who had been killed in a motoring accident; a private aircraft stood by to rescue Beauchamp if the police suddenly appeared with a warrant. The truth, or otherwise, of Westminster's allegations has never been established. One theory was that Westminster, probably the richest and certainly the most unpleasant man in England, was motivated by jealousy: Beauchamp had had seven children while he had had none. Westminster was rumoured to write to Beauchamp: 'Dear Bugger-in-law'.

Waugh met Beauchamp's children when he was at Oxford in the 1920s, and the house and family inspired his novel *Brideshead Revisited*. Sebastian Flyte is said to be partly modelled on Hugh Lygon, the son who was killed: a feckless youth for whom Waugh conceived a great affection. Brideshead bears some resemblance to Madresfield. Thus Beauchamp might be said to be the best known of all state governors, because he became the model for Lord Marchmain, the owner of Brideshead, who lived abroad with his mistress. Laurence Olivier, who played him in the celebrated television series, milked every part for the last drop and enjoyed upstaging all competitors, boasted that he had exploited Marchmain's deathbed scene so effectively that he had died through two commercials.

Hilaire Belloc wrote a famous Cautionary Verse about little Lord Lundy, and how his aged grandfather the duke, disappointed beyond bearing by Lundy's lachrymose habits, summoned him and spoke the following lines:

> We had intended you to be
> The next Prime Minister but three:
> The stocks were sold; the Press was squared;
> The Middle Class was quite prepared.
> But as it is! . . . My language fails!
> Go out and govern New South Wales!

This more or less describes what happened to Beauchamp. When he first arrived in Sydney as governor, in 1899, he set out to keep a diary, now in the Mitchell Library, in the belief that that would help him to write the 'book which is now in my mind about Australia' (he never wrote it). An early entry referred to the Transvaal crisis and 'the excitement of speeding out our own contingent . . . very loyal feeling shown as usual throughout the colony'. He then, in a hair-raising entry that shows how these things were managed in the good old days, describes how he got the job. A year earlier, he noted, he had been making a tour of Greece; in Olympia he had viewed the *Hermes* of Praxiteles and sighed, in a sentence that the Duke of Westminster would have regarded with deep suspicion, 'Alas that in Greece we saw no one who for face or figure compared with this.' (Waugh saw the statue in 1927 kept in a garden shed and looked after by the village idiot and thought it 'quite marvellous'.) Back in Athens, Beauchamp found a pile of letters awaiting him. 'In the course of these I came upon one from Mr Chamberlain [Joseph Chamberlain, Colonial Secretary] in which to my enormous surprise he offered me the Governorship of New South Wales – I scarcely knew where was the colony and certainly nothing about it . . . The offer was very nearly forthwith refused so ridiculous did it appear to me . . .'

Back in London, he called at the Colonial Office. One reason for the offer now became clear. In a room next door to the Colonial Secretary, an official read him the letter of resignation sent to Chamberlain by Lord Hampden, the retiring governor, in which he complained about the expense of the governorship: it had cost him some £12,000 a year, a fortune in those days. Such complaints did not impress the Colonial Secretary; as he wrote to Beauchamp later, 'I imagined that it was generally known that the acceptance of an Australian Governorship involved considerable personal expenditure.' So Australia was to be governed by the rich. Luckily, an intolerable burden for Lord Hampden was a tolerable burden for Lord Beauchamp. He wrote a note of acceptance to Mr Chamberlain, then 'fled' home to Madresfield. Next comes the endearing entry: 'Lady Mary Villiers and her younger sister were at Middleton [Middleton Park, Oxon, seat of the Earls of Jersey] and the peals of laughter with which they received the news was not very gratifying to my vanity.'

His next stop was Windsor Castle, where Queen Victoria invested him with the KCMG. The room was small. 'The Queen inaudibly murmured something which I took to be "Arise Sir William",' and those present then assembled for dinner, at which 'the conversation was subdued'. Beauchamp noted, 'The Queen never sits next to a stranger.' What should he say to his sovereign? 'Having thought of her anxiety to be called Empress of India, I expressed some hope that Her Majesty should honour the various colonies by assuming some such as Empress of India, Canada and Australia.' To this initiative the Queen made no response, but instead 'complained of a lack of good modern hymns and prayers'.

Thus Beauchamp left for his post, on the eve of Federation, without a word of instruction either from the sovereign whom he represented or from the politician responsible for the colony to which he was being sent.

The governors formed their own network. 'Any chance of you and your party coming to pay us a visit here?' wrote Lord Lamington from Brisbane. Lord Tennyson sent an invitation from Adelaide to a formal occasion: 'I fear that it is a tall hat business.' The idiom was English; Lady Tennyson wrote from Marble Hill, South Australia, 'a perfectly delicious place'. But, to be fair, Tennyson and Beauchamp were not really, or not entirely, P.G. Wodehouse characters. They compared observations of the educational systems of New South Wales and South Australia. Tennyson told Beauchamp that he was 'just off to address a large corroboree of natives at Oonadatta in Central Australia and I have been reading Jenner and Lillens' book about them. A really solid excellent fine piece of work.' They were acutely aware of the sensitivity of their elevated positions:

I quite realise all you say about the troubles of Gov. House . . . impossible to please everyone . . . I think the 'fierce light' beats harder on a Governor's chair than on any 'throne', for the Monarch has so many lightning-conductors to avert the flashes from him or her, whereas the lower [rank] has to bear the brunt almost unsheltered . . . Lady Onslow used to say, 'One cannot turn one's head without their attributing a motive and it is generally a wrong one.'

Beauchamp made some shrewd and disinterested comments on politics:

On the whole question of the politics of the country I must confess I am disappointed. There was one admirable feature indeed in the absence of bribery . . . on the other hand, the standard of the average member was distinctly low. Socially and intellectually they were quite uneducated. The best class of lawyer or merchant or squatter held himself aloof and scornful of politics and politicians alike . . .

However: 'That the democracy do recognise a good man is happily shown by the list which was chosen to represent the colony at the Melbourne conference.'

Sending out to Australia as governors stray members of the upper classes, with no obvious qualifications for the job apart from an ability to incur 'considerable personal expenditure', had one advantage: because they were not part of any career system, they could take up a cause purely because it appealed to them personally. In January 1900 Beauchamp received out of the blue a letter from the writer Henry Lawson. He had heard that the Governor had spoken kindly of one of his books and was therefore seeking his help. He was broke. 'The oldest and wealthiest Daily in Australia fills its columns with material clipped from English and American magazines' and there was thus no market for would-be Australian contributors. 'Nothing goes well here that does not come from or through England.' Such contributions as he could get published were miserably paid: 'I send you specimens of the work I am now doing for £1 per column.' He had tried hard to get sent as a war correspondent to South Africa with the New South Wales contingent, but could not get any journal to pay his expenses. 'Will you help me out of the miserable hole I am in? I heard you were rich. All my friends are as poor as myself – I know none of our scrubby aristocracy, nor do I wish to know them. If you cannot help me, kindly destroy this.'

Beauchamp could and did help, while asking Lawson not to tell anyone. Lawson said he would 'endeavour to thank you in person for your generosity', would be able to get away in early April and added, 'your wish re keeping the matter private has of course been respected'. Beauchamp confided in Tennyson, who evidently with a touch of pride reminded Beauchamp that it was he who had recommended to him the Lawson book *While the Billy Boils*, and asked, 'How are you sending him home?'

Thus the central figure of a scandal of the 1930s (kept very quiet at the time) linked two wholly disparate national literary icons, the reactionary Englishman Waugh and the republican Australian Lawson – inspiration to one, benefactor to the other.

One footnote remains to be added. In November 1931, after the homosexuality scandal had broken, Buckingham Palace sent a cyphered telegram to the Governor-General, Sir Isaac Isaacs. It read: 'As circumstances do not admit of Lord Beauchamp being received at court it would be undesirable that he should be received at Government Houses should he visit Australia.' The word 'circumstances' was cleverly chosen.

Royal Budgerigars

Have governors ever been useful? In a spare upstairs room of the present Lord Gowrie's house in Wales is a glass case displaying the full ceremonial uniform of his grandfather, former Governor of South Australia and Governor-General of Australia. It is an impressive object, glittering with imperial nostalgia, and liable to keep guests awake at night as they reflect on their own drab inadequacy. Even in his own lifetime, few people were able to match the record of Alexander Hore-Ruthven, the first Earl Gowrie. Born in 1872, he went into the army and won a VC in the Sudan, aged twenty-six, for rescuing a wounded Egyptian officer from the legendary Whirling Dervishes, like a hero in the *Boy's Own Paper*. He fought at Gallipoli and was wounded; back in action in France, he won a DSO and bar. By the time he was appointed governor of South Australia in 1928 his proper mode of address was Brigadier-General the Honourable Sir A.G.A. Hore-Ruthven, VC, KCMG, CB, DSO, etc. Among the letters of congratulations was one from a friend in Moss Vale who wrote (too optimistically): 'You will be able to lead the life almost of a country gentleman and will have plenty of leisure.'

The Agent-General for South Australia in London wrote (more accurately): 'You will find South Australians an hospitable people with unquestionable loyalty to the Crown and to His Majesty's representative in residence.'

His predecessor as governor sent practical advice: 'Footmen

with us never lasted very long and we eventually had parlourmaids and were happier.'

Of the gubernatorial papers I have looked at, those of Hore-Ruthven are the best-written, in straightforward, military prose, and illuminate most clearly the nature of the imperial relationship and the attitudes of the best sort of old-style governor. Never, in private letters or state documents, such as the reports he made to the Dominions Secretary at three-month intervals, is there a trace of condescension: it was not in his nature, his training or his experience to be patronising; and he was better qualified for the job than plenty of other governors – Beauchamp for one.

But what exactly was the job? Hore-Ruthven was not without experience of politics or of Australia. He had been military secretary to Lord Dudley when he was Lord Lieutenant of Ireland between 1904 and 1908; he had been to Australia before, on Dudley's staff in Sydney when Dudley was appointed Governor-General. The fact that he had been wounded at Gallipoli was in his favour. Even so, Hore-Ruthven evidently arrived at Government House in Adelaide misjudging his role, and it was not long before he was compelled to recognise the limits of his powers. He attempted to mediate in a dispute between the shipowners and the Waterside Workers Union. He scrupulously informed the government of exactly what he had been up to. Nevertheless back came a sharp memorandum from the Premier: the Governor had done some good, but ministers 'view with considerable apprehension the possibility of the introduction of the King's representative into the dispute . . .' Would he please not do it again?

In 1930, after the start of the Great Depression, the Premier told Hore-Ruthven that ceremonial was to be cut down when the governor opened Parliament. Hore-Ruthven believed in gubernatorial ceremony, not for its own sake but because it drew attention to the imperial connection, particularly important at a time of crisis. He reminded the Premier that a procedure for opening Parliament was laid down in Colonial Office instructions. Nevertheless, the Premier replied, the governor on this occasion would kindly follow the South Australian government's wishes, not those of the Colonial Office. Hore-Ruthven complied.

His job often enough was to be a post-office, and as a man of action he must have felt the frustrations of this modest role, although he did not allow them to show. Soon after he arrived he received a petition from 600 British migrants, who begged to be sent back to England. They had been 'promised unlimited opportunities' by Australia House in London and felt that they had been misled. Now the boom that had been in progress when they had emigrated was at an end, and they were destitute. Could the Governor arrange for a ship to take them home? Or could the King do so? Hore–Ruthven replied with compassion and passed on their request to Buckingham Palace, but no ship came. Sometimes he was irritated by what he took to be the casual behaviour of the British government. In 1931 the Colonial Secretary, J.H. Thomas, announced that he would be coming to Australia and visiting South Australia on his way to the Imperial Economic Conference in Canada. Everyone was gratified to hear this. Next he said that he might not have time to come ashore and might have to see ministers on board his ship while it was in Port Adelaide. At that Hore–Ruthven sent Thomas a sharp personal letter saying that his 'hurried rush' would be seen as a slight: it would prevent the Colonial Secretary from acquiring a true picture of South Australia's problems and would be 'interpreted as a failure to appreciate the importance of the primary producing states which are the backbone of the country'. In the event Thomas 'reluctantly' never came at all.

But the main source of Hore–Ruthven's frustration was inherent in his position. He was the governor, the sovereign's representative, and *ipso facto* above party. He was also a soldier, and trained to be subordinate to the civil power. Running throughout his official reports and personal letters is the conviction that Australia could be the most wonderful country in the world, if only the politicians would pull together, like members of a decent regiment. Their views were far too often narrow and parochial: they had to understand that their problems were not local problems, and that 'until they can cultivate a more thorough grasp of economic facts and Imperial policies, and realise that their progress and manner of life will to a great extent be affected by the interests and aspirations of their neighbours, their commercial prosperity will not increase at the rate one could wish for'. He wrote:

> Australia should be the easiest country in the world to live cheaply in and in comfort. She can produce in profusion everything that she requires for the support of human life. She is under-populated and under-developed; there should be work, and to spare, for every able-bodied man and woman, and yet unemployment is rife and thousands are on the starvation line. Inefficient and extravagant management in national affairs are, in the main, responsible for this situation, added to which the people have wandered from the more simple pleasures of life and have demanded greater social services, and more costly amusements and more leisure to enjoy them.

Hore-Ruthven was not the last person to fret about this persistent state of affairs.

He went on: 'Besides being a rich and fertile county, which with the advance of agricultural science has limitless possibilities, she had a greater asset still: an intelligent, enterprising, robust and loyal people.' All that was needed was for the people to be wisely led, and for the leaders to refrain from petty bickering and domestic strife. He wrote these words at the height of the Great Depression, when unemployment had risen to around 30 per cent, the country was in turmoil and everywhere there was a general feeling of helplessness and hopelessness. Hore-Ruthven's own confidence in the future, and in Australians' ability to find solutions to their problems, did not waver.

He blamed the businessmen and well-off graziers as much as the politicians:

> Unfortunately the Australians of the better class are themselves a good deal to blame for the present state of affairs. They will not, as a rule, bother to take an active part in politics or in any form of public life. 'We hate politics', they say, 'and despise politicians'. But the present crisis will, it is hoped, make them realise that, whether they like politics or they do not, it is by politics that the country has to be governed, and if they decline to take an active part they have no right to grumble if things go wrong.

At the height of the crisis he set off on two morale-raising tours, first to the wheat-growing districts where 'I found a well-established and loyal community, who in a few years have brought many areas into profitable wheat production.' More land would have been cleared, he reported, had not labour costs been so high. After that he toured the farthest north-eastern districts, finding some of the most inhospitable country he had ever seen, and being reminded of the Sudan (without the Nile) more than anywhere else. No rain to speak of had fallen up there for five or six years. The salt bush was nearly all dead. The stock had been reduced to a minimum, and he thought he had seen more kangaroos than sheep:

> The people are wonderfully plucky and optimistic and a few light showers that they have had in the last few weeks have heartened them considerably, and I am told, though it is hard to believe, that after a few inches of rain the country would be unrecognisable. Of course large profits are made from this country in good or even average seasons, but the last few seasons must have absorbed the profits of many previous years and unless a continuation of good seasons comes about now the losses will not be recovered.

Hore-Ruthven used the word 'loyal' about the wheat-growers. Regarding himself as a representative of the imperial connection, he kept a sharp eye out for 'loyalty'. His reasons were not entirely sentimental. Australia was deeply in debt. 'The present depressed state of our credit has been largely due to our attempt to isolate ourselves from the rest of the world.' It followed that Australia, to improve its credit and to effect a reduction in the rate of interest charged on the national debt, must stick more closely to Great Britain and the rest of the empire. Any further separation would have 'disastrous reactions overseas'. Any anti-empire talk or actions would only further alarm foreign creditors and cause them to raise interest rates.

So he constantly used his limited powers and imposing physical presence to promote the imperial bond and national unity. He welcomed a visit from Lord and Lady Baden-Powell, which drew 40,000 people to watch a display by the Boy Scouts and Girl

Guides. His unveiling of the State War Memorial on Anzac Day attracted the largest crowds seen in Adelaide for many years. On the King's birthday 'the opportunity was taken' – taken, that is, by the Governor – 'to hold a King's Birthday Parade of 2,000 troops of the Citizen Forces . . . it proved a good opportunity of showing the Communists that we had an army, and the material which composed it was loyal and patriotic to the core'.

The Communists, then prospering, held a noisy but not very determined demonstration in Adelaide in January 1930, some of them armed with sticks and spanners. During a miniature riot, arrests were made. The demonstrators sent a message to the Premier refusing to disperse until the men who had been arrested were freed. 'The Premier happened to be with me at the time,' Hore-Ruthven wrote in his best regular officer manner, 'so we sent a message back saying that we were afraid they would have a long wait as the rioters had rendered themselves liable to a sentence of two years. The crowd then dispersed.'

It was during the misery and unrest of 1930 that Hore-Ruthven received his only direct request from the sovereign whose representative he was. The request, made on behalf of the King by a Mrs Featherstonehaugh, was unusual, and Hore-Ruthven passed it on to the director of the nascent Adelaide Zoo, A.C. Minchin, a forebear of the later senator Nick Minchin. On 24 June back came Minchin's puzzled reply:

> Your Excellency,
>
> In reference to the brown or cinnamon budgerigars that you are anxious to procure for His Majesty the King, I might state that personally I have never heard of this variety. Inquiries have been made from several aviculturists including Dr A.M. Morgan who is the honorary ornithologist at the South Australian Museum, but I can gain no information as to the variety contained in Mrs Featherstone-haugh's letter.

Hore-Ruthven was equal to the problem, however. Following further consultations with the bird experts, none of whom wished to disappoint their sovereign, he sent off – free of charge – a couple of somewhat similar creatures, and word eventually came back that His Majesty the King had received them safely and was most grateful for the present.

The Game Episode

If that was the most trivial example of Hore-Ruthven doing his duty as governor, the most important was his role in the dismissal by the Governor of New South Wales of J.T. (Jack) Lang, the state Premier, in 1932. Only once in a combined total of some 500 years of gubernatorial office since Federation has a governor made a serious political move, and this was it.

Sir Otto Niemeyer, who visited Australia from London in 1930 at the (Labor) Prime Minister's invitation, proposed a deflationary plan to deal with the Depression that involved balanced budgets and cuts in wages and government expenditure. Niemeyer, of St Paul's and Balliol, was a senior ex-Treasury official and Bank of England adviser − not the 'British banker' he was often represented as being, then and since, a description that makes him sound like a Rothschild capitalist, red in tooth and claw. Lang, an awkward cove at the best of times, took the contrary view; he proposed an inflationary plan, which included the suspension of interest payments to British bond-holders. He could not see why his constituents should be made to suffer dole cuts so that the British could continue to draw interest on their misguided investments. The crunch came after the Federal Government used its powers to take over the revenues of New South Wales. The Governor decided that a Lang circular instructing public servants not to pay money into the Federal Treasury broke the law. Accordingly on 13 May 1932 he dismissed Lang − acting in accordance with his mysterious 'reserve powers', which are not mentioned (still less defined) in the Constitution. Even this bold action proved unnecessary, since in June Lang was over-whelmingly defeated at the polls.

The Governor of New South Wales was a retired Air Vice-Marshal, Sir Philip Game, who had had a brave career in the Great War (five times mentioned in dispatches, and a DSO) and later became the Commissioner of the Metropolitan Police, which showed that the sacking of Lang by no means harmed his career prospects.

Hore-Ruthven, evidently untroubled by the notion that he was an unelected Englishman sticking his fingers into Australian elected politics, gave Game advice from the wings. He thought that Lang's plan to suspend interest payments to London would have disastrous repercussions on Australia's credit rating overseas. The spine of the Governor of New South Wales apparently needed to be stiffened. Hore-Ruthven wrote to him on 13 February, 'The consensus of opinion appears to be that provided you are satisfied that Lang's proposed action involves repudiation, whatever else he calls it . . . [and] that no other alternative exists to save the situation, then, but not till then, you would be justified in dismissing Lang . . .'

He added, 'You would have to be assured that the people were thoroughly dissatisfied with Lang's policy before you could act . . .' Hore-Ruthven had talked to the editor of the *Adelaide Advertiser*, Lloyd Dumas, and to his patron, Keith 'Murdock [*sic*] who controls a large number of papers in Australia'. Murdoch ran the powerful *Herald and Weekly Times* group based in Melbourne. Their view was that the 'drastic step' of dismissal should be taken only when there was no alternative; but if that condition was met, then, Sir Alexander Hore-Ruthven assured Sir Philip Game, 'you would have whole-hearted support from the press . . .'

Thus was Lang dismissed. Some quarter of a century later Paul Keating came to view him as his hero (despite Lang's lifelong belief in the White Australia policy), partly one may suppose because of the circumstances of his dismissal – the only time since Australia became a Federation with a written Constitution that a state governor has taken such a 'drastic step'.

The Game decision proved to be a severe complication in the debates of the late 1990s about the powers of a head of state in any future republic. Governor-General Kerr had sacked Prime Minister Whitlam in 1975 because he could not get appropriation bills through the Senate; Game had sacked Lang in 1932 because he acted unlawfully. It followed therefore – said the lawyers in the 1990s – that if you favoured a 'minimalist' solution to the crafting of a new Constitution, you would have to accept that the head of state's powers must include the power to follow these two highly exceptional precedents, particularly the Game precedent.

When the Constitutional Foundation appeared before the Republic Advisory Committee in 1997, its chairman Malcolm Turnbull said to Sir Ninian Stephen, the former Governor-General and High Court judge, that it was surely important for an Australian head of state to have the power to dismiss a Prime Minister who was acting unlawfully. Sir Ninian was bemused; he replied that it had never occurred to him that as Governor-General he needed any such power; he thought that allegedly unlawful actions could be dealt with perfectly adequately by the courts. Looking back, it is easy to see that that is what should have happened in the Lang case – it was the courts that had the duty to determine the legality of Lang's actions, and not the governor. 'It is a real issue in Australia,' said Professor Cheryl Saunders of the University of Melbourne in 1997, 'and it all stems from Game.'

I remained unpersuaded that six governors and their staffs were indispensable accretions to the already overpopulated, and over-privileged, layers of Australian government. I used to think, and may even have written, that Government House in Melbourne would make an excellent state casino. Had that idea been adopted, the present casino that disfigures the banks of the Yarra would never have been built. Another suggestion was made, more recently, that also fell by the wayside: that Government House should be turned into an annexe of the Victorian State Gallery in order to house the outstanding Joseph Brown collection of works of art, which he had promised to the state, provided that an appropriate and mutually acceptable home for it could be found in Melbourne. Alas, this ready-made, convenient and elegant solution to the problem was considered frivolous, and the governor remained *in situ*.

4

Royal Romances

It was the arrival in Australia of a member of the royal family that led to my next visit to Government House and prompted me to give a little thought to a recurrent gubernatorial headache: how to handle The Royal Visit.

In 1979 the Prince of Wales arrived in Australia for his fourth visit in a dozen years. Charles liked Australia; his spell at Timbertops, Geelong Grammar's outpost in the Victorian bush, had given him a lasting affection, apparently, for Australian openness, informality and lack of bullshit. Nevertheless, informality was not the keynote of this visit. Along with hundreds of others, we were in due course bidden to a reception for HRH at Government House, Melbourne; my wife was advised that she should not fail to wear long white gloves. After a lengthy wait in a queue of cars, we fought our way into the celebrated white-and-gold ballroom, whose dimensions would have dwarfed those of Osborne itself, had Queen Victoria not let it be known that she would disapprove of such grandiloquence in a colonial copy. In the crush, my abiding memory is of a small, anxious-looking, red-cheeked Prince, his stubby hands extended to the eager grasp of the throng, bobbing along on a tide of social rapture.

There were three other royal visits in 1979; the Duke and Duchess of Gloucester, Princess Anne and Captain Mark Phillips, and Prince Philip. The purpose of these visits was not always entirely clear, nor was it clear whether they achieved what they were presumably intended to: reinforcement of the ties of affection and respect between Australia and the monarchy.

As the chief chronicler of the phenomenon, Philip W. Pike, has pointed out in his book *The Royal Presence in Australia: The Official Royal Tours of Australia 1867–1986* (produced by the aptly named Royalty Publishing, based – equally aptly – in Adelaide), the show was initially slow to get on the road. By 1986 there had been over fifty visits; but until the Second World War there had been only six. The post-war explosion could not be attributed wholly to the speed and ease of air travel; it looked as if someone had decided that frequent royal appearances must be a good thing. Certainly that was the view of Mr Pike and his publishers: the blurb on the cover of his large, lavishly illustrated book says, 'This increased contact has served to endear members of the royal family more strongly to Australians.'

But has it? From the beginning, the Royal Tour has contained as much potential for disaster as for triumph, and nothing shows this better than the tale of the very first visit of all.

'A New Era . . .'

On 31 October 1867 Prince Alfred, Duke of Edinburgh, the second son and fourth child of Queen Victoria, disembarked from the steamship *Galatea* at Glenelg in South Australia. He was twenty-three. The Melbourne *Argus* regarded the arrival on Australian soil of a genuine royal prince as a sign of 'a new era in the history of the world'. Prince Alfred was met (as well as by dignitaries) by a choir of women dressed in white and men in black who sang 'God Save The Queen' with a special verse about the Prince, followed by the 'Song of Australia', which began: 'There is a land where southern skies/Are gleaming with a thousand eyes.' He was then driven into and around Adelaide beneath flags, garlands and portraits of himself, while women and children threw flowers into the open carriage. He was admired for the amiable way in which he remarked that he was not sure his mother would recognise him from some of the portraits, and even more for being polite about his first swig of Australian wine: he compared it to Muscatel or Madeira. Local delicacies that he purported to enjoy included wallaby pie and an omelette made with emu eggs.

He performed the royal duties expected of a prince, then and now: he laid foundation stones, danced with society matrons and attended the opera. His hosts staged a possum hunt by moonlight, and his sporting prowess at massacring native Australian wildlife was much acclaimed. It was not until 1978 that the republican-minded Manning Clark in his *History of Australia* took a different view: 'the air filled with the cries of wounded animals . . . birds were lying bleeding and dead in the bush . . . victims of the guns of the Prince and his friends . . . baby birds, the mating season being then in full swing, called for their mother's food, not knowing that now they would never be fed.'

In Melbourne the French Consul reported, 'the people, despite their deep-seated democratic feelings, are wild with joy'. Some of them were wild with rage: hostility between Irish Catholics and Protestants flared up over decorations that showed William of Orange triumphant; there was fighting in the streets on the night of the grand Royal Ball; shots were fired and one Irish Catholic boy was killed. The next night, 28 November, the mayhem spread. The organisers, keen that the Prince should meet the people as well as the élite, had planned a Free Public Banquet on the banks of the Yarra River; 10,000 people were expected; 40,000 turned up. It had been a sweltering day in Melbourne, with temperatures in the nineties, and the 'wine fountains' (also free) proved too tempting. The revellers grabbed the food before it could be laid out; the wine fountains were drained into fire-buckets. As for the Prince, he never appeared; the Police Chief had advised him to keep away. Next day *The Age* was stern about the 'drunken debauch'; the *Argus* called it 'the most miserable day in the state's history'.

A public banquet in Geelong, where the royal party shot 400 rabbits in three hours, was another rowdy fiasco; by the time the Prince reached Ballarat, the temperature had risen to 100 degrees Fahrenheit. After enduring a very loyal and very long address by the mayor, the Prince retired with heat exhaustion. In Bendigo a firework display ended in tragedy when three boys were killed. In

Tasmania, although he expressed approval of the Englishness of the landscape, scenes of public drunkenness did not go unnoticed and the rain was torrential. In Queensland there was more fighting in the streets between Catholics and Protestants. The royal patience was by now wearing thin. After a muddle over his accommodation, he declined to dine with the Mayor of Brisbane. Even so, the tour was thought to be going well. The press was almost uniformly positive; even the sceptical Bohemian journalist Marcus Clarke, to his surprise, found himself affected by the popular mood.

Clarke was born in England and arrived in Australia in 1863 at the age of seventeen; he was writing a weekly column in the *Australasian* by the age of twenty-one. To the end of his brief life — he died at thirty-five, having written one of Australia's great early novels, *For the Term of his Natural Life* — he was, according to L.T. Hergenhan, editor of his journalism, 'in two minds about staying in Australia'. Despite his doubts, or perhaps because of them, he was perceptive about Australian society. He had been at school in Highgate, north London, with Gerard Manley Hopkins and his brother Cyril, to whom he wrote in 1864, 'I am glad on the whole I came out. One gets such an immense amount of humbug forced out of one by the force-pump of society . . . I have found there is quite a deal to do before I can cry quits even with a colonial.' During the Prince's time in Melbourne, Clarke kept a cool eye on the more fawning officials and journalists, teased them for their 'tender flunkeyism' and was almost alone in making mild fun of the drunken excesses and social hysteria aroused by the royal visitor everywhere he went. He also alluded, discreetly, to rumours of the Prince's taste for gambling and prostitutes. When he left Melbourne, Clarke wished him 'God speed' and reflected, 'There has been little absolute snobbery here. Some few persons, of course, indulged in all that frantic and preposterous adulation of Royalty which is so charming a trait in the character of the British Snob.' Clarke was at his fiercest on the sensitive topic of class distinction in the colony. 'The sham aristocracy of a country like this is pitifully absurd,' he wrote. 'Every man has it in himself to make himself respected, honoured and enobled, If he does not do it, let him take it for granted that nature did not intend him for an aristocrat, and be content.'

On 12 March 1868 Prince Alfred arrived in Sydney. His programme included a picnic at Clontarf on the harbour to raise money for a sailors' home – then, as now, royalty made the best fundraisers. The Prince duly arrived by steamer and joined dignitaries for lunch; as he left the marquee to mingle with the crowds, a man stepped forward and fired several shots from a pistol at his half-turned back. The wounded victim was removed, amid scenes of hysterical confusion, to Government House, while the crowd tried to lynch the assassin. He turned out to be an Irishman, a religious fanatic and a drinker called James O'Farrell. (There is nothing like an assassination attempt to turn a royal visitor into an instant hero, as Prince Charles found in 1994.) Farrell's achievement was to create a tidal wave of sympathy and support for the Prince and the Crown. Fortunately the injury was not grave and three nurses trained by Florence Nightingale herself were on hand. By 3 April, the bullets having been removed, the Prince was able to appear again in public. Huge crowds attended a service of thanksgiving. Nevertheless, after this narrow escape it was decided to cancel the rest of the tour to New Zealand and on 4 April the *Galatea* bore the Prince away to England. He was to marry the Tsar of Russia's daughter in 1874 and died in 1900 at the age of fifty-six.

Thirteen years passed before the next royal visit. In 1881 two of Queen Victoria's grandsons, Prince Albert and Prince George, arrived at Albany in Western Australia. They were aged seventeen and fifteen respectively and as part of their education were in training as midshipmen. A further twenty years then elapsed before the first royal visit of any constitutional importance. In 1901, the year of Federation, the Duke and Duchess of York (the future King George V and Queen Mary) arrived on a Jubilee tour of the empire to be present at the inauguration of the first Australian Parliament in Melbourne. The tour had been announced by Queen Victoria shortly before her death; by the time it took place Edward VII was King and the Duke of York was therefore heir to the throne.

The royal presence at this significant moment was generally

regarded as a compliment, though the *Bulletin* warned of 'the coming crawl' and took to referring to the smallish Duke as 'The Mighty Atom' or as a fabulous beast, 'The Jookayork'. The Victorian socialist journal *Tocsin* was more savage, referring to 'class-conscious legislative councillors . . . the sad catspaws of ambitious title-hunting women, lickspittle junior officials, developing fungi from the university . . .' Huge sums were spent on appropriate decorations and illuminations, and when the Duchess herself pressed the magic button on 9 May 1901 that opened the first Federal Parliament in the magnificent Parliament building at the top of Spring Street, a message was telegraphed instantaneously both to England and all round Australia, accompanied by pealing bells, waving flags and countless bursts of the national anthem.

David and Mollee

It was again nearly twenty years before another heir to the throne arrived in the Antipodes for one of the longest and most elaborate of royal visits – one, moreover, that was still being talked about sixty years on. In 1920 George V's eldest son, Edward, Prince of Wales (known to his family and friends as David), was dispatched at the age of twenty-six with his cousin and close friend Louis Mountbatten in the battle cruiser HMS *Renown* for a five-month journey to New Zealand and Australia. It was the Prime Minister, Lloyd George, who came up with the idea of a series of princely tours around the empire, to signal the gratitude of the monarchy and the motherland to the colonial forces for their heroism during the First World War; he hoped thereby to defuse some of the growing agitation within the empire for constitutional reform. In Lloyd George's view, 'The appearance of the popular Prince of Wales might do more to calm the discord than half a dozen solemn Imperial Conferences.' Asquith, Lloyd George's predecessor, approved the plan; the Prince, in his view, was 'not sorry to be off again in March, even to so dismal a goal as Australia'.

In fact the Prince left England with great reluctance. He found formal royal duties a strain, and he had been home for only three months after a demanding trip to Canada; moreover, his first real love affair, with a fashionable young married woman, Freda Dudley Ward, was only a year old. 'He's as lonely and homesick as can be and is at present HATING this trip,' wrote Mountbatten to his mother from *Renown*. 'He says he'll cheer up later.' Like all royal visitors, the Prince of Wales knew that he was not going to Australia to enjoy himself; he had a job to do.

Now that the story of his aborted reign is so familiar, it has become hard to remember how much hope and adoration swirled around the Prince of Wales in the 1920s. On slight evidence (he had expressed his sympathy for ordinary soldiers and working men; he liked to smoke, dance, stay up late and wear casual clothes) he was thought to stand for youth and idealism, a new and better world, a more democratic and casual monarchy. He was boyishly handsome and golden-haired, and carried a hint of star quality. His tours of the empire had their ups and downs, especially in India, but have generally been regarded as a triumph – not least in Australia where one of the legacies was a lingering tale of romance.

We heard the rumours soon after we arrived in Melbourne in late 1977, for the simplest of reasons: my second wife shared her maiden name with the alleged object of the Prince's affections. 'Chisholm?' said a Melbourne hostess keenly. 'With any Australian or royal connections?' At the time this meant nothing to us; but a little later we learned that somewhere out in the bush was a household of Chisholms who kept a signed photograph of the former Prince, subsequently the Duke of Windsor, prominently displayed on a grand piano. Furthermore, one of the family, we were told, had borne a most striking resemblance to the royal person himself. It all seemed most unlikely. One day, we thought, we should sort it all out.

Twenty years later, over lunch in Melbourne with Patricia Guest, the city's leading *grande dame* of the old school and an elegant, humorous eighty-year-old living in a substantial house in Toorak with an enormous garden, we raised the matter of the princely visit of 1921. She remembered well how, as a small girl, she was taken aboard the *Renown* and allowed to sit in his very chair; how dashing he had appeared; and how she had always understood that his tour of Australia had done nothing but good. As for the Chisholm connection, she was blunt. It was common knowledge that the Prince was said to have had a fling with a Sydney girl called Mollee, who had subsequently married a man called Chisholm and produced a son with a strong resemblance to the House of Windsor; moreover, the boy was the former Prince of Wales's godson. The Chisholms kept a royal photograph prominently displayed and had never tried, our hostess reckoned, to discourage the rumours; in her view the alleged connection was socially useful. 'It explains why they were always asked to Government House for the Melbourne Cup when the Dela-combes were there,' she remarked. (Major-General Sir Rohan Delacombe, the last of the state's British governors, was Governor of Victoria from 1963 to 1974.) But did she believe the tale herself? Yes, on the whole she did; the likeness really was striking. 'It must have been a bit of luck,' she admitted, 'as everyone knows the Prince wasn't much good at it.'

It was not long before we learned of a further twist to the tale. A part-Aboriginal football player based in Perth called Scott Chisholm, whose sporting success had drawn the attention of the press in the mid-1990s, had aroused even more interest when it was claimed by his family that he might have royal blood, through his grandmother's relations with the owners of the station where he grew up. This curious ramification clearly merited looking into.

Meanwhile, contemplating the official record of the Prince's tour, it was hard to imagine that he had found time or energy to spare for dalliance. He was in the country between late May and mid-August, travelling from one side of the continent to the other. Although there were no drunken riots to contend with, huge crowds turned out everywhere to greet him. On occasions the enthusiasm was downright alarming; the Prince was several times plucked from his open car by excited 'diggers' and, he wrote in his memoirs, 'tossed excitedly about the streets'. By the end of each day he was covered with bruises. He attended race meetings and agricultural shows, Government House balls and Returned Soldiers Smoke Nights; in Ballarat he was presented with yellow silk pyjamas made by local girls who had each put in one stitch. In

Sydney thousands of children stood in formations representing the Prince of Wales's Feathers. When he drove into Queensland, it was across a carpet of wattle blossoms. He crossed the Nullarbor Plain *en route* to Western Australia by train, alighting at Ooldea to greet the legendary anthropologist Daisy Bates and her Aboriginal companions. On the next leg of the journey torrential storms damaged the track and his train was derailed; it was reported that the Prince was found waving a cocktail shaker out of the window of his carriage to reassure frantic officials. Such sang-froid went down well with the Australian public. The only dissenting voices came from predictable quarters. Radical newspapers wrote of the 'nauseating drivel' poured out in his honour and of the 'sordid extravagance' of his welcome, and the Trades Hall Council in Sydney passed a resolution enjoining members to boycott any royal function to which they might be invited. But it was generally agreed, and has been accepted ever since, that when he sailed away in August 1920 he left behind him a major popular success.

Behind the scenes, however, there was another story to tell. In Canberra, at the National Library, I came upon the papers of Lord Novar, who as Sir Ronald Munro-Ferguson served as Governor-General of Australia from 1914 to 1920. On the point of returning to England, he had stayed on especially to play his part in support of the Prince, and his papers provide an unusual insight into the amount of frenetic paddling beneath the surface, which no doubt has always been – and always will be – necessary to ensure the reasonably smooth progress of any royal visit.

In January 1920 the Prince's political adviser, Colonel Grigg, wrote in some detail to the Governor-General about the sort of tour that the young Prince of Wales had in mind. He hoped, Grigg emphasised, to see the people (underlined) of Australia and to meet as many returned soldiers and sailors as possible. He wanted there to be, in the cities and larger towns, 'a popular reception to which the general public will be admitted without ticket or social selection of any kind' and he hoped that only one speech would be required in such places. He would prefer no breakfast engagements and no engagements at all before 10 a.m.; and for either the morning or the afternoon of each day to be free 'for work or exercise'. And, Grigg added, the Prince did not care for too much exclusively male company. 'He likes women present as well as men.' All of which reads endearingly now, and provides confirmation from the inside of the Prince's relatively informal outlook; but at the time it was more like wishful thinking. As Novar's papers show, two problems bedevilled the tour from its inception to its final moments: precedence and exhaustion.

The trouble about having a royal Prince in Australia to represent the monarch was that he made the Governor-General, the monarch's full-time stand-in, redundant. Colonel Grigg spelled out the implications well beforehand: 'In view of difficulties created by precedence, the King considers that during the Prince of Wales' visit to the Dominions the Governor-General and His Royal Highness should appear in public together as seldom as possible.' Munro-Ferguson knew what the form was and accepted it; but it proved trickier to get the same point across to the state governors. The Governor-General did his best, as instructions and advice flowed on from London through him to the outposts. With the Prince's arrival imminent, he informed all the state governors that Admiral Halsey, the Chief of Staff, had cabled that 'HRH is very grateful to you for your arrangements which will make him the central and only figure on all ceremonial occasions'. Even so, some furious manoeuvring was going on. Both the Governor and the Premier of New South Wales, having tried and failed to get the Prince to take his steps on Australian soil at Sydney rather than at Melbourne, then took grave exception to the arrangements made by Government House for his arrival in New South Wales. 'It might almost be deduced,' wrote the Governor, that 'the outstanding question in your Excellency's mind was how to frame the functional ceremonials so as to arrogate all authority and position to the Governor-General of the Commonwealth and belittle the Governor of the State.' Munro-Ferguson was unmoved.

As the tour ground on, it turned out to be the Governor of Western Australia who was the most recalcitrant. Far from hovering in the background, he was determined to be prominent on all occasions. His method was simple: he waited until the last minute and then inserted himself alongside the Prince, knowing that it would then be too embarrassing to eject him. Irritated cables and letters flew backwards and forwards between the royal party and the Governor-General's office; one of the ADCs regarded it as his duty to report every move in the game. The final tussle occurred over the Prince's departure from the state; although he had specifically been instructed to stay away, the Governor insisted that his Premier had especially requested him to perform this final courtesy; he intended, therefore, to accompany the Prince to Kalgoorlie and see him off. Further representations followed; when they proved successful, a note scribbled in red conveys the triumph at HQ: 'Choked off at last!'

Meanwhile, those in charge of the Prince found that their pleasure in his evident popularity among Australians was eroded by increasing concern about his health and state of mind. By mid-June there was talk of somehow carving out a week's rest for him, as he was suffering from 'nervous fatigue'. The Governor of South Australia, Archibald Weigall (whose wife happened to be a friend of Freda Dudley Ward and therefore someone in whom the Prince of Wales could confide), was especially outspoken. The Prince, he felt, was 'overwrought' and in danger of breaking down. There was a real possibility, 'if not a probability, of ruining his nervous system for life'. Everything should be done to avert such a disaster: 'His personality is such a priceless posession to the Empire as a whole . . . the one thing he wants is healthy relaxation and a respite from public adulation and ceremonial.' The royal archives contain several similar reports; but George V, whose relations with his eldest son were famously difficult, was not sympathetic.

A handful of letters from the Prince himself to the Governor-General have survived. He wrote from the *Renown*, at sea, on the way back from Western Australia to Sydney, several handwritten pages of amiable, juvenile, slightly anxious and above all dutiful remarks, dismissing all apologies for the Western Australian railway drama, 'tho' it was a providential escape'; admitting to feeling 'depressed' that he had lost his voice in Tasmania and that he had been 'rather worn out so that I haven't been in the best of form this week!! . . . What a lot of trouble and worry I've given you and everybody else out here the last two months; I'm sorry and do apologise very sincerely tho' it's not my fault!!' When Munro-Ferguson wrote back, it was with shudders at the thought of 'what might have happened when the Royal train was derailed'. 'That terrible accident in WA filled me with despair.' In his view, the journey should have been cancelled when the weather broke. He commiserated with the Prince over the jockeyings of the local bigwigs in New South Wales and Canberra; the Prince's reply was self-deprecating. 'Personally I can't fathom any of it tho' perhaps that's just as well and it's easier for me to be able to drift along in a haze of political ignorance, tho' I seize every chance of talking to these politicians!!'

It had been arranged that the Prince should have the badly needed week's respite from his public duties in New South Wales, once the official round of ceremonies and parties in Sydney was over. 'I'm looking forward to my week in the backblocks,' he wrote 'if only the weather is decent as I'll get all the riding I want there and a chance of getting really fit again!!' Here, perhaps, my wife and I speculated, was the opportunity for romance, maybe with a pretty daughter of a well-connected property owner roped in to entertain him in the bush, away from officials and the press?

It was with this idea in mind that we learned, in Sydney, the true story of the Prince of Wales's Australian romance. A Mrs Judith Chisholm, who resides in the heart of the Eastern Suburbs on Bellevue Hill, having lived for most of her life with the rumours about the family into which she married in 1951, had recently written a memoir (since published by Northern Territory University Press) setting the record straight. Even so, it became clear to us that she remained highly sensitive on the whole matter, which was clearly a source of both pride and embarrassment.

Like other Highland Scottish clans, the Chisholms spread around the world in the late eighteenth and early nineteenth centuries. This particular branch arrived in Australia with the second fleet in 1791. James Chisholm was an army officer who settled in New South Wales, where just over a century later his descendant Harry was still living near Goulburn with two sons and a daughter called Sheila. During the First World War Sheila and her mother travelled to Egypt, where the two boys were serving with the Australian army; there Sheila, who was blonde, high-spirited and beautiful, captivated an aristocratic young British officer, Lord Loughborough, whose grandfather was the Earl of Rosslyn. They were married in 1915 and after spending the war in London, Sheila and 'Loughie' were among the fashionable young friends of the Prince of Wales and his brother Prince Albert. When the Prince set off for Australia in 1920 it was only natural for Sheila to introduce him to her family and her circle, including her great childhood friend, a doctor's daughter called Mollee Little. Sheila's brother Roy Chisholm and Mollee were romantically involved at the time.

When they met in Sydney, Mollee and the Prince took to each other at once. His staff had already observed that his passion for 'darling Fredie' did not mean that he was uninterested in attractive young women whom he met along the way. Like Sheila, Mollee was not only very pretty but light-hearted, outspoken and easygoing. It was evidently a great relief for the Prince and his friend Lord Mountbatten to meet a girl of their own age, connected to their social set and someone with whom they could relax; Mollee and her group in Sydney knew how to have fun and they were not overawed by royalty. Soon the Sydney gossips spotted that the Prince sought out Mollee on every occasion and danced with her as often as possible. Nevertheless, he sailed away in August 1920 and she duly married Roy Chisholm in 1922; their eldest son, David Anthony Bruce (who became known as Tony) was born in October 1923. Mollee and the Prince had kept in touch; she asked him to be Tony's godfather and he accepted.

One thing is clear from the dates alone: whatever went on in Sydney between the Prince and Mollee, he could not have been Tony's father unless they managed to meet again in secret in early 1923, as some eager journalists – unwilling to let drop the possibility of a royal cuckoo in an Australian nest – have suggested. This seems most unlikely, and the handful of letters and cables between the two that the family has carefully kept possesses a cheerful, impersonal tone that is hardly indicative of an illicit love affair. The correspondence, and the friendship, gradually petered out.

Why, one may well ask, did the story about Tony Chisholm being the son of the Prince of Wales linger on? This was partly because, as he grew up, he did look rather like his royal godfather. Had he been stout, dark-haired and hawk-featured, the story would probably have faded away; instead, when Tony turned out fair and slim, with a wide mouth and slightly snub nose, it gathered momentum. Even so, it was not until he was a young man himself that Tony Chisholm heard the rumours about his parentage. On a visit to England he went to see his Aunt Sheila, who had divorced Loughborough in 1926 and married Sir John Millbanke; she was still a society beauty and much sought-after. She told him that the rumours were untrue and he believed her, but the story has never quite gone away. It is as if some Australians still want to believe it; they rather like the fairy-tale notion – no matter how far-fetched – that a royal prince once fathered a secret Australian bastard.

A couple of years ago a book called *Letters from a Prince* was published in London that added fresh substance and detail to the lingering legend of the royal Australian romance. By a peculiar chain of circumstances an English marketing executive, Rupert Godfrey, had come upon a collection of love letters written by the Prince of Wales to Freda Dudley Ward between 1919, when their affair began, and 1921. A large number of the letters were written during his tour of Australia, and thus it was possible for the first time to read the Prince's own account of what went on.

The letters show that the Prince left England not only dreading his separation from Freda, but secretly hoping that she might be pregnant. Already, at the age of twenty-six, he clearly had strong reservations about the pomp and ceremony of the British monarchy and his own capacity to play his part in it; he referred to his public appearances as 'stunts' and told Freda that he had even begun to think that 'the day for Kings and Princes is past . . .' As for his views on Australia, he was wary of politicians and especially of Labor governments, trade unionists, Irish agitators and 'bolshies' in general. 'I don't think I'll get much respect in Australia, sweetie,' he wrote to Freda. 'Anyway I'll be very surprised if I do.' Throughout his travels he waited with impatience and anxiety that bordered on the hysterical for Freda's letters: his staff dreaded the days when he did not hear from her.

One real scoop in the newly discovered royal love-letters

concerned not the man who was to be so briefly King, before abdicating for love in 1936, but his younger brother Bertie (the future George VI) who, it now turned out, had an Australian romance of his own. While David was carrying on with Freda, his brother was becoming romantically involved with her best friend, Lady Loughborough, the former Sheila Chisholm from New South Wales. Before the Prince left London they would sometimes make up a foursome; they called each other the 'Dos'. In May 1919 David wrote to Freda from 'Buckhouse' that 'Do no. 2 [i.e. Bertie] is writing to Sheila, which won't surprise you . . .' When his brother borrowed his car to drive down to see Sheila in the country he remarked, 'I don't expect to see him tonight!!!!'

Before Bertie fell in love with his future wife, Lady Elizabeth Bowes Lyon, his name was linked with several girls, some more suitable than others; and it was almost inevitable that, like princes before and since, his early love affairs should be with married women. Sheila's marriage to Loughborough was not going well; the Prince's letters to Freda are full of sympathy at her friend's plight, but at the same time he plainly did not regard Bertie's romance as nearly as important as his own. Even so, it was causing concern at the Palace: 'Now as regards old Bertie and Sheilie,' he wrote to Freda *en route* to Melbourne, 'B talks a lot of hot air about HM making him a duke on condition that his name ceases to be more or less coupled with Sheilie's . . .' David and Freda knew that by this time Sheila was interested in someone else, but even so the romance had been serious enough for a while to worry the King. Here we have the full explanation for what has hitherto been regarded as an obscure reference in the letter that George V wrote to his son when he did indeed create him Duke of York in June 1920: 'I know that you behaved very well in a difficult situation for a young man and that you have done what I asked you to do. I feel that this splendid old title will be safe in your hands.'

It would appear that poor Bertie, more naturally dutiful than his glamorous and self-absorbed elder brother, realised quite quickly that he had best avoid getting too involved with someone whom he could never hope to marry. Soon after he was made Duke of

York, he saw Lady Elizabeth Bowes Lyon at a ball and fell truly in love. Unlike his elder brother, Bertie then went on to make a famously happy and successful marriage, which no doubt accounts for the fact that the name of Sheila Loughborough, née Chisholm, does not feature in any of his biographies.

As for what went on in Sydney, even allowing for the fact that he was writing to his own true love, the Prince of Wales's letters about his meetings with Mollee do not indicate a love affair. After their first meeting at a ball in Sydney he wrote: 'I met Sheilie's great friend Molly Little and had 2 dances with her and of course we talked about S the whole time!! S writes to her a lot and so she's heard about you and Bertie . . . She seems a nice girl and she dances well and she certainly has a look of Sheilie, particularly about her mouth!!' As the tour continued, he saw as much of Mollee as he could; the fact that this annoyed the stuffier officials made it all the more appealing. Mountbatten was also 'rather smitten with Moll', according to the Prince, 'though he doesn't often get her to himself as she is really my little "bit" or rather friend, as I've only got one "bit", my Fredie . . . Moll is just crazy to meet you and I'm sure you would love her, Fredie darling, as she has so much in her that is of our atmosphere and ideas . . .'

His last letter before sailing from Sydney on 19 August started with a wail of disappointment at 'no Fredie letter . . . what can have happened' and then went on to describe the farewell party on the *Renown*, featuring 'Mollee Little and 8 or 9 other girls, all bits belonging to and asked for by various members of the staff and ship's officers and they lunched on board and didn't leave the ship until about 5 pm'. Here, perhaps, we have the origin of whispers still current in Australia fifty years later about the conception on board *Renown* of a royal bastard; even at the time the Prince for once felt it necessary to justify himself:

> I've got a terrible haunting feeling that all I've said about Moll and seeing so much of her these last five days might make you thulky, sweetie . . . although we may have got ourselves talked about a little in Sydney, beloved, everyone knows it's because of Sheila Chisholm and consequently because of Fredie!! The only thing I fear is giving you a false impression of it all though I don't think I have really!!

Anyway, he added, Mollee was 'rather fond' of Roy, Sheila's brother. 'But enough about Mollee, angel; she shoved off with the rest of the women and we sailed at 9.00 pm.'

As for the connection with the part-Aboriginal football player, Scott Chisholm, this appears to be just another variation on the old gossip. The Chisholms moved away from New South Wales to run a series of large properties in the Northern Territory. In the 1950s, when Tony and Judith Chisholm were living at Anningie, 130 miles north of Alice Springs, relations between the boss and his wife and the Aboriginal workers were still feudal. They all knew their place, but they lived together on close terms. One day one of the housemaids produced a dollar note, pointed to the picture of the Queen and said, 'Him Boss's Auntie, in'it?' When told this was not so and asked where she had heard such a thing, the answer was 'All-about bin talk'.

The story among the Chisholm household servants that led to a renewed spate of royal cuckoo stories – this time with a fashionable inter-racial ingredient – was that, as a youth, Tony Chisholm had made one of the Aboriginal maids pregnant. It is certainly true that in those days, if one of the women working on a property had an illegitimate child, she would often give it the owner's name, which did not mean that she claimed he had fathered the baby. Nevertheless, to the family's embarrassment, an Aboriginal woman called Barbara Chisholm started to claim that she was Tony Chisholm's daughter; and when her son Scott began to make a name for himself as a footballer, she told journalists she had always known that he was special because he had royal blood. During the royal visit in 1987 the claim was repeated on television; the Darwin press even sent Barbara Chisholm and her mother to London and took their pictures outside Buckingham Palace. The British press picked up the story and printed photographs of Tony Chisholm, pointing out the resemblance to his alleged father. Judith Chisholm and her family were, and remain, unamused by this variation on the tale.

As for the question of why she and her husband were for many years on the visiting list at Government House in Melbourne, there is a simple explanation. From the 1950s on, whenever a distinguished visitor came to Australia and a visit to a property in the Northern Territory was on the agenda, the Chisholms would be asked to entertain them; the regular invitation to Melbourne for Cup Week was simply an official return of hospitality.

There was one last, poignant encounter, as Judith Chisholm recounts in her memoir. In 1970 the Chisholms were in Europe, and a visit was arranged to the Duke and Duchess of Windsor at their house in Paris. Once again the intermediary was Tony's dashing Aunt Sheila, by now herself a princess by marriage to her third husband, an émigré Russian called Prince Dmitry Obolensky, a nephew of the last Tsar and hence himself related to the Duke. The erstwhile Prince of Wales, once so golden and glamorous, but now wizened, elderly and leaning on a stick, produced photographs of his old dancing partner Mollee Little, taken in Australia half a century before.

Royalty Worship Continues

There were two further royal visits before the Second World War and before air travel to and within Australia changed everything. Neither of them was as fraught with tension as the Prince of Wales's visit in 1920, and certainly neither left behind such a tantalising whiff of scandal, but both made their mark in a way that the spate of later royal arrivals never did. In 1927 the Duke and Duchess of York (the future George VI and his wife) opened the newly built Parliament House in Canberra. After all, his father George V, when still Duke of York himself, had opened the first Parliament of the Commonwealth in Melbourne and his brother had laid the foundation stone in Canberra in 1920. It was the Australian Prime Minister, Stanley Bruce, who had proposed the visit; according to one of the Duke's biographers, he had hoped for the Prince of Wales again and was not best pleased when he heard that the Duke of York had been chosen, for he feared that the Duke's bad stammer would ruin his public appearances. However, the Duke had been having treatment with a leading speech therapist, Lionel Logue (himself an Australian), and to general relief the stammer was greatly diminished.

During the two months they were in Australia between late

March and late May, the Yorks too had their difficulties. It poured with rain for much of the time; the crowds at a Sydney ball were such that the couple could only dance together if aides cleared a space, and then kept the crush physically at bay by linking arms; and their arrival in Melbourne was overshadowed by an appalling flying accident that killed four men. But the huge crowds were gratifying, and they were able from time to time to escape to the races, then – as ever – the future Queen Mother's favourite sport. There was little sign in 1927 of any diminution of the royalty worship that had marked the visit of 1920; indeed, the presence of a royal couple, and the knowledge that they had left their baby daughter Elizabeth (just nine months old) behind, raised loyal fervour to new heights. One of the press corps was an Australian journalist, Taylor Darbyshire, 'Special Correspondent for the Australian Press Association', who managed to get a book entitled *The Royal Tour* out before the end of the year. An unabashed piece of propaganda for the empire and the monarchy, it boasted a flat but amiable introduction by the Duke himself: 'I much hope,' he wrote, 'that this book will be the means of inducing English men and women to take a yet greater interest in the Dominions and Colonies than they do at present.'

The tone throughout is one of breathless admiration and shameless sentimentality. In Sydney, Darbyshire relates, hundreds of returned soldiers, many of them badly disabled, were assembled in special stands alongside an enormous statue of Queen Victoria in Queen's Square, and the Duke was able to meet eleven of New South Wales's fourteen VCs. As for the bad weather, 'Rain spoilt silk hats and dainty dresses alike, but the guests seemed compensated for their discomfort when the Duke and Duchess walked on the lawns among them.' According to the *Sydney Morning Herald* – 'not,' wrote Darbyshire primly, 'a journal given to exaggeration' – the assembly crushed itself into 'one enormous phalanx of impatient adorers and swept across the lawn to the Duchess . . . she swept into the hearts of the crowd, leaving a trail of madly delighted faces . . .' Even Brisbane, 'supposed to be rather radical in tendency' in that it had a Labor government, 'set itself lavishly to establish once and for all that political creeds have no part in the minds of those anxious and eager to do honour to a King's son and his wife'. When the Yorks mingled with the race-going public on The Hill at Flemington in Melbourne, 'a mighty roar went up'; in the Duke's speech at the Anzac Day ceremony, 'one of the most emotional speeches of the tour', he spoke of 'traditions of loyalty, fortitude and devotion to duty . . . on the preservation of which the whole welfare and security of the Empire depend'. Sir John Monash, in his reply, pledged that '"Remember Gallipoli" is destined to become the watchword of the Australian people'.

In South Australia the Duke went hunting; he got a fine bag of rabbits and, 'crowning excitement of all, ran down a kangaroo, the Duchess following the galloping horsemen in a car'. In Canberra, the culmination of the tour, 'not one hitch took place', according to Darbyshire, 'but for another unfortunate flying fatality at the military review in the afternoon of the day on which Parliament was opened'. Of course he nowhere mentioned the Duke's stammer. In Canberra, in a temperature of eighty degrees, the Duke of York spoke to 20,000 people without hesitation and wrote afterwards to his father, 'I was so relieved as making speeches still rather frightens me, though Logue's teaching has really done wonders . . .'

There was one more royal visit before the Second World War when, in 1934, the Duke of Gloucester followed in his older brother's footsteps. Once again a royal train stopped at Ooldea for a meeting with Daisy Bates; in Canberra a tree was planted at the War Memorial, grown from a seed taken from Gallipoli; and in Brisbane the Duke inaugurated the first airmail service between Britain and Australia. The Duke of Gloucester was a bluff, straightforward character, less glamorous but less nervous than his brothers; it was observed in polite society that he greatly enjoyed the company of pretty women and copious amounts of drink. Well-connected Australian women of a certain age still recall merry tales of how the Duke would rattle their doorknobs after dinner, or even try climbing in through bedroom windows. He took two terriers home with him.

It was to be this Duke of Gloucester who, in 1945, became Australia's first and only royal Governor-General; but by the time he arrived the old order had been irrevocably altered, first by the abdication and then by the Second World War. At first the accession to the throne in 1936 of the Prince of Wales, whose 1920 visit had given Australians renewed confidence in their special bond with the monarchy, was greeted with the usual loyal outpourings, which were more swiftly than usual made to look foolish. When the *Women's Weekly* offered 'Intimate glimpses of our Bachelor King' it did not, of course, refer to Mrs Simpson; newspaper proprietors knew all about her, but their readers did not. 'He will maintain the domestic ideals of his father' was a prediction hardly borne out by events of late 1936. It fell to the former Alexander Hore-Ruthven, now Baron Gowrie (who was given the title when he became Governor-General in 1935), to deal with the aftermath of the abdication, which in Australia − as everyhere else in the empire − was generally regarded as the only way out of the mess. Gowrie was able to write to Lord Wigram, one of the royal secretaries, that 'the general feeling appears to be one of relief . . . it has been all for the best'. The Australian government, led by Joseph Lyons, was well aware that 'the prestige of the throne was the one thing that mattered'. It was a good sign that cricket was now back on the front page, he went on, and that the new Queen, also remembered fondly from her 1927 visit, was widely admired. 'Respectability and family life mean more than anything in the people's estimation of the Royal Family' was his prescient conclusion. When George VI and Queen Elizabeth were about to be crowned, he wrote them a heartfelt, if slightly exaggerated, message: 'I can say with confidence that Your Majesties will be in the thoughts of all sections of the community, of all classes and creeds in every part of Australia on that day . . .'

As Gowrie approached the end of his time as Governor-General − and acutely feeling the expense − he pushed hard for the appointment of a member of the royal family to succeed him. He said as much in his regular letters to the royal household. Australia 'feels a little neglected', he wrote in the summer of 1938, pointing out that both Canada and South Africa had already notched up two royal G-Gs. When it was agreed that he would be succeeded by the Duke of Kent, Gowrie was delighted and hailed it as 'a very important landmark in the history of Australia'; but when the Second World War broke out and the Duke of Kent wanted to remain in Britain, Gowrie agreed, with some reluctance, to continue in the job himself. The war that caused the death of the Duke of Kent in a flying accident also took the life of the Gowries' only son on active service in the Western Desert; with great gallantry the Gowries stayed on in Australia, and were only released when the Duke of Gloucester arrived in 1945 to take his brother's place. Thus the first royal Governor-General of Australia coincided with the arrival of the post-war world, which was to bring enormous changes to both British and Australian perceptions of the role of the monarchy.

5

Bodyline

Whenever I mentioned to people that I was writing a book about Anglo–Australian relations, half of them at once exclaimed, 'Bodyline!'

'I was there!' added Jeffrey Smart, the painter from Adelaide, long resident in Tuscany. 'Jardine, Sardine! Jardine, Sardine!' Instantly the words came back to him, among the olive trees and cypresses, sixty-five years on. Aged eleven at the time, he remembered arriving at the Adelaide Oval in 1933 at seven o'clock in the morning in order to get a good place on the pickets. 'Everyone in trilby hats,' he said. That was certainly true: I had seen the photographs. But in all the millions of words written about bodyline, most of which I seemed to have read, I had never before heard about that 'Jardine, Sardine' chant; it sounds like the sort of simple rudery that eleven-year-old schoolboys would have invented. How that crowd hated Jardine, as the England captain flaunted his social and national superiority in a white silk choker and a multicoloured Harlequin cap; and how he hated them.

'Bodyline' – to take pity on the non-cricketing reader – was a tactic originally called 'leg theory' whereby the English fast bowlers, particularly the exceptionally quick and accurate Harold Larwood, aimed at the batsman's upper body; the batsman, in defending himself, was liable to give a catch to the ring of close-in legside fielders. When Larwood hit the Australian captain Bill Woodfull in Adelaide and sent him reeling, the crack of the impact did not echo round the world, but it certainly echoed round Australia and has never been forgotten or forgiven. Douglas Jardine, the architect of bodyline, was a cheat. At that moment Australia finally lost respect for the English gentleman.

Non-sporting people have never quite grasped the psychological significance of the bodyline tour as a landmark in Anglo-Australian relations. They think of cricket as a game, and not, as the late Ian Peebles was the first person to remark, a way of life. The ill-feeling and mistrust engendered by bodyline, which rumbles on even today, did not come out of nowhere. Anglo-Australian competition at cricket has always caused bad blood.

W.G. Grace, the great panjandrum of English cricket, was the hero of the Victorian industrial working class in England, but he was no hero in Australia. At the end of the first of his two Australian tours in 1873–4 Grace imperiously led his team off the field in Sydney after a disputed umpiring decision. 'There were plenty of Australians who were sensitive to any hint of arrogance by visiting Englishmen,' said Grace's biographer Robert Low. 'One reporter wrote at the time: "Tonight we shall see the last of the English Eleven – at least such is the fervent hope of all in this city who care to see the game played in a courteous and manly spirit . . . in this colony at least, we have an intense distaste for bumptious and overbearing captains."' In 1878–9 Edmund Barton, the only Australian Prime Minister to act as a first-class cricket umpire, had to quell a riot in Sydney during an Anglo-Australian match. And in 1891, on his second tour, Grace again made himself unpopular, after persistent disputes with the umpires. He was too keen on winning at any price. Australians preferred the gentlemanly type of amateur captain who got beaten with style, such as A.N. Hornby, the Harrovian, who – 'true sportsman that he is,' wrote the Australian player Tom Horan – came into the Australians' dressing room after their famous victory at the Oval in 1882 and congratulated them on their 'splendid uphill game'. This was the victory that inspired the Ashes, the match when one spectator dropped dead and another gnawed through the handle of his umbrella. When Lord Sheffield, the sponsor of Grace's second tour, arrived at the Melbourne cricket ground, the band struck up 'A Fine Old English Gentleman' to the applause of the populace. Nobody thought Grace a gentleman, with his gamesmanship bordering on sharp practice, his demand for vast playing fees and his high West Country voice. Spofforth, the greatest bowler of all time, used to caper down the wicket in glee whenever he dismissed Grace.

In those days Australia was looking for sources of pride and unity. Melbourne was thought by some to be the finest Victorian city in the world; but that sounded like an empty boast when compared with, for instance, the Victorian grandeur of Manchester. And with whom were Australians to compare themselves, if not England? Literature: Henry Lawson versus Shakespeare. Painting: most of the best-known Australian painters were in any case from England; and who had heard of Tom Roberts outside Australia? Politics: Gladstone, Disraeli, Lloyd George versus . . . who? But sport: that was a different matter; and sport in those days meant cricket. The great batsman Victor Trumper did not quite fill the bill as sporting hero; his universal popularity depended to a degree on his modesty. 'Tiger' Smith, the young English wicketkeeper who toured Australia in 1911–12, described Trumper as 'a most un-Australian person'. But at last there appeared an Australian counter to English superiority: W.W. Armstrong, a huge, confident, powerful figure whose personal and sporting dominance gave all his fellow-countrymen someone to admire and applaud at an anxious period in the fortunes of Australia itself, as it struggled to deal with the consequences of the First World War.

If that sounds exaggerated, we can call Manning Clark as a witness. According to *Wisden*, he would have got a cricket blue at Oxford in 1940 but for the Second World War. He has written:

> The horrors and the casualties of the First World War had conferred on the heroes of the cricket field the role of taking revenge on the English for their alleged indifference to the lives of Australian soldiers in the war. Experiences at Gallipoli, the Somme, Pozières, Ypres, and Passchendaele had planted the idea in some Australian minds that the English upper classes were prepared to use Australians as cannon fodder to preserve their own privileged position in the world.

Australians suspected that their own soldiers were vastly superior to the English; that the Digger had the courage, the resources and the initiative so lacking in the Tommy. The first cricket test series in Australia in 1920–1 degenerated from a trial of strength and skill into an occasion for settling such scores. The Australians won the series easily, and the Australian captain emerged as a national hero.

Armstrong looked the part: over six foot six tall, twenty-two stone when he was aged forty-two and winning his eighth consecutive test match against England. Australians loved him because of his will to win. 'He bore himself in a way likely to cause offence,' stated his obituary in *Wisden*. Once he deliberately provoked the England captain, the Hon. Lionel Tennyson, a grandson of the poet and son of the former Governor of South Australia; bored at the prospect of a draw, Armstrong 'actually picked up and read a fully extended newspaper that was blown from the crowd' – a famous insult.

The Background to Bodyline

But Armstrong fades into insignificance beside Donald Bradman, and not only because Bradman was a better player. 'The Boy from Bowral' started to acquire national status in 1928–9, when an Australian crowd gave him such an enthusiastic reception that the English eleven sat down in the field and waited for the racket to stop. He became a permanent hero. Part of the South Australia State Library in Adelaide has been turned into a shrine to him, with items of his clothing behind glass and volume after volume of his press cuttings carefully bound and preserved; a poster for the late extra edition of the *Star*, the London evening paper, dated 20 August 1930 is wonderfully nostalgic, reading simply: HE'S OUT. In 1996 the Royal Australian Mint produced a 'special uncirculated coin', worth five dollars, 'as a tribute to Sir Donald' – 'greatest cricketer ever to play the game'. On 1 January 1997 Australia Post made what it called an 'historic stamp issue'. Australian stamps had featured famous Australians before then – Caroline Chisholm and Kingsford Smith, for example – but now Australia Post was featuring 'a living Australian for the first time. As part of Australia Day celebrations, Australia Post has instituted the Australian

Legends Award to honour a prominent Australian. Sir Donald Bradman, considered the greatest cricketer ever to play the game, is the first Australian to be honoured as an Australian legend.' A special stamped envelope showed Bradman, on his first tour of England, going out to bat on the first day of the third test at Leeds, when he scored 309 not out during one day. On the back of the envelope, Australia Post noted: 'A few years later, during the English tour of Australia in 1932–33, the English team introduced bodyline bowling to combat his remarkable talents. Even Bradman's retirement from cricket in 1949, after achieving an extraordinary test average of 99.94 runs, seemed only to increase his fame and the admiration of his fellows.'

Why did Australia have no other heroes? Manning Clark, in a rather overheated essay, makes the unspoken assumption that Australia defined and chose its heroes entirely in relation to England. The early colonial phase, when the settlers drank toasts to Pitt, Nelson and Wellington as 'the victors in the titanic struggle between liberty and despotism', soon passed. The great explorers were heroes in their day, with highways, streets, suburbs and federal electorates named after them; but at the end of the nineteenth century, in the eyes of the new nationalists, the explorers were found wanting: many of them were not democratic; some were army officers; some had 'modelled themselves on the English governing classes'. The bushranger Ned Kelly 'embodied the aspirations of those who resented British condescension towards the colonials', but scared 'the Anglophiles'. The First World War produced the unsung heroes whose statues and memorials are to be found in virtually every Australian city and town, but there is a marked absence of memorials to named heroes – no generals or admirals; no Australian politician qualifies. Alfred Deakin was a hero to the conservatives; but he was an 'Australian Briton'. Billy Hughes, another Prime Minister, started as the soldiers' hero, but after he 'made a bargain with the traditional enemies of the Australian working classes ... the English governing establishment, to introduce conscription', the 'little digger' was transformed into a Judas. Between 1925 and 1932 Jack Lang was the people's hero, but only in New South Wales, as 'he held up to ridicule and hatred the imaginary enemies of the people – the Jewish overseas bankers, especially in London, the coloured peoples of the western Pacific, and all effeminate Englishmen'. Not a very secure base for a lasting reputation, one would hope. The Labor Prime Minister John Curtin 'dropped his sword before the giant of British philistinism', while Robert Menzies was 'an apologist for British civilisation'. That ruled him out.

Australia has no Lincoln or Washington, no Nelson or Churchill, no Lenin, no Gandhi. Charles Williams – Lord Williams of Elvel – wrote a biography of Bradman in 1996 and called him both 'without exaggeration . . . the greatest of all Australian heroes' and an 'icon'; and he justified these descriptions by fitting Bradman into his context – the only biography of the cricketer to do so.

Williams, born in 1933, captained Oxford and played first-class cricket for Essex. He then became a prominent merchant banker, with left-wing leanings; the Labour Party made him a life peer and deputy Labour leader in the House of Lords. In the biography his sympathy with the Australian officials at the time of bodyline, who felt they were dealing with a lot of stuffed shirts at Lord's, comes through strongly. Bradman, he argues, originally became a national hero because, as the scourge of England, he was the sole source of hope and pride in the depression of the late 1920s and early 1930s – a depression that the City of London had helped to produce, as Williams the banker stresses.

My own prejudice had long since led me to the same conclusion, and I was gratified to have it supported by a professional. Bradman the fresh-faced boy from the bush moved to Sydney – the move that opened his glittering career – in 1928. The year before, at the opening of the new Federal Parliament building in Canberra, Prime Minister Bruce had announced that Australia was 'on the threshold of achievement'. For dud prophecies, this took some beating. In fact, it was on the brink of the worst depression it had known. Throughout the 1920s Australia, and especially New South Wales, had overborrowed in London. By the spring of 1928 the price of wheat and wool was falling sharply. A loan issue for the Commonwealth of Australia in January 1929 fell flat – 84 per cent was left with the underwriters.

Australia, said the financiers, must put its house in order: which meant a deflationary and monetary squeeze. This was the very period in which, in the test series against England between October 1928 and March 1929, Bradman first became a household name and national champion – already, and rather absurdly, compared to W.G. Grace.

The recession that was already under way developed into the Great Depression in 1929, after the Wall Street Crash. James Scullin, the Labor Prime Minister elected in 1929, was scarcely up to coping with a worldwide slump. His first reaction to the crash was to announce that it would benefit Australia – another dud forecast. On the contrary, Australia was particularly badly affected. Externally, wool and wheat prices collapsed and overseas loans dried up. Internally, droughts and the existing recession made things even worse. By 1932 unemployment stood at 30 per cent and many others were only partly employed: wages, prices, company profits, dividends and interest rates all fell. The social cost was high: divisions caused by the uncertainties and suffering ran deep; violence was in the air, and sometimes on the streets; politicians seemed to the ordinary voters to be more interested in faction-fighting than in the general welfare; irregular political movements surfaced.

Bradman's early triumphs of 1928 were repeated still more emphatically in England in 1930; as the country went down, so Bradman went up. In him alone could Australia take pride. The Adelaide test that brought the bodyline crisis to a head came after the visit of Sir Otto Niemeyer, representing the London bankers – the villains of the piece, from the point of view of many Australians – and the sacking of Jack Lang. In his biography Williams, writing as a banker, agrees with those Australians.

Soon after his biography came out, I talked to Williams in the Long Room at Lord's, the most beautiful room (to cricketers) in England, overlooking the sacred turf on a glorious summer morning. No game was in progress; the Long Room was empty; and we were conscious of the all-seeing eye of Sir Donald himself, whose portrait looks down the length of room, smiling faintly – just as he used to smile, both maddening and terrifying opposing bowlers, when he took his motionless stance at the crease.

103

Coming into the room, Lord Williams sniffed. He remembered how he always used to be conscious of the distinctive smell of its floor polish when he walked through on his way out to bat. When did he last play? Four years earlier the annual Lords v. Commons cricket match had been revived and played at the Foster's Oval (as it is now called). Williams captained the Lords. 'It's an argument for a hereditary peerage,' he said laughing. 'We had four former captains of Eton.' One of them was a duke. The Lords could have won easily but Williams, who made forty before retiring, contrived a draw.

Bradman, he said, was the outstanding example of a sportsman who played 'an iconic role' in the history of his country. 'Perhaps Jesse Owens had had a similar status among black Americans; but it's very difficult to think of any other sportsman who occupied that role.'

The connection between sporting performances and national status was becoming more and more exaggerated. Nigeria had declared a national holiday when one of their team won a gold medal at the Atlanta Olympics. This connection was not new. Williams referred to the epigraph of his book, a quote from Pindar about Xenophon of Corinth, who in the Olympic Games of 484 BC won both the short sprint and pentathlon on the same day: 'he achieved things that no mortal man had achieved before,' Pindar wrote. Xenophon's feat transformed Corinth's reputation: until then, said Williams, Corinth had been 'just a boring old town'.

One point about Williams's performance particularly interested me, and this was how he had penetrated Bradman's notoriously elaborate defences and secured an interview. I had had one or two failures myself over the years. In 1959 I was in the lobby of the Windsor Hotel in Melbourne when Bradman walked in through the front door. It was a tense moment in Anglo-Australian relations, since the touring England test team was convinced that one of the Australian fast bowlers, Ian Meckiff, was a chucker. Bradman was a member of the Australian Board of Control. As he approached the lift, I approached him, identifying myself and my newspaper and asking an anodyne introductory question that I thought any decent Aussie would be bound – if only out of politeness – to pause to acknowledge. He did not pause. The

Windsor then had one of those lifts with open, see-through metal doors. Bradman stepped in, pushed the button, the doors clanged shut and, as the lift began its ascent, he rapped out in his high voice, 'No comment,' leaving me to watch his trousers disappear smoothly upwards.

Twenty years later I pursued him again. In 1978 *The Observer* in London asked me to try to arrange a conversation between Bradman and Sir Leonard Hutton in Melbourne. Hutton was ready to fly out. I wrote a careful letter to Bradman in Adelaide, designed to dispel any possible reservations he might have: he would see final proofs, have a veto over the text and headlines, and so on. Then I rang him up. I do not believe that any of his answers to my increasingly desperate questions was longer than a polite monosyllable. He would not do it, and that was that. It was, as R.C. Roberson-Glasgow wrote about playing against him, 'like bowling to God on concrete'.

Williams arranged his own meeting through his old Oxford cricketing contemporary, Colin Cowdrey, who approached the South Australian Cricket Association, which in turn gave Williams precise instructions about when to go to which gate at the Adelaide Oval; how he should then proceed to the Committee Room; and how Sir Donald would arrive at a certain time by walking up certain stairs. It sounded like having an audience with Louis XIV. The House of Lords seems to have played its part. A meeting with Lord Williams may have struck Sir Donald as more worthwhile than a meeting with a plain Mr Williams.

Bradman, it appears, has never particularly relished his iconic standing; but, having been placed on a pedestal, he has been determined to stay there. Williams sent his manuscript to Bradman, whose most serious objection was to Williams's account of the notorious incident during the first test of the 1946–7 Ashes series, which soured the rest of that tour. The Englishmen were convinced that Bradman had been caught in the slips when he had scored 28 (he went on to make 187); Bradman did not leave the crease, and the umpire gave him not out.

It was suggested that he must have known he was out and should have walked, without waiting for the umpire's decision. Bradman always said he did not think he had given a catch, and neither did the umpire; and so of course he batted on. But he felt that his honour had been impugned. Fifty years later, reading Williams's account, Bradman was evidently still sensitive on the topic. He thought the book had exaggerated the incident's importance; and he also thought Williams made too much of the English witnesses and not enough of the evidence of Lindsay Hassett, batting at the other end, who agreed with Bradman.

Williams's published account states cautiously that of course Bradman did not think he was out (that is, he acted honourably); and that the truth will never now be known.

The English Gentleman Cheats

Jeffrey Smart was not the only spectator-survivor of the Adelaide test to whom I talked sixty-five years after that disastrous match. Ian McLachlan belonged to a substantial property-owning family; was later the friend and golfing partner of Bradman; and father of Ian junior, Cambridge and South Australian cricketer, grazier-politician . and member of the 1996 Liberal government. McLachlan was in the Members Stand on the electrifying Saturday when one ball from Larwood brought bodyline to a climax. After Larwood hit Woodfull, the Australian captain, over the heart, making him stagger as if shot, the crowd erupted in a storm of shouting and abuse. Jardine then behaved in a way that was barely rational. First, he visibly congratulated Larwood. Then, at the beginning of Larwood's next over to Woodfull, who was still plainly groggy, he swung the field into the bodyline setting – in effect announcing, as Robert Menzies, who was sitting in the Committee Box, later wrote, 'that bodyline was designed as a physical attack, no more, no less' – and a clear warning to Bradman, who was batting at the other end. At that, it looked as if the packed, enraged crowd might storm the pickets and invade the ground.

At the end of the day's play McLachlan walked back to dinner at the Adelaide Club, where he found the members taking the view that bodyline was a criminal offence and that Jardine was the arch-criminal. McLachlan, a loyal son of empire, did not agree – almost alone in all Australia.

'The next day was Sunday, and a party of us went off that night to Victor Harbour,' he told me. 'I slept in the same room as Jardine. When we were going to bed, Douglas said, "Well, it was an interesting day, laddie." And I said, "Well, we weren't going to talk about cricket, but, Douglas, I do want to say this. If this goes on it's going to muck up cricket because you're going to have cricketers playing in things like baseball masks." And he said, "Oh, don't be silly, laddie. It'll be stopped. I've got an instrument in my hand whereby I can win a series against the little man." The little man was Bradman. "It's good for England to win a series against the little man. But don't worry. It'll be stopped."'

This story powerfully suggests that Jardine knew perfectly well that the intimidatory tactics he was using, though within the laws of cricket, were unfair, destructive and, indeed, 'unsportsmanlike'. This was the word used in Australia's official complaint cabled to London, which caused such offence that it almost led to the cancellation of the rest of the tour. Had Jardine thought otherwise, why would he have been so sure that his tactics would be 'stopped'? The Australians, faced with what soon became a semi-political and not merely a sporting crisis, were made to withdraw the offending word; but its use, though tactless, was justified.

Adelaide is the only city in Australia possessing what could – and to an extent still can – be described as a clearly defined upper class: the well established, well off, often landed, with the odd title. St Peter's School was (and still largely is) its private breeding ground; the Adelaide Club was (but is no longer) its power base. McLachlan apart – who thought there was nothing in the rules that said Jardine could not do what he did – its members all thought Jardine disgraceful.

The crowd had no doubts about what they had seen. They took Jardine to be the symbol of an English upper class. Jardine played up to that image, with his silk choker amd multicoloured cap. The irony was that he was a bit of an outsider himself, despite Winchester and Oxford. Born in Bombay, the son of a Scottish lawyer, he was brought up by an aunt in a bleak mansion in Scotland. Rumours at Winchester told of how his will to win a school cricket match had come perilously close to sharp practice. He said 'orf' for 'off' and 'gorn' for 'gone', in the manner of some upper-class English; but he lacked gentlemanly instincts. No gentleman would have allowed himself to be so provoked by the barracking of Australian crowds that he would have openly referred to Australians as bastards, as Jardine did. Rockley Wilson is often quoted as having said, when Jardine was appointed captain, 'We shall win the Ashes but may lose a Dominion.' It is less often explained that this remark was not a witticism: E.R. Wilson had been a star all-rounder at Cambridge, an outstanding cricket coach at Jardine's public school, Winchester, a member of the England tour party to Australia in 1920–1, and a Yorkshire county cricketer. Like all Yorkshiremen of that era, Wilson knew that cricket was more than a game, and he also knew all about Jardine's ambition and will. Nothing was more typical of Jardine than the way he persisted with his tactics, regardless of the danger they involved to limb (if not to life), even after the rubber had been won. P.F. Warner, the team manager and himself a former England captain, asked Jardine to abandon bodyline for at least the last test, as a gesture of goodwill, but Jardine refused: 'We've got the bastards down there, and we'll keep them there,' he said. That attitude made Bradman even more of a national hero, since he still managed to average 56.57 in the series.

What did the lasting damage to Anglo-Australian relations was the British reaction to events in Australia. It was loftily assumed that the Australians were complaining about England's 'unsports-manlike' tactics because they were being beaten. 'Undignified snivelling,' said the *Daily Herald*. 'Cheapest possible insult,' said the *Star*. In a leader about 'what has begun to be called body-line bowling', published the day after the Australian cable of protest arrived, *The Times* said that it might not be amiss:

> to give some idea of how the matter strikes the average Englishman. First of all, there is nothing new in the kind of bowling to which exception is now taken ... It is inconceivable that a cricketer of Jardine's standing, chosen by the MCC to captain an English side, would ever dream of allowing or ordering the bowlers under his command to practise any system of attack that, in the time-honoured

English phrase, is not cricket . . . In all probability the present difficult and delicate position would never have arisen but for the irresponsible chatter of elderly critics in the pavilion and in the Press, and the craving in some quarters for sensational news stories . . .

The Times did not mention that it might have been better placed to judge whether there was anything new in this kind of bowling, and to provide its readers with non-sensational news stories, if it had not been too tight-fisted to send out its own correspondent. The MCC Committee, cricket's ruling body in England, instinctively and with equal ignorance took the same view as *The Times*. Class, one cannot help feeling, played a part. Viscount Lewisham, who happened to be MCC President, more perhaps because of his social and political connections than because of his knowledge of the game (he was a former Conservative MP and the current Lord Great Chamberlain to George V), cabled back, 'We deprecate your opinion that there has been unsportsmanlike play . . . fullest confidence in captain . . .' And so the cables went to and fro – twelve in all between 18 January and 14 December 1933 – and the governments of both countries became involved as did Governor Hore-Ruthven of South Australia, on leave in London, until the MCC climbed down, bodyline was effectively banned (just as Jardine had predicted), Larwood was made a scapegoat, and Jardine – though greeted as a hero when he first arrived home with the Ashes – announced that he never wished to play against Australians again.

His distaste for Australians seems to have been pathological – a fact that the MCC must have known, or should have known, before they appointed him captain. On the 1928–9 Australian tour Jardine had been subjected to merciless barracking; to placate the crowd – not usually beyond the wit of an English cricketer with a sense of humour – went against his nature. Fielding near the fence, he once turned and spat on the ground to show what he thought of his tormentors – not a wise gesture. 'They don't seem to like you out here, Mr Jardine!' said Patsy Hendren, who was liked by everyone everywhere. 'It's fucking mutual,' said Jardine. Warner said, 'When he sees a cricket ground with an Australian on it, he goes mad.' His vice-captain, R.E.S. Wyatt, commented,

'He disliked the Australians, which was unfortunate.' Gilbert Mant, the Australian who was the Reuters correspondent on the tour, introduced himself to Jardine on the boat going out. Jardine looked up from his deckchair and said, 'I see.' Those were the only words Jardine spoke to Mant during the whole seven-and-a-half-month tour, although the two men were constantly in the same hotels, trains and buses. When Mant was married at the end of the trip, Jardine was the only member of the English party who did not congratulate him and his wife. Mant could only conclude that Jardine saw him as an Australian mole in the English camp.

At this point I can reveal a fact that I have long kept quiet about in polite (and especially Australian) company. It is that I played cricket with Jardine. In the 1950s a man at William Collins, the publishers, used every year to organise a Publishers v. Authors match on the Westminster School ground in Vincent Square. This had started as a purely social match between two scratch sides, but the Collins man became ambitious and turned it into an 'occasion', by pressing serious cricketers to play, some of whom had never been near a book in their lives, and by laying on lunch in a tent, with self-congratulatory speeches by publishers; the players had to pay for their part in this commercial event. One year I was fielding at second slip when Jardine came in to bat. He looked, in his early fifties, just as he did in pre-war photographs: six foot tall, beaky nose, silk choker, Harlequin cap. Heaven knows how long it had been since he had walked on to a cricket ground; his bat was brown with age. First ball, medium pace, goodish length, just outside his off stump: he had all the time in the world, and hit it off the back foot with the greatest of ease for four past extra cover. He turned to the wicketkeeper, smiled and made some agreeable remark. For the rest of the day I watched him closely, unable to connect this sociable, if slightly remote, figure with the haughty and brutal architect of bodyline. Three or four years later I read that he had died of tick fever contracted in Southern Rhodesia; the obituary said that in later life he had taken up Eastern religions.

Forty years on, in the Mitchell Library in Sydney, I examined the bundle of letters written back to 'Darling Dad' in England by G.O. Allen during the bodyline tour and presented to the Library in 1992. Allen was the amateur fast bowler on the tour, and his venom towards Jardine sizzled off the page so strongly that I was surprised the letters had not self-combusted. At first, all is sweetness and light, and lunches at Government House in Adelaide, where Allen thought Hore-Ruthven charming; unfortunately the governor and Lady Hore-Ruthven were going 'home' on six weeks' leave in December and 'will not be here during our next two visits' – meaning no more lunches at Government House. 'So many people ask after you both,' Allen wrote, which was not surprising, since Darling Dad was Sir Walter Allen, Commandant-in-Chief of the Metropolitan Special Constabulary, son of the late Sir Wigram Allen of Toxteth Park, Sydney, and husband of Pearl, the daughter of the late Edward Lamb, Minister of Lands, Queensland. In Sydney, G.O. Allen's uncle was a partner in the leading law firm of Allen, Allen and Hemsley. G.O. Allen himself had been born in Sydney and educated at Eton, but given that during the tour he was regularly consorting with his cousins, and staying with prominent families such as the Baillieus at Sorrento, he could be described as an Anglo-Australian, or an Australian-Anglo, and thus immune from the irrational hatred of Australians that gripped his captain, and from the disdainful attitudes towards the colonial whingers displayed by the Committee of the MCC.

On the eve of the Adelaide disaster Allen wrote to say that he had been picked to play again tomorrow; but he had had a big row with Jardine, who had tried to get him to bowl leg theory, and he had refused. Then followed a general point about his captain: 'DRJ asks for it with his offensive manner and is then hurt when they [the newspapers] say nasty things about him.' Nevertheless, Allen added, he was 'still hugely enjoying every minute of the trip'.

His enjoyment did not survive the test, even though England won. It had been, he wrote to his father from the Pier Hotel, Glenelg, a 'most unpleasant match . . . nothing but rows and barracking until I am fed up with everything to do with cricket . . . both the press and more especiallly the public are taking their set-backs very badly. (Douglas Jardine is loathed &, between you and me, rightly, more than any German who ever fought in any war.)'

If the Australian Board of Control, 'that famous band of muddlers', protested to the MCC about leg theory:

> I forecast the following: I think MCC is sure to cable Jardine to abandon it. If they do he says he will resign . . . I have not changed my mind in any way about the leg theory and all the side is aware of the fact. I just hate it and will not do it.
>
> There is no getting away from it, Jardine is a perfect swine and I can think of no word fit for Mum to see which describes him well enough. Plum [P.F. Warner] simply hates the sight of him and so does everyone else.

The tyranny of distance played its part. Only three British newspaper correspondents were covering the tour; the other papers relied on Reuters. Of those three, Bruce Harris of the *Evening Standard* knew nothing about cricket and was in any case in Jardine's pocket; the great Jack Hobbs, hired by the *Star*, was still playing county cricket for Surrey under the captaincy of Jardine, and never said a word either for or against bodyline (although in private he was profoundly against it), because, as he said later, 'I did not want to embarrass Jardine or his men by giving the Australians another peg on which to hang their fierce attack'; and a cheerful sports writer called Jack Ingham of the *News Chronicle* – from the same group as the *Star* – was Hobbs's ghost and delighted in filing stories about Australian 'squealing'. Gilbert Mant, the Reuters correspondent, in a book published when he was ninety, finally explained that he had never filed a word of cricitism of bodyline in case his employers in London thought that he, as an Australian, was biased and fired him. His silence, he wrote, had been on his conscience ever since.

Ignorant of the true nature of the leg-theory attack – ignorant too of the fact that half the English team, let alone the Australian team, thought that bodyline would destroy the game if it was allowed to continue – the MCC reacted instinctively to the 'unsportsmanlike' charge. In much the same way that it did not occur to Sir Otto Niemeyer that there might be two sides to the problems of Australian indebtedness to the London banks, so it did not occur to Lord Lewisham and his fellow-committee members that the Australians might have a case. The fact that Rockley Wilson's prophecy could imaginably have come true is invariably attributed to Allen's 'famous band of muddlers', the Australian Board of Control, and their tactless insult about 'sportsmanship' – the word that nearly lost a Dominion. But should not some of the blame attach to Warner? 'Plum has had a terribly worrying time and has aged a lot, poor fellow,' Allen wrote home in February. Though universally popular, Warner was not a forceful character. 'Like Bismarck, I can be silent in six languages,' he liked to say to press inquiries. He asked to see the fateful cable before it was sent, but his request was ignored. He disliked Jardine and clearly foresaw (as he conceded later) the mayhem that Jardine's methods would cause. But he neither used the telephone (which was admittedly primitive, but more or less worked) nor the cable (which worked perfectly well) to tell the MCC the true state of affairs: namely, that bodyline was deliberate intimidation and physically dangerous. They would have been bound to listen; Warner was a member of the MCC Committee, and nobody knew more about the game – certainly not Lord Lewisham – or more transparently had its interest at heart. His speeches on the tour constantly talked about 'British fair play', boring the reporters. Suppose the MCC had told Jardine to stop bodyline and he had resigned, as Allen predicted? His vice-captain, R.E.S. Wyatt, who had already captained England against Australia in 1930 and who did not approve of bodyline, would have taken over; and, as it happens, England would still have won the series. In the test after Adelaide in Brisbane, which on its very eve Jardine thought might be called off, the wicket was soft and unsuited to bodyline; yet England still won the game and with it the series.

English talk about fair play and sportsmanship had proved to be fraudulent. It was Woodfull, the Australian captain and head-master, who had turned out to be the gentleman, and Jardine in his Harlequin cap was the cad. By 1936 bodyline had been more or less outlawed as a tactic and Allen, the England captain on the Australian tour of that year, had made friends with Bradman, even feeling 'very sorry' for him; 'I like him enormously and I don't think he is getting the full support of the Roman Catholic element in the side' (Allen was right). The two captains dined together in Adelaide during the test – an inconceivable event in 1932–3. The alliance thus formed made the Allen–Bradman axis the most important influence on cricket for decades to come. But the public remained hostile. Allen dreaded the Melbourne test, with 100,000 people present every day and 'about 99,950 there simply to scream for Australia'.

When the England team and its attendant handful of corrrespondents sailed away from Sydney at the end of the 1936 tour, 'like a party of transported convicts', wrote the Reuters correspondent decades later, 'nobody from Australian cricket officialdom and not one member of the Australian team saw us off'.

At the centre, the wounds were patched up. After Jardine's death his portrait was hung up in the Long Room at Lord's next to Bradman's; someone must have thought he was making a conciliatory gesture. Larwood, having emigrated to Australia, was eventually made an honorary member of the MCC. In Australia he was given an award on the same day as James Fairfax, the chairman of Fairfax newspapers, whose sister later presented the G.O. Allen letters to the Mitchell Library. On the periphery, bodyline became a potent myth, full of symbols.

The story refused to die. Bruce Beresford set out to direct a film about it, to be produced by David Puttnam in the wake of his Oscar-winning *Chariots of Fire*; but Australian Equity insisted that all parts must be taken by Australians, and so Beresford, who thought it essential for Jardine to be played by an Englishman, abandoned the project. Instead, in 1984, along came a television miniseries, a popular success that confirmed every Australian prejudice. It was full of blunders. Aboard the RMS *Orontes*, on which the England team sailed for Australia (leaving Tilbury with two funnels and arriving in Fremantle with three), the amateurs were shown in dinner jackets on the ship at night and the professionals in daytime suits. All in fact wore dinner jackets. Jardine was a caricature; while poor modest Warner was turned into, as Mant saw it, 'a half-drunken scowling introvert'. A Union

Jack was burned on top of the Adelaide Oval grandstand: a complete invention.

Australians always tended to see bodyline as a matter of class — English snobs, led by the MCC, putting the colonials in their place at the one activity in which they had challenged England with success. Eventually the man in the stocking mask struck back.

Packer Beats England

The riposte came to a head in the High Court in London during the autumn of 1977. On the surface, the case was about cricket or, as some thought (correctly), the whole future of the traditional game. Below the surface, deeper currents were at work. Formally, what had happened was that the man in the stocking mask, the Australian media tycoon Kerry Packer, had sued the Test and County Cricket Board — by this time the controlling body in the UK — for banning his players. He had secretly signed up thirty-two first-class cricketers to play a series of 'super-tests' arranged by himself. The English authorities replied by banning the cricketers from county and test cricket. 'Lock-out,' cried Packer. 'Self-protection,' replied the Authorities. They felt threatened, understandably. They feared that the Packer enterprise would wreck the existing game by (a) stealing its revenue, and (b) creaming off the best players as fast as they were produced by the current system.

There could have been no greater contrast between two groups than between the Packer men and the Authorities. Would-be impartial observers, such as myself, sensed at once a different view not only of the Noble Game but of life itself. The Authorities appeared in the court room in sober dark suits. The Packer men were a riot of colour: Packer in a pale-blue suit with a multicoloured tie; Richie Benaud, the former Australian captain recruited by Packer, in a polychromatic costume with crocodile shoes; a Packer partner in primrose yellow; another fellow in orange leather. They were dressed as if for a studio in Burbank, Los Angeles, rather than the Committee Room at Lord's.

The case coincided, as it happened, with a highbrow piece in the *New York Review of Books* entitled 'The Corruption of Sport'.

Its writer went back over the history of sport, taking his cue from the classic work *Homo Ludens* by Professor J. Huizinga, a study of the 'play' element in culture. Huizinga, who published his book in 1938, saw the history of civilisation in terms of the steady decline of 'play'. The *NYRB* writer developed the thesis with reference to the impact of television on sport. Television distorts sport, he argued, changing its very nature. The whole point of sport – or 'play' – is that it should be pointless: an escape from reality (although it is, of course, deeply serious). Once sport is put into the service of some ulterior purpose – profit-making, or the sale of products – it becomes degraded.

I did not swallow the thesis whole, but I kept being reminded of it as I listened to the case in court. The hearing was full of talk of deals, contracts, incomes, accountants, tax liabilities and tax-avoidance schemes. Mr Packer referred to an England–Australian test series as 'the product'. It was a long way from Huizinga's notion of useless play as a primary human need. However, the men in dark suits did think in Huizinga-like terms. To them cricket was, as one of them remarked to me, stumbling over his words, 'about, well, it's about the human spirit'. He obviously regarded Packer as an Australian from outer space, a destroyer of tradition and ritual.

Packer, it was true, did look a shade forbidding. One of his own lawyers described him to me as 'the sort of man you wouldn't want to meet on a dark night'. But he spent two and a half days in the witness box, and even under extended cross-examination from a clever opposing QC had plenty of time for his shots, like Jardine in Vincent Square. Here was yet another instance, I thought, of the English misjudging an Australian – assuming that, because an Australian looked like one of the boys and behaved like one of the boys, he really was one of the boys. The Authorities underestimated his intelligence, his determination and possibly his wish to teach his English would-be saboteurs a lesson.

People used to make the same mistake with his father, the late Sir Frank Packer, who built up the newspaper group that his son later sold in order to concentrate on television. They saw a fellow who looked like a retired boxer (which he was), and who liked a bet on the horses (which he did), and they thought his brain would match his manner (which it did not). He was tough as well as shrewd, and sometimes ruthless, so that Kerry grew up in a hard school, which to their cost the Authorities failed to understand.

Packer got into the dispute because he wanted to make money by putting cricket on his television network. He tried, and failed, to buy exclusive rights to televise test matches in Australia. So, thwarted, he bought up the best players and set out to stage his own matches. His 'super-tests' were to be given American-style television treatment. The aim, as his partner John Cornell explained to me outside the court room, was to make the game more exciting to the viewer than to the spectator at the ground. Technology, combined with American-inspired showmanship, would do the trick: more cameras, microphones in the stumps, zoom lenses to show the expressions of players and umpires, split screens, day–night games under floodlights, coloured clothing, an American name – World Series Cricket. Cornell might have been supplying material for a supporting footnote in 'The Corruption of Sport' article: that television turns sport, which used to be for the participants, into a professional spectacle for a mass audience, who then have to be fed with sensations extraneous to the sport itself in order to hold their attention and keep them alert for the advertisements.

All the ambitions of the Packer people came true. They won the court case. Packer secured the right to televise test matches. His technicians transformed the way cricket was televised, and thus the nature of the game itself. As time went by, winning became still more important, and the game more and more of a business, until in 1996 the English cricket authorities actually brought in a businessman, Lord Maclaurin, the head of a supermarket chain, to reorganise the time-honoured structure of cricket in such a way that England would produce an all-conquering team. Following the blow dealt by Packer, the English romantics – who, consciously or not, had always seen cricket as the 'play' element in English culture – were routed. 'The Australians are a very, very pragmatic people,' an Australian academic once told me. Australian pragmatism routed English romanticism.

One point that became obvious in the High Court was that – as the 'Corruption' writer in the *NYRB* observed – the sportsperson had ceased to be a hero. To achieve heroic status, the hero must put something ahead of his own personal interests. But the cricketers bought up by Packer had all put their own interests first. One poignant example was that of Derek Underwood, the England bowler, who said in the witness box that it had always been his ambition to take more test wickets than any other England cricketer, but he had sacrificed this ambition in order to play for Packer; the attraction was, he candidly explained, the 'financial reimbursement'. His decision was understandable, but not heroic. And so the decline of 'play' continued. In 1990 the editor of *Wisden*, Graeme Wright, lamented the way that cricket had become a business. He recalled that the late Sir George Allen (formerly G.O. Allen), who after his playing days were over became one of the game's foremost administrators, had resigned in 1982 from all his administrative roles on the grounds that a national game had been virtually taken over by the full-time professionals. A former editor of *Wisden*, John Woodcock, had warned at the time that in Australia the say of the marketing people took precedence over that of the cricketers. 'Beware the small, executive sub-committee of businessmen,' Woodcock wrote, 'to whom the charm of cricket is little more than a technicality: that was the burden of Mr Allen's message.' Graeme Wright concluded his lament: 'The game is no longer an end in itself. It has become in many respects the means to an end.'

In 1997 Australia's leading cricketers – the 120 top players represented by the Australian Cricketers' Association – threatened to strike for more money, refusing to play for Australia until their demands were met. Mr Packer, at least, must have sympathised. In a twenty-years-on anniversary piece in the *Sunday Telegraph*, Scyld Berry noted that the effects of his revolution, which 'launched the game into the modern era of professionalism, popularisation, and player-power', were still being felt. Left to the old Authorities, said Berry, the game might have become 'a grey ritual' watched only by a few elderly spectators. Thinking back, however, to the days when words like fair play, unsportsmanlike, bodyline and the

Ashes could arouse genuinely deep – and shared – emotions, both in England and in Australia, the Englishman who mumbled that cricket was 'about, well, it's about the human spirit', must have wept.

6

The Colonial Mentality

E.W. Swanton, doyen of cricket writers (and the most prolific: on his eightieth birthday in 1987 it was calculated that he must have written eight million words about the game, and he was still at it in his nineties), used to give readings from *Wisden* to his fellow-inmates of a Japanese prison camp in the Second World War. The readings helped them to keep the war in perspective. Even Swanton, though, would probably have admitted – if pressed – that the bodyline crisis faded into relative insignificance by comparison with what happened to Anglo-Australian relations while he was suffering the horrors of the camp. In 1988 the historian David Day published a book which stated that 'the Anglo-Australian relationship went through its greatest crisis in World War Two'. Not many people would disagree with that statement, especially if they had read the book. Day's argument is that the British deliberately deceived Australia about the help it would provide them with in the event of war, and that this deception meant that – when the Japanese drove south, capturing the prize base of Singapore, and Swanton with it – Australia was virtually unprotected. Day gave his book the challenging title of *The Great Betrayal*.

But he also argues that Australia to some extent connived in this deception. Throughout the 1930s it almost wilfully failed to recognise the peril it might face, and spent only trivial amounts on defence. When the war started, in September 1939, Australia possessed six cruisers, five elderly destroyers, practically no air

120

force and a largely unmechanised skeleton army. It knew of course that Japan was the most powerful nation that might threaten Australia, but assumed that in the remote event of this threat becoming serious, the Royal Navy would steam instantly to the rescue. How could Australia's leaders have been so short-sighted? Day's answer, or part of his answer, is that underlying their easy, misguided and nearly fatal assumptions about the protection that Britain could, or would, give to Australia was what he calls the Colonial Mentality.

From our distant vantage point, he explains, it is easy to ignore an essential fact about inter-war Australian society: an underdeveloped sense of Australian nationality caused by the country's incorporation within a wider and powerful empire. Those born in the British Isles formed 10.7 per cent of the population. Most Australians were probably far from clear whether their primary allegiance lay with Australia or with Britain. Even the allegiance of many second-, third- and fourth-generation Australians remained undimmed by time, distance or immediate ancestry. The epitome of this sentiment was R.G. Menzies, Australia's most notable political figure of the twentieth century, the son of native-born Australians, who nevertheless developed such an abiding attachment to Britain and her institutions that it provided the core of his existence throughout his long life.

Australians in the grip of the 'colonial mentality' knew, or thought they knew, that Britain possessed the power, through her navy, to defend any part of the empire against attack; and they further assumed – the assumption that very nearly proved fatal – that the mother country possessed the will to undertake that defence, come what may.

As it happens, we are in a position to examine this 'colonial mentality' in some detail. In the National Library of Australia in Canberra is an enthralling document: the private diary, written in pencil, that Menzies kept on his first visit to the UK in 1935. Why the diary has never been published in full I do not know. It would confirm his critics in their opinions, and arouse nostalgia in those who regard Menzies as the last Prime Minister to stand for good, solid values – family life, hard work, independence, Parliament and the Queen.

121

He was aged forty, the newly appointed Attorney-General in the Federal Government, and his mission was to represent Australia at the Jubilee of George V, to monitor some trade negotiations then in progress between the UK and Argentina, and to appear in a patent case before the Privy Council. His character and ambitions were already formed. Critics such as Donald Horne have complained about the way that he, as Prime Minister, still clung to the provincial ideas prevalent in Melbourne at the turn of the century, particularly loyalty to Great Britain, and thus held back the development of Australia during a time when it should have been opening up to Asia and to a new technological future. It seems hard on Menzies to complain about the importance of Britain in his cosmography. He was born in the flat outer limits of settled Victoria, the son of an upwardly mobile coach-painter and store-keeper descended from Scottish crofters. 'The Scottish farmer,' he said in a speech in 1946, 'ponders upon the future of his son, and sees it most assured not by the inheritance of money but by the acquisition of that knowledge which will give him power, and so the sons of many Scottish farmers find their way to Edinburgh and a university degree.' Much the same happened to Menzies. His world was circumscribed by Britain. At the University of Melbourne he studied law that derived from England; he became Victoria's youngest KC in a city where the street containing barristers' chambers was known as Chancery Lane. As a young man, he read English history and literature; he could quote chunks of Wordsworth's *Prelude*. At sea, as he set off for England, he was reading *Macbeth* and *King Lear*. He had already played a part in state politics; and he seems to have been fully aware that his greatest asset was a strong, melodious voice and an exceptional talent for making speeches and holding an audience – aptitudes originally developed as an aspiring young politician from the back of a lorry at Melbourne street corners. Command of the English language was a source of political power. Radio had started in 1923, and by the mid-1930s it was spreading everywhere, taking the voices of politicians into living rooms.

Here then are the most amusing or pertinent extracts from the diary of the man who dominated Australian post-war politics: a rather orthodox and humdrum, but nevertheless alert, mind at the very moment that it experiences the wider world. And, after all, it is this mind that has been blamed for holding Australia back, for smothering Australia and failing to perceive its true Asian destiny – not historical necessity, not economics, but Menzies's anachronistic attitudes.

He sailed on 19 February 1935. On 24 February he wrote: 'Perhaps it is mere fancy, but British ship's officers give one a feeling of security. They have an air and a carriage which suggests (as the fact is) that their ancestors have been ruling the waves so long that rough seas mean nothing to them.'

This was precisely the feeling, as David Day might have commented but did not, that caused Australian political leaders to trust Britain's assurances that she would of course continue to rule the waves, and thus protect Australia, in time of war.

3 March: 'Earl of Wicklow speaks to me in the swimming bath. Note the levelling effects of water. Ditto Lady Beatrice Wilkinson who wears only neck to knee bathing costume in the world.' He quotes Noël Coward's song 'Mad Dogs and Englishmen'.

In 1935 every convenient maritime stepping-stone between Australia and England was British territory: Singapore, Colombo, Bombay, Aden, Port Said, Malta, Gibraltar. Menzies admired the English he met at Government House in Colombo and Aden, remarking on 'the persistent Englishness of the English: here is a golf course, there is a soccer football ground (in this climate!), there a cricket ground'. The more he saw of the English, he reflected, the more satisfied he was that they ran these places and gave 'these people' what they could obviously never give themselves. In Colombo, the governor prided himself on never having worn a white dinner jacket (no doubt because he regarded this garment as an American invention). In Aden, Menzies lunched at the Residency with Sir Bernard Reilly (a soldier), and met the 'usual bright young Englishmen who carry on their business of ruling the earth and with all the usual attitudes of cleanness, good manners, an interest in Test Matches and the championships at Wimbledon'.

He was astounded by Cairo. He had thought it was 'a broken down village surrounding some place called Shepherd's Hotel', and found it to be a city of a million. The museum was 'staggering'; he had expected a 'crude and barbarian' display. Instead he doubted whether any modern craftsman could do what these 'poor savages' did in the thirteenth century BC.

'We travel like Royalty,' he wrote, which inspired a 'melancholy reflection upon the meagre and mouldy way in which we treat distinguished visitors to Australia. If we were really a grown-up nation we would understand and practise these courtesies much more adequately.' He complained about the way Australians dressed.

Of the 'natives', he took a poor view. In Aden, he found them 'experts in idleness' and in demanding baksheesh. In Cairo, the 'gyppos' were no better.

He disembarked in Italy and took a thirty-two-hour train journey to Calais. He was constantly aware of the beauty of the landscape through which he passed and of the 'perfect proportions of the houses – many of them shabby but all showing more than a trace of that widespread artistic judgement which is so rare with us'.

Whatever he saw – clothes, the reception of foreigners, artistic judgement – Menzies made comparisons with Australia. In Cairo, he observed 'the true Australian touch' – a fellow-countryman 'who attended everything dressed in a white (or near white) panama hat, a baggy grey suit held together by a white belt, and a pair of white tennis shoes. Our dislike of dressing up properly on proper occasions is a queer form of inverted snobbery, and the sooner we realise it the sooner will English people cease to regard us as a set of outlandish Yahoos.'

He talked to a German Jew about Germany and Hitler: the more he reflected on what he had heard, 'the more one realises that the English notion of freedom as the object or end of government is the best'.

Crossing northern France, he thought of the Roman legions and realised with a thrill that he was not more than twenty miles from Crécy. 'The whole of this part of France has over a period of centuries been one of the great battlefields of England.'

Then comes the one diary entry that does get quoted occasionally, and mocked: 'White cliffs on our right, and crowning them the Dover Castle. At last we are in England. Our journey to Mecca has ended, and our minds abandoned to those reflections which can so strangely (unless you remember our tradition and upbringing) move the souls of those who go "home to a land they have never seen".'

Very soon Menzies was in Westminster Hall, standing beside the plate marking the spot where Warren Hastings stood trial nearly 150 years before, 'recapturing the great description by Macaulay, and listening for echo of ringing tones of Burke's great denunciation. For the moment almost imagine I am Hastings (*mens aequa a arduis*) until I remember that his person was "small and emaciated" and realise I am not cast for the part.'

He thought the London streets and buildings drab. In the Temple church, he found 'a brooding atmosphere. English history becomes a new thing; it comes nearer to you.' In the Cabinet Room in Downing Street, he thought of the men who had worked there: Walpole, Chatham, Pitt, Disraeli, Gladstone, Asquith, Lloyd George.

25 March: 'In afternoon see Sir Henry Batterbee of Dominions Office and tell him that quality of speeches made in Australia by visiting princes must be improved if prestige of Crown is to be maintained; very important if Imperial Unity's last link is to be unbroken.' This was bold advice; Batterbee had been political adviser to the Duke of York during his visit to Australia in 1927, and would have been one of his speech-writers.

Menzies always commented on the speeches he heard; when he went to see Gielgud as Hamlet, he remarked that Gielgud 'rants a little'. (Jessica Tandy, who played Ophelia in that famous production, starred half a century later in the Australian Bruce Beresford's Oscar-winning film *Driving Miss Daisy*.) At a Mansion House dinner he saw the Prince of Wales, then at the height of his affair with Mrs Simpson, 'who now has a real sense of the platform. He looks small and restless. I meet him and speak with him. He is not a regal person.'

He went to the Grand National: 'All the women were plain and ill-dressed. No wonder any Melbourne girl can snap up a peer on sight.' After another social occasion: 'The women of England may have big feet but they understand training servants.'

He met the loquacious politician Brendan Bracken: 'I am still looking for the reserved Englishman.' He met law lords and the Dominions Secretary Jimmy Thomas. He attended an empire banquet at the Grosvenor House hotel for the Duke of Gloucester: 'Speeches bad and I longed to make one'. He noted the dog mess on the streets.

Oxford lost the Boat Race and Menzies made a shrewd observation: he suspected that there might be a 'little cleverness which I perceive in so many young Oxford men who prefer an epigram to the truth and an attentuated intellectuality to reality. These states of mind do not produce crews or teams.' It would not have surprised him to find Australians occupying a leading role in many subsequent Oxford eights, and five Australians, including the captain, in the Oxford rugby XV in 1997 (they still lost).

He spent a day in Buckinghamshire: 'What a day!' It encompassed Runnymede, where he thought about the barons; Chequers and a letter in the 'very handwriting' of Cromwell 'whose sword and character made England a free country'; the great John Hampden, whose house and church 'would stir the soul of an Australian trade union secretary!'; and Milton, 'the greatest poet of liberty'. Parliament, he told himself, did not spring from a political theory, as it did on the Continent, but from the very roots of English life.

A tour further afield produced thirty pages of description that showed a keen interest in architecture and building materials. On 25 April Menzies attended Anzac Day at St Clement's Dane church: 'a poor service' taken by a 'posturing and irritating' clergyman.

Soon he noted that after-dinner speeches in England were 'too stilted'. In the House of Commons he listened to Churchill: 'The idol has feet of clay. His language is good, but his expression hesitating, and he practically reads what he has to say . . . constant repetition of "I told you so" . . . impression that Winston has become an entertainer rather than a leader.'

He attended all the main events of the London season. The annual show at the Royal Academy was a 'great disappointment and not unlike Victoria artists!' At dinner at Buckingham Palace he took in Mrs Churchill, 'bright and talkative'. They swapped stories of Billy Hughes and Lloyd George. The King exchanged

Billy Hughes stories 'with obvious gusto'. Visiting Cambridge, Menzies quoted Wordsworth to himself in King's College chapel; at Granchester, he observed that the church clock had alas got itself going again. He said he was 'beginning to understand the secret springs of English poetry'.

On 18 May, at All Souls College, Oxford, he wrote: 'I am ashamed (or almost ashamed) of our Australian vice of censoriousness and uncontrollable itch to regulate the lives and conduct and thought of others. In England they know better.' On 3 June he appeared before the Privy Council, and soon afterwards the diary ended.

So far as I am aware, the one person who has used the diary effectively to illuminate Menzies's attitudes and beliefs is Judith Brett. She said in 1992, with every justification, that Australians had shown a general reluctance to re-examine the political representations of Menzies that had been current in his lifetime; both historians and commentators, she noted, were 'freezing him as some felt he once froze the culture'. So in her book, *The Forgotten People*, she set out to give an account of him that included both his merits and his demerits.

Most Australians' experience of England, she remarks, begins as an experience of an entirely imaginary place. When they come up against the reality, they often react either with aggression or with the notorious cultural cringe. But, as his diary shows, Menzies reacted in neither of these ways. He passionately wanted his vision of his England, the source of his spiritual and intellectual nourishment, to be true; and that is what happened. He saw only what he wanted to see: green fields and villages of Cotswold stone, not the slums and the industrial heartland. Nor was he disappointed or angered by the locals – unlike Deakin, for instance. He did not feel inferior to the people he met; on the contrary, he seems to have been perfectly at ease with everyone from the King downwards. He felt that Australians could pick up a tip or two from the English whom he came across on the trip over, both in the matter of dress and in the way they received distinguished visitors; but on the whole the difference between being Australian and being British was not one of his preoccupations. The notion that loyalty to Australia and loyalty to Britain might possibly conflict would not have entered his head; imperial unity under the Crown was not merely the main foundation of national politics, but the only conceivable foundation. The diary shows too that the criticism made of Menzies later, that he was a philistine, was wide of the mark; his love of English poetry, though conventional, ran deeper than an affectation trotted out to decorate his speeches.

He wanted to make his mark and to be accepted at the imperial centre. It gave him immense satisfaction when he was made an Honorary Bencher of Gray's Inn, 'an honour usually reserved for Prime Ministers!!!' But, as Judith Brett observes, it is easy to miss an anxious note in the diary; a hint that, for all the warmth of his reception – the invitations everywhere, the honorary member-ships of the Carlton and the Athenaeum – he is wondering whether he is not really regarded as an outsider. He was, after all, Scottish; and thus, in some English eyes, doubly an outsider. Is it possible that the English he meets are only interested in the material benefits that can be extracted from Australia, as if it was just a market? Recognise that 'our common destiny is not just pounds, shillings and pence', he told one audience. Do not treat us Australians of British birth simply as strangers with whom you will be perfectly friendly, he told a Chatham House audience (that is, a politically informed and influential audience): friendship is not enough. Warren Hastings is 'my Hastings, not merely yours'; the empire is 'my Empire, not merely yours'; England is 'my England, not merely yours'. It is not difficult to understand why, when Britain declared war on Germany on 3 September 1939, Menzies as Prime Minister instantly did the same, without consulting Parliament.

A large section of Australian society has always found this hanging-on to the imperial coat-tails unacceptable, although this section is not easy to define. American newspapers sometimes employ the term 'left-leaning' to describe anyone whose politics are to the left of the prevailing orthodoxy. It avoids the ambiguous word 'radical', which has come to be used both for the right and the left; and it is less emphatic than 'left-wing', which might attract writs. Almost nobody in Australia is left-wing any longer – certainly not members of the Labor Party, which has scrupulously avoided the word socialist at least since Bill Hayden was the party leader. The term 'liberal', since it was hijacked by Menzies and his Conservatives, can be confusing. Left-leaning, in Australian political discourse, would be applied these days to people who are convinced republicans, pro-Aborigine rights, sympathetic towards Asian migrants, but not necessarily sympathetic to the machine politics of the Labor right, especially the NSW Labor right, and who are hostile to the concentrations of power in the Australian media or the great mining and pastoral companies.

A person's instinctive reaction to the word 'Menzies' would be a sure test of left-leaningness. In the UK, the name evokes a typical, old-style Australian: physically large, supremely self-reliant, proud of his Australianness, an accomplished speaker, keen on cricket and the company of cricketers, loyal monarchist and all-round good bloke. He damaged his reputation as a statesman by his overambitious attempt to solve the Suez crisis, but nobody in the UK took much notice of the incidents that caused teeth-grinding in Australia: Menzies's clumsy attempted compliment about seeing the Queen passing by, and yet he'd love her till he died; and his satisfacion in dressing up in a cocked hat as Lord Warden of the Cinque Ports. The British are more used to seeing distinguished old men looking absurd in the antique costume that in Britain still often accompanies state preferment; the Knights of the Garter *en grande toilette* who merely attract stares on their annual procession to St George's Chapel in Windsor would excite derision on Pitt Street.

To the left-leaning Australians, Menzies is anathema. To them, he personifies everything that was wrong with Australia before the advent of Whitlam. At the heart of this objection lies what they see as his subservient or colonial attitude to Britain. Subservient is a strong word, however; and the evidence of the diary is against them. Nor did he think of himself as a colonial. 'Displaced Briton' would be nearer the mark. David Day speaks of Menzies's *Boy's Own* outlook. Again, the evidence is not there. The sort of history of which he was intensely conscious in his maturity was not *Boy's Own* adventure-story history – not Nelson's death at Trafalgar or Wolfe storming the heights of Abraham – but Whig history: the growth of Parliament and the rise of English liberty. A left-leaner can with self-respect tip his hat to Cromwell or Milton, and even the Runnymede barons may be said to have done the Aussies a good turn.

Defenders of Menzies, however, have a more difficult brief when considering his performance as Prime Minister during the northern spring of 1941. The war was going badly in Greece and North Africa. Churchill's leadership was under pressure, and his strategy was being questioned. Japan appeared to be preparing to enter the war with an attack on British possessions in the Far East. Menzies flew to London via Singapore and the Middle East, and in two and a half months of effort failed to secure any of the military equipment that Australia would desperately need in the event of war with Japan. More important in Menzies's own mind, evidently, was the thought (encouraged by Lord Beaverbrook) that he could balance Churchill's dominance by playing the same sort of role, as a representative of the Dominions in the War Cabinet, that Jan Smuts had played in the First World War. He may even have toyed with the idea that he might himself replace Churchill. If so, it was a fantasy; but it is hard to quarrel with Day's verdict that 'Australia had become saddled with a Prime Minister who had more concern with political intrigue against Churchill than with the security of the country in his charge'. But again, it was not Menzies's feelings of colonial inferiority that led him to think that he was equipped to play a central role in the direction of the war. He thought in imperial, not colonial, terms. The empire – not just separate allied countries called Britain, Australia, and so on – was at war, and it was therefore appropriate for him to seek to use his talents wherever they could best be deployed. He would have been bewildered to be told that fifty years later he would be regarded in some quarters almost as a traitor to Australia because he went off to London instead of staying in Canberra. Nobody in London, least of all Churchill, supported his ambitions. It was a critical psychological turning point in Anglo-Australian relations when Menzies discovered that politics was the one calling in which it was impossible to transfer successfully from Australia to the UK.

Japan Attacks

Most Britons are, I think, wholly unaware that in recent years many Australians have come to believe as an article of faith that Britain betrayed Australia in the Second World War. On 7 December 1941, Japan attacked and destroyed the United States fleet in Pearl Harbor. In February 1942 Singapore surrendered. Thus Britain's promises to defend Australia had come to nothing; Australia lay open to attack. Churchill had tried to prevent American forces being sent to the Pacific, and to delay the repatriation of Australian forces needed for their country's defence. 'Thus Britain deliberately left Australia at the mercy of Japan, using her to divert and delay the Japanese thrust westwards to India and the Middle East.'

That is the David Day thesis in outline. Now let us look at the story in greater detail.

Throughout the 1930s Australia's relations with Britain were characterised by dependency. Economically, Australia was inextricably tied to Britain. She scarcely possessed a foreign or defence policy of her own; she scarcely possessed a foreign service: only a High Commissioner in London and a Counsellor attached to the British Embassy in Washington. The High Commissioner represented Australia at the League of Nations; elsewhere Britain represented Australian interests. In addition, the Federal Government in Canberra was almost entirely dependent on the British Dominions Office for information and intelligence; the External Affairs Department relied on the BBC news.

Australia showed little interest in pursuing its own foreign policy. Nor was it much more interested in its own defence. It preferred to rely on British assurances. Singapore began to be turned into a great base in 1921: it was designed to harbour a fleet large enough to frustrate Japanese ambitions and thus became the cornerstone of Australia's defence thinking. Britain and Australia, however, viewed Singapore in different ways. Australia, looking northwards, saw it as a shield, a forward base that the Royal Navy could use as a springboard into the Pacific; for Britain, looking southwards, it marked the outer limit of British naval power, at the end of a chain of British bases – Gibraltar, Malta, Port Said,

Aden, Bombay, Colombo, Singapore – whereby the navy could protect the Indian Ocean.

Throughout the years after construction of the base began, the Australians repeatedly questioned the capacity of Britain to dispatch a fleet to Singapore if there was a war on two fronts, in Europe and in the Pacific. They were invariably reassured. The mother country would protect her children. Australia's fatal illusion was to suppose that Australia bulked as large in British minds as Britain bulked in Australian minds.

Now it is at this point that the embarrassed and potentially ashamed British reader of Day's thoroughly researched and annotated book begins to have doubts. 'Britain had her own good reasons for deceiving Australia about her capacity to fulfil her defence guarantee,' Day writes. In the sentence quoted earlier, he uses the word 'deliberately'. Here the important word is 'deceiving'. Day says that if Britain had admitted that it lacked the capacity to defend Australia, British power worldwide would have been called into question, and the shrinking tentacles of her navy exposed, since the British Empire was held together by a belief in the navy's ability to patrol and control the seven seas.

But he does not produce any evidence, despite the range and comprehensiveness of his research, to show that Britain deliberately deceived Australia. He quotes the former Prime Minister, S.M. Bruce, now High Commissioner in London, complaining that it was very hard to discover what British policies were until they were 'almost unalterable'. He says that British officials 'occasionally admitted that Britain would have problems in fulfilling her guarantee'. The assurances may in the event have proved worthless; and Day is at liberty to ascribe to Australia's colonial mentality its failure to recognise the peril that it faced. But he fails, on my reading, to supply evidence to support the charge of deliberate deception. Self-deception, not the deception of others, was Britain's abiding error in the 1930s.

Now for Day's main charge: betrayal. Naturally the British hackle is inclined instinctively to rise at this strong word, and equally naturally it must be at once suppressed by the disinterested reporter.

From the start of the war British interests and Australian

interests diverged, although the Australians were desperately slow to recognise this fact. Self-protection is the first duty of a state: a point missed by Australia because its leaders thought in imperial terms, and assumed that, since Australia was part of the empire, it would automatically be protected by Britain.

This did not mean that Australia failed to worry about its own security. At the start of the war Australia sent troops to the Middle East, ships to operate with the Royal Navy in the Mediterranean and aircrew to train with the RAF. But it was not long before a persistent theme emerged: in order to keep Australian troops coming, Churchill had to keep up the reassurances. As the Battle of Britain began, in mid-1940, Australia was worried about Japan. Suppose Japan attacked the Dutch East Indies: what would Britain do then? Churchill, preoccupied with the defence of Britain, failed to see any urgency in the question. Lord Caldecote, the Dominions Secretary, told the War Cabinet that the urgency arose not so much from the likelihood of a Japanese attack as from the need to reassure Australia: 'Certain important convoys were shortly due to leave Australia. Caldecote thought that Australia and New Zealand would only be prepared to agree to the convoys sailing if they knew we had reached a decision to resist by force Japanese aggression in the Dutch East Indies.' A Chiefs of Staff report gave the game away; it was not communicated to Australia. British forces in the Far East were not strong enough 'to give any appreciable assistance to the Dutch'. Then it stated that 'any attempt to produce an adequate naval concentration at Singapore in the present world situation would be unsound'. The most that the British could do would be to 'send one battle cruiser and one aircraft carrier to the Indian Ocean to be based at Ceylon for the purpose of protecting our vital communications and those around the Cape to the Middle East'.

That was a plain enough assessment of British weakness, and a plain enough statement of British priorities: the Middle East before the Far East. But it would scarcely quieten the fears of Australia. In stepped Churchill, with a cable to Prime Minister Menzies. Britain had 'always in mind [Australia's] interests and safety'. Britain would 'of course defend Singapore which, if attacked, which is unlikely, ought to stand a long siege'. He undertook to 'base on Ceylon a battle cruiser and a fast aircraft carrier which . . . would exercise a very powerful deterrent upon hostile raiding cruisers'. (The Chiefs of Staff had said that the Ceylon force, if sent, would be intended for the protection of the Middle East and the Cape sea route, rather than Australia.) Churchill added that if Japan set about invading Australia on a large scale, 'I have the explicit authority of the Cabinet to assure you that we should then cut our losses in the Mediterranean and proceed to your aid sacrificing every interest except only [the] defence position of this island on which all else depends.'

Australia was satisfied. Menzies appreciated the British position in the Middle East. He understood that 'Britain's expulsion would give spectacular and far-reaching results, involving not only our elimination from a vital sphere but endangering our interests in Iraq, Iran, and India, as well as giving encouragement to Japan for acts of further aggression.'

Here, with the war barely a year old and Churchill in power scarcely three months, the divergence of interests between the two countries was plain. Churchill said that he would rescue Australia if it was invaded on a large scale. But what exactly did that mean? The Australian Chiefs of Staff had reported that Australia could hold out in the event of a Japanese invasion for one month. How could Britain possibly prevent a total occupation? Even so, Australia complied with British strategy. In return for Churchill's optimistic reassurances, Australia gave him what he wanted: troops for the Middle East and the defence of Malaya, with its vital tin and rubber. It was as if Australia too failed to recognise the peril that threatened her.

Churchill's fundamental strategy, before Japan came into the war, was to defend the British Isles and to protect the Middle East, India and Burma. Japan was thought highly unlikely to go to war unless Germany successfully invaded Britain. Australia therefore did not need defending; she could best serve the cause by supplying troops, ships and aircrew in support of British strategy.

On 7 December 1941 the whole course of the war was transformed when Japan bombed Pearl Harbor – a 'supreme world event', in Churchill's phrase – and the United States declared war. Then Germany declared war on the United States.

Churchill was elated: now we had won the war. Australia was less elated; now they urgently needed to look to their own defence. They assumed that British and Allied strategy would change to take account of Japan's entry into the war. Fundamentally, however, it did not. Churchill's triumph, after he had sailed to the United States a week after Pearl Harbor in Britain's newest battleship, the *Duke of York*, was to persuade Roosevelt and his defence chiefs to maintain a Germany First strategy. (The Australians would have been happier had the *Duke of York* sailed east to Singapore, instead of west to Washington.)

From that decision all else flowed. But the Australians were not told of it. Curtin did not learn the full terms of the Anglo-American agreement until 28 May 1942.

Thus UK policy towards Australia remained constant both before and after Pearl Harbor: secure the use of Australian manpower, while reassuring them that Britain would come to their aid in the event of a serious crisis; treat their requests for supplies with sympathy, but in fact put them well down the list, well after other supplicants, such as Russia. The result was to leave the Dominion practically defenceless.

Day attributes the mistreatment of Australia in part to British snobbery; New Zealand and Canada were both better treated. Some of the quotes dug up by him are incredible. We knew that Churchill, when he was in a bad mood, once told his doctor Lord Moran (who made a fortune by ignoring the Hippocratic oath and publishing Churchill's indiscretions after he was safely dead) that 'the Australians came of bad stock'. Oliver Harvey, Eden's private secretary, described Curtin in his diary as 'a wretched second-rate man'. Oliver Lyttelton, Britain's minister to the Middle East, described General Blamey in a cable to London as 'little short of being insufferable'. Britain's High Commissioner to Australia, Sir Ronald Cross, criticised the Australians just before the fall of Singapore, in a letter, as an 'inferior people' with poor nerves.

Eventually the Australian worm turned. In the aftermath of the surrender at Singapore, Curtin insisted that Australian troops return from the Middle East to defend their country rather than be diverted in a desparate attempt to save Burma. Here, it is usually said, was an assertion of Australians' right to control their ultimate fate. Even so, Curtin allowed part of the Australian contingent to be off-loaded in Ceylon at Churchill's insistence, so his action was not quite such a proof of independence as has sometimes been stated.

One other myth is modified by Day. Curtin's celebrated New Year message of 27 December 1941 has been taken as an historic turning point in Anglo-Australian relations. It challenged Churchill's central strategy, which made the Japanese war an incident in the war against Germany: Curtin refused to 'accept the dictum that the Pacific struggle must be treated as a subordinate segment of the general conflict', and now looked to America 'without any inhibitions of any kind' and 'free of any pangs as to our traditional links or kinship with the United Kingdom'. However, Day claims that the true realignment of Australia's position in the world came much later. At the time Australia thought she was seeking only the temporary protection of the United States, and continued to believe that the imperial relationship could be resuscitated after the war.

And now that shocking word 'betrayal'. The general application of the word is clear enough: Britain promised to defend Australia and betrayed her by not providing help, leaving her at the mercy of Japan. But where does this word come from? Was it used at the time by Australia? It occurs six times in Day's text. The *Prince of Wales* and *Repulse* were sunk by Japanese torpedo bombers off the Malayan coast on 10 December. Singapore surrendered on 15 February 1942. On 23 January Sir Earle Page, Australia's envoy to London, cabled Australia to say that Churchill planned the evacuation of Singapore. Curtin was in Perth. In his absence an emergency meeting of the Australian War Cabinet met and agreed that the strongest representations should be made to Churchill. The Deputy Prime Minister, F.M. Forde, presided over the meeting but, says Day, it was probably H.V. Evatt, the Attorney-General, who composed the strong cable to Churchill saying that any evacuation of Singapore would be 'an inexcusable betrayal'. When Churchill got the cable he rounded on Page, reminding him that Britain was not planning to evacuate Singapore, only to divert its reinforcements to Burma. That is the first mention of the word 'betrayal'.

The next mention occurs when Day describes General Percival, the British commander in Singapore, walking down the road to the Japanese lines in his long baggy shorts and carrying a white flag, in a tableau that summed up the ignominious defeat. 'What it did not and could not reveal was the history of British neglect and betrayal that had made that lonely march inevitable.'

The third reference occurs when Churchill blames Australia for the loss of the British 18th Division, which he would have preferred to divert to Burma, but which went to Singapore because (according to Churchill) of the Australian accusation that its evacuation would constitute 'an inexcusable betrayal'.

In April 1942, as the Japanese advanced through the Solomon Islands and New Guinea, London dismissed Curtin's appeals for assistance. Lord Cranborne, the Colonial Secretary, privately noted that Australia had been wrong to assume Britain could protect them in all circumstances. Day goes on: 'He regarded with considerable equanimity the consequent Australian anger at Britain's betrayal of her defence pledge.'

Then we come to Day's concluding summary:

> The Australian Government claimed that Britain's threatened decision not to reinforce Singapore would be classed as 'inexcusable betrayal'. Churchill relented on that occasion and sent a British division which was uselessly added to the prisoners of war captured by the Japanese. Though the Australians accused the British of betrayal over Singapore, there were no such open accusations over Britain's long-promised assurances regarding Australian defence. Ironically it was left to MacArthur to make the allegation of British betrayal of the Dominion.

But did MacArthur make any such allegation? On the eve of the naval battle of Midway in June 1942 he advised Curtin that Australia's fate would depend on the result. Australia could not influence the battle, but it could protect itself against an adverse result. Accordingly MacArthur recommended that Australia insist on the return of the 9th Division from the Middle East and obtain Britain's support for the supply of aircraft to the RAAF. He observed that 'in Australia's hour of peril she was entitled at least to the use of all the forces she could raise herself'. He strongly criticised Britain for not returning in kind the 'assistance Australia had rendered overseas with naval, military and air forces'. By 11 June, after Midway had put the Japanese on the defensive for the rest of the war and assured Australia's survival, MacArthur was saying that 'it would now be interpreted as a timid cry for help, if we were to persist in demands for assistance for the defence of Australia'.

So Britain's betrayal of Australia is a conclusion reached by Day, rather than an accusation made by anyone in the Australian government at the time. Evatt's use of the word referred to a possible future event, and was in any case based on a misunderstanding. MacArthur thought Britain had mistreated Australia, but did not speak of betrayal.

I met Day, a bearded, quietly spoken man, born in 1949, in Melbourne and asked him how it was that he had been virtually the first person to dig up such rich material on a subject that had been sitting there for forty years. He told me that questions of war – military history – had been sidelined by comparison with social history; besides, Australians were either staying at home to do their PhDs or going to the United States rather than to London. You needed money to be able to work in the British archives for any length of time.

Why was he different? 'I simply wanted to go overseas and look into Australian history. The Second World War seemed to be a critical period – a period when you could latch on to a topic and say something significant about Australia generally. I applied to American universities, but only Cambridge would help with funding. The subject I chose seemed to be a time when Australia changed allegiances. I wanted to understand modern Australian history for myself.'

Where did the word 'great' in his title come from? 'I don't know; it seems to be not a minor betrayal, but a betrayal of historic proportions. Evatt used the word. If Britain abandoned Singapore, he said, it would be an inexcusable betrayal.'

But Britain did not 'abandon' Singapore, did it? 'Well, it cut its losses. It left it largely undefended.'

Could it have done otherwise? 'It had choices. Singapore was very low down in the priorities. That was something that Australia wasn't particularly privy to, until too late in the day.'

But what were we doing in the area – me and my mates aboard HMS *London*, and the rest of the 5th Cruiser Squadron – if we were not fighting the Japanese and thus defending Australia? 'Well, you were protecting British interests in the Indian Ocean. That's exactly what Stephen Roskill said.' Day was referring to Captain Stephen Roskill, DSC, a prolific and distinguished naval historian and a Fellow of Churchill College, Cambridge. 'I was at Churchill, where he was, and one of the other Fellows said to me, "Oh look, you should give Stephen your paper to look at." So I gave it to him, and he called me into his house, and he thumped the table.' Day laughed. 'This was only a very preparatory draft that I'd written based on secondary sources, and he said, "What do you mean we weren't there? I was there!" He was in command of a British cruiser they'd given to the New Zealand navy – *Leander*, I think it was [it was] – and this was the sole British cruiser in the Pacific Ocean.

'It's the same as Geoffrey Blainey. He says Britain didn't betray Singapore and didn't let Australia down because they sent out the *Prince of Wales* and *Repulse*. That's just nonsense. They weren't coming out to Australia; they were only coming out to Singapore on a tour, and they weren't going to stay there until the Japanese came in.'

What surprised him about his research? 'I had the notion, which most Australians have, that Australia during the Second World War switched from Britain to America because Britain couldn't defend us; they wanted to, but they couldn't. It was a bit different to that. Australia did switch to some extent, briefly, for no more than a year; but by 1943 they were seeing that their interest really lay in being back within the British Empire.'

The Australians thought they could succeed Britain as an imperial nation: 'kingpin, within the Empire, in the Pacific. Right back to the 1880s Australia had hankered after a southern empire. The ambition seemed to be realistic for a while; in 1943–4 Britain simply wasn't there' – except of course for me, and my regular naval brother, and Captain Roskill. 'Britain seemed to lack the will to recapture her empire, but there seemed no way that her empire could become independent. Somebody had to take control of those territories; nobody foresaw decolonisation coming so fast.'

Day said that one person in particular, W.S. Robinson (who was very big in the metals industry), was advising Evatt that Australia would have to create an arc of control from Malaya right round to Indonesia, New Guinea and Fiji. The idea was that Australia would draw on its raw materials; and Australian ex-servicemen, instead of being sent into the bush, as they were after the First World War, would be put into these territories to set up plantations and otherwise take control.

I asked Day how *The Great Betrayal*, and his earlier book, *Menzies and Churchill at War*, had been received. Funnily enough, he said, the more adverse reactions came in Australia. 'There were people here who just wouldn't have a bar of it; they couldn't credit that Menzies had ambitions in London. They didn't like the idea of him turning his back on Australia.'

More recently Day had been taken aback to discover that Paul Keating, when he was still Prime Minister, had been interested in his work. An invitation to tea had followed, served by an English butler, at which Keating supplied two hard-to-believe chips of Anglo-Australian news. He told Day that his own hero was Churchill. He also claimed that Robert Hawke had appealed to him to allow him to stay in power a bit longer – after Keating had displaced Hawke as Prime Minister – because he was about to be given the Freedom of the City of London.

Before we parted, and wishing to test the Day chip-on-the-shoulder factor, I said that Alexander Downer, about whom I had written a long profile shortly before, was by no means a fully paid-up Anglophile, in my opinion, largely because he had been maltreated and looked down on at an English public school because he was Australian. Had Day ever felt he was being looked down on? 'I think all Australians have that experience. They say that when an Australian walks into the room you can hear the chains clanking.

'I went to England very much with the idea that Australian Prime Ministers and politicians had had during the war: that Australia bulked large in the British mind. But when you got to

Britain you could see how small Australia bulked in the British mind. Corelli Barnett [military historian, and Keeper of the Churchill Archives at Churchill College, to which Day was attached for three years while working on his book] came to dinner once; and I made some offhand comment about Britain letting Australia down during the war, or words to that effect, and he said, "Well, you know, what was in it for Britain? It was only lamb chops – and Britain could get them cheaper and closer from the Argentine.'"

Day paused. He had reason to feel a shade resentful, I thought. Then he said, 'So it's interesting seeing these places from different ends of the telescope.' So: *no* chip on this historian's shoulder, I concluded.

Nevertheless, I cannot swallow the word 'betrayal'. The historian Geoffrey Serle has written, 'I deplore extreme assertions of British betrayal over Singapore – foolishness enough, surely, but betrayal is ridiculous.' In early 1943 Serle was in the army in Port Moresby, faced with the prospect of Japanese invasion and thinking hard about his country's basic situation. This led him into what he called 'insistent Australianism' after the war, in charge of Australian history and 300 students at Melbourne University: an active Fabian wanting to drag Australia out of colonialism towards self-respect, independence and effective nationality. His view on the matter must be said to carry weight.

7

The Republicans Stir

Of all the *grande dames* of Adelaide, the late Mrs Dutton was one of the grandest. One day at luncheon her clever son Geoffrey said that he had heard something funny about Government House.

'Geoffrey,' she said, '*nothing* about Government House is funny.'

Under those circumstances it is not altogether surprising that Donald Horne, professor of political science, inventor of the phrase 'The Lucky Country', prolific author and sometime chairman of the Australia Council, says that the person who started the modern republican movement was Geoffrey Dutton, who died in 1998.

I first encountered Dutton at the front gate of Patrick White's house Dogwoods (formerly The Glen) at Castle Hill in 1960 or 1961, where White lived with his friend Manoly, a few acres of what to me looked like unpromising scrub and a pack of intrusive schnauzer dogs. I was there to write a profile of White for the London *Observer*, just at the time when Britain – some people in Britain – was beginning to notice that White's novels, Sidney Nolan's paintings and Ray Lawler's plays seemed to constitute an Australian cultural awakening from the long Menzies sleep. I knew Dutton's name, because as part of my researches I had read his recent little book on White, and was aware that he was a poet, literary journalist and man of letters. I was also aware that he came from a grand South Australian family; indeed, White was interested in him partly because he was an exception to the rule laid down by *his* mother, namely that nobody of their class ever wrote books. White was just saying goodbye at his gate to Dutton, and it struck me that they could both be said to come out of the same Anglo-Australian box: tall and self-assured, one educated at Cambridge, the other (Dutton) at Oxford, both from old, well-established grazier families. Years later I learned from David Marr's biography of White that the two men had a furious falling-out; one of the many causes of White's fury was that Dutton had described him in print as an 'aristocrat', a classification that had made him hit the roof.

At all events, both men could fairly be described as privileged, with not a clanking chain within earshot. Dutton's father went to Magdalen College, Oxford, in 1898. Dutton himself belonged to the generation who still, if they had the money, went as a matter of course to Oxford or Cambridge; in his time there were heavy infusions of Australians in the Magdalen cricket XI, the rowing VIII and the tennis team.

A quarter of a century after the Dogwoods encounter, when I called on Dutton (known to his friends as 'Geoff'), he seemed physically to have changed less than most. The family home of Anlaby and its 8,000 acres sixty miles outside Adelaide had been sold long since, and Dutton was now living in a comfortable apartment in a modern block of flats in Melbourne, near the Victoria Market. He was wearing a blue denim shirt, tan trousers and good-looking brown shoes; and was full of bounce and gossip, and as busy as ever, reviewing here and there and working on a book about three nineteenth-century writers, all of whom had sadly died in their thirties: Marcus Clarke, Henry Kendall and Adam Lindsay Gordon.

Dutton remembered exactly how his republican views had taken wing; and if Horne is right in crediting him with starting modern republicanism, then it must be worth describing in some detail how this happened, since Dutton never wrote his own account.

But he did keep an intermittent journal. In March 1958 he wrote:

The Royal Visit of the Queen Mum – the heartburn over invitations. We saw the 'Royal Progress' from a stand in front of the Town Hall – good Australian touch provided at last moment by City Council garbage truck driving through massed crowds, manned by three hairy-legged blokes in shorts, one of them giving a regal wave to the crowds. Refusal of intellectuals like Max [Harris] to take any part – what social comedy they miss!

In England the writer and mischief-maker Malcolm Muggeridge, lately retired from the editorship of *Punch*, had been enjoying himself with an anti-royal tease that had provoked abuse and controversy. Two months after the Queen Mother's visit he came to Adelaide, and Dutton dined with him, Rohan Rivett, editor of the Adelaide *News*, and the young Rupert Murdoch, proprietor of the Adelaide *News* and, at that stage, little else. Dutton's journal notes: 'M.M. genuinely concerned at bad effect on Australians of worshipping image of power that had no power.'

To me Dutton said, 'I remember that dinner very well, in a rather nasty, smoky restaurant on the Anzac Highway. Muggeridge said: "Geoffrey, what are you doing about a republic?" and I to be honest hadn't thought about it. My mother was an ardent monarchist – friends with all the governors who used to come up and stay and all this sort of thing. I wasn't an ardent monarchist; I was busy thinking about other things and the status quo didn't worry me. Then Rupert and Rohan charged in, and Rupert was very strong. He said: "Well, I think it's really ridiculous there's not a republican movement here." Rohan said he felt strongly about it too, but he didn't think the Adelaide *News* could be pushing it; and Rupert said: "Oh well, yes, the time's not quite right, but it certainly should be coming." So I went away and thought.'

That was the start of it all. His first thought concerned his possession, like all Australians, of a British passport. 'I wrote something for Tom Fitzgerald at the *Nation* about how cheesed off I was about this British passport business. For instance, I had travelled through Persia in 1952–3 at the time of the great Mossadeq oil crisis and the frontier official – a charming, well-educated man – said, "You know, you British are doing bad things to us here." I said, "No! I'm Australian!" He said, "But you're a British subject," and I had to explain the whole rigmarole. In several places where the British were unpopular and the Australians were totally out of it, I had to explain that I wasn't British.'

The trigger for the subsequent article credited by Horne with starting the modern republican movement was a spell in the United States as a visiting professor (Dutton was nothing if not mobile). 'This university I was lecturing at was way out in the sticks in Kansas, so it was pretty authentic Middle America, it wasn't sophisticated New York, and some of these people really thought Australia was an offshore island of England; Australia had no identity at all, just part of the British Commonwealth. I thought: this is ridiculous. So I wrote an article saying that Australia should rid itself of the monarchy and sent it off to Tom Fitzgerald and he published it. The headline was "British Subject", a reference to the fact that Australians were still "British" on our passports.

'That was the article which Donald Horne very generously identified as the start of modern republicanism. The reaction absolutely amazed me, because the *Nation* was a highbrow fortnightly, not the sort of thing that the man in the street reads, but when I got back to Australia six months afterwards it was amazing the way people talked about it, even taxi drivers.' Soon after the article first appeared, Fitzgerald rang Dutton in Kansas from Sydney to ask if there was such a person as L.M. Dutton. There was: Dutton's sister-in-law Peg, President of the Liberal Country League of South Australia; she had written to the *Nation* dissociating the Dutton family from Geoffrey's 'attitude to our Queen'.

The *Nation* article was published in 1963. In June 1966 Dutton edited a book entitled *Australia and the Monarchy*. 'I think in the interval *Quadrant*, an Australian quarterly review, had a pro-monarchy blast. There were a few things like that. The adult-education organisation in Victoria and the Fabian Society staged a combined symposium on the republic, with an academic from Melbourne University who was the hired gun for the monarchists;

145

he was a bit of a turncoat, that one, because he became a back-door republican.'

The reference to this event in his journal is dated 18 April 1965: 'Lecture to Fabian Society in Kew Town Hall. John Button chairman . . . Fantastic furore in *News* when home. "SA Poet Tilts at Queen. Floods of Letters." People stopping me in street and saying "I agreed with every word you said" . . . Mrs M. saying did I know, as friends of hers had told her mother, that Queen descended from David.'

Australia and the Monarchy was by no means an undiluted call for a republic. The monarchists were given their say. One of the contributions, by the journalist Don Whitington, entitled 'The Liberal Party and the Monarchy', quoted the Liberal Member of Parliament William Charles Wentworth, great-grandson of the nineteenth-century New South Wales politician ánd landowner and, like him, educated at Cambridge. A member of the House of Representatives since 1949, Wentworth was known as a 'red baiter', but he was also regarded as intelligent and well informed. 'It is not so much the abstract idea of an Australian President which is repugnant to us,' he opined, 'rather it is the idea of an actual Australian as President. The Monarchy helps us resolve this innate dilemma.' He added, 'There is virtually no republican sentiment in Australia.'

Nevertheless, Dutton recalled, 'when the book came out we were amazed at what we'd stirred up. I was sprinting all over the place doing radio and television.' The Adelaide *News* serialised the book in June. Dutton noted in his journal on 10 June: 'Melbourne for pub. of Monarchy. TV Meet the Press. Too polite.'

He was not polite enough for the South Australia establishment. 'A storm broke out in Adelaide. I remember Donald Horne [one of the republican contributors to the book] writing to me and saying, "I had lunch at Government House in Sydney yesterday and you've been kicked out of the Adelaide Club! That's the difference between Sydney and Adelaide." Actually I wasn't kicked out. I resigned. The story made front-page news.'

It was a defining event. The public learned about it on 8 July: 'Monarchy Critic Resigns. Leaves Club,' stated the *News* headline. The story read: 'Adelaide's critic of the monarchy Mr Geoffrey

Dutton has resigned from the Adelaide Club after an influential and senior member suggested this to him in a letter . . .' Dutton was forty-three and had been a member of the Club for twenty-two years. His statements to the *News* were low-key. 'I am not squealing about it,' he was quoted as saying. 'I still firmly believe that the internal affairs of clubs should remain absolutely the concern of members. I would not want to cause embarrassment to others in the Club by intruding as an alien.' Asked for his reaction, the Club president, Sir Brian Swift, had declined to discuss the matter.

The letters columns of the *News* remained silent for six days, although there was plenty of alarmed coverage about a falling concrete block that had narrowly missed the Queen in Belfast. On 8 July the paper told its readers which South Australians had attended a royal garden party at Buckingham Palace; those present included the newly knighted High Commissioner to London, Sir Alexander Downer, and Lady Downer, who wore 'a flower-printed silk jersey dress in blue and yellow with a white picture hat'. On 12 July the paper reported that two unnamed Australians had been in a 'royal car crash' with Prince Richard of Gloucester. It looked as if W.C. Wentworth was right about the paucity of republicans, at least in the *News* circulation area. (Its more conservative rival, the *Advertiser*, had not deigned to report the story at all.) Finally, on 14 July the *News* published a single letter defending Dutton. The writer had read with disgust about the row: 'a typical example of the bigoted nonsense and snobbery that exists particularly in South Australia. Surely Mr Dutton is allowed some freedom of thought and expression . . .'

Behind the scenes, despite his public calm, Dutton was extremely angry, and he remained so thirty years on, even though the movement he had allegedly started appeared to be rolling ahead on an unstoppable wave.

'The thing that incensed me, and my colleagues, was the line that one was unpatriotic! This is absolutely true: you were thought to be unpatriotic if you were a republican. If you said, "My loyalties are to Australia, not to the Queen," it was disgraceful. That was the basis of the letter I had from this old brute, this lawyer in Adelaide, Collier Cudmore, who was actually up at

Oxford with me, and I rowed with him, and he was my sponsor or whatever you call it for the Adelaide Club in 1944. He wrote me this letter, beginning "Dear Sir", saying it was disgraceful that I should be so unpatriotic and that he didn't see how I could remain a member of the Club. He had been President of the Club, an old warhorse, and I wrote back and more or less said he could stick his club up his arse, I was so annoyed. I resigned instantly.'

His journal reads: 'June 25–July 10: The Club row . . . sorted out my mates . . . Dick and Chris [Christopher Legoe, later a member of the Supreme Court of South Australia] resigned from the Committee in protest – no one would support even a mild letter to Collier Cudmore. Ian Thomas, Chairman, had already written accepting my resignation. Chris furious – he tore up letter. Jim Hall denounced me . . . Only supporter Jack Rymill.'

Several members thought it ridiculous that Dutton should have resigned, including 'old Archie Price' – Sir Archibald Grenfell Price, head of St Mark's College, Liberal MP and a staunch monarchist. His brother-in-law, the 'Dick' who resigned from the Committee – Dick Blackburn, chancellor of the Australian National University and a chief justice of the Federal Court – thought the same. He told Dutton there were lots of members of the Club who would have supported him. 'So there were a lot of members who weren't republicans, but wouldn't have thought it unpatriotic to hold republican views.'

Dutton's wife (his journal notes) went to dinner with some friends who had their own answer to this apparent conflict. 'Well,' they said, 'he can be a republican as long as he stays loyal to the Queen.' His sister-in-law, Peg, was less tolerant, 'saying this was the end, my telling the Press. Why hadn't I said "No Comment" like B. Swift – when I'd been defending the bloody Club. Poor Collier,' she had said, 'he just loves his Club, your father, and John [John Dutton, Geoff's brother and Peg's husband] and the Queen.'

One national organisation with which Dutton had a series of brushes after he declared his republicanism was the Returned Services League. Although his four and a half years in the air force had entitled him to join the RSL, Dutton had not done so, because he found them intolerably reactionary. (He did join during the Vietnam War, however, so that when he mounted an anti-war platform he could wear an RSL badge alongside his air-force medals.) It so happened that at about the time of the Club row, Dutton persuaded the Russian poet Yevgeny Yevtushenko to attend the Adelaide Festival. His presence had not been welcomed by all. Dutton treasured two phrases resulting from the visit, one from either side of the Iron Curtain. In Adelaide the head of the local branch of the RSL, a ferocious anti-republican, recommended that Dutton should be sent back to Russia where he obviously belonged. 'Send Dutton Back To Russia' read the *News* poster. The other phrase cropped up the following year when, in return for the Yevtushenko visit, Dutton attended a 'cultural' event in Georgia; Yevtushenko used to introduce him as a 'former member of aristocratic club'.

Dutton edited a follow-up volume in 1977 called *Republican Australia?* and asked Sir Zelman Cowen to contribute. 'I knew he'd sit on the fence. That was one of things that amused me: the fury of the monarchists because neither of these books was purely republican; in the second, as in the first, we allowed monarchists to have their say. In *Republican Australia?* we had Daniel O'Connell, the great expert on international law, Chichele Professor of International Law at Oxford and a tremendous monarchist, arguing that republicanism would weaken the Federation. Anyhow I asked Zel to do a chapter, which he did, and his appointment as Governor-General exactly synchronised with the publication of the book; totally unexpected. So that was a nice touch.'

Who, I asked, were his allies? 'Richard Walsh, the young demon, as he was then. Max Harris; he and I were co-editors of the original *Australian Book Review*. And of course Donald Horne. Robin Boyd; he drove me out to that Fabian Society function in a very nice car, a Studebaker. Jock Marshall the scientist. Surprisingly, *The Bulletin* was on side, too. Kerry Packer was the proprietor and it wasn't his official line, but of course it had had a tradition of republicanism going back to Archibald's day; they asked me to do a big piece when the second book came out.

'Patrick White was a flaming republican, but not originally. I first knew him in about 1957; his partner Manoly was a terrific snob, being descended from a Byzantine emperor or something, and both he and Patrick were terribly conservative. When this article of mine came out, they went into a deep think about it, but Manoly's line was that no Australian was up to the job of being President. Patrick didn't explode; he said, "Oh well, well yes." Patrick subscribed to the airmail editions of *The Observer* and the *Sunday Times* and used to take their line, not just on literature. He had a residual "British-is-best" attitude. Eventually Patrick became one of our best supporters. But it was not a rapid conversion.

'None of my allies was Irish. Daniel O'Connell, as I say, was a staunch monarchist. Henry Lawson wasn't Irish. But there was a powerful Irish interest. The great Melbourne journalist Marcus Clarke edited several magazines that came and went; I found one the other day in the Mitchell Library, about 1870, saying the child must leave mother eventually, but little Victoria wasn't old enough to leave big Victoria – Queen Victoria – yet.' Here was a classic example, I thought, of 'separation anxiety'. 'That was pre-Federation of course, so they had a point; but I hadn't realised that that was stirring along well before the *Bulletin* in the 1890s.'

I could remember no fall-out from the 1977 book by the time I arrived to work for *The Age* in the autumn of that year. This surprised me, because the passions aroused by the sacking of Whitlam by Governor-General Sir John Kerr in 1975 were still raw; on the left, arguments were still going on about the extent to which Buckingham Palace might or might not have been involved. During the federal election campaign of 1980, Michelle Grattan, the paper's Canberra bureau chief, and I – in an interview with the leader of the Labor Party, Bill Hayden – asked him what he thought about a republic. As I recall, he kicked for touch; and throughout the campaign he certainly never mentioned an issue that I had supposed, in my innocence, might have been a vote-winner for a halfway radical Labor Party. At any rate, Hayden lost.

I asked Dutton why republicanism, after the flurry of 1977, died away. 'The whole story, right up to John Howard today, is terribly indicative of the conservatism of Australians. A combination of Mummy Knows Best and a sort of easygoing "Oh, yeah, well things are rolling along and we'll do something more urgent." The *Bulletin*, after the 1977 book came out, did quite a few republican stirs. I saw the editor, Trevor Kennedy, soon after I did my piece and he said, "Oh, there's just a lot of apathy. It seems to be a dead issue." And it was, for an awful long time. For all his faults, and the way he tried to take it over, Paul Keating shoving it on the front iron is what really got it going again. Australia's got an enormously slow-moving pulse, and of course John Howard is completely plugged into that; listening to that pulse is his life. That's how he operates.'

The Clubs

That a club was the opening battleground of modern republicanism is not at all surprising. The most prominent Australian clubs, even now, are shrines of Englishness – or, if their members object to that notion, were within living memory shrines of Englishness or Britishness.

Consider the following statement: 'Where is the heart of the British Empire? . . . in the Adelaide Club you will find the answer. Here, far removed from any suspicion of the idea that Queen Victoria is not still on the throne you will find something that I thought had ceased to exist – the England we were taught about at school, the England of Kipling, or even of Dickens!'

This is an extract from Boyd Neel's *The Story of an Orchestra*, published in 1950. It might be supposed that most organisations, eager to present themselves as forward-looking, would buy up all available copies of Boyd Neel's book containing this wounding statement and hide them in a cellar. On the contrary, the quotation stands as the epigraph to the official history of the club: *The Adelaide Club 1863–1963*, privately printed for members and friends, by E.J.R. Morgan. The introduction to the book is by C.R. Cudmore, President – the fellow whose letter to Geoffrey Dutton caused him instantly to resign. Cudmore writes: 'None of us would claim that this Club is unique. But we would all hope by our daily lives in this place to substantiate the claim that here we carry on the kind of Club life that has been the joy and relaxation of English gentlemen, wherever they may be, during the nineteenth and twentieth century.'

The text describes the British connection. It argues that from South Australia's earliest days, probably because of the way the colony was founded and the class of people who came there as founders, a certain number of the second, third and now the fourth generation of those founders' families have finished their education at the old 'Oxbridge' universities. The 'vast majority' of those young men, after returning, 'and becoming established, in the professions, or on the land, joined The Adelaide Club . . . This almost continuous infusion of the mellow thought, as well as the latest ideas, from the English seats of learning has, I am sure, had a profound influence on this Club.'

The class of people who comprised the Club's founders were, the history tells us: first, pastoralists; and, second, men in commerce. There were no members of the retail trade. Many were members of the legislature. In all, the Club has included six Premiers, past and present. Most of its members were Protestants, 'but at the beginning and thereafter Club members have included some belonging to the Roman Catholic faith and some of the Jewish faith'.

Not all students of Adelaide society, naturally, take quite as sunny a view of the Club as the contributors to its centenary history. In the city's library is a copy of a Melbourne thesis dated 1973 by D. Van Dissel. It is called *The Adelaide Gentry, 1880–1916*, and observes: 'Essentially it is a story relating the success of eighty or so families in achieving the status, rank and position to which they had aspired, but had been unable to attain, in the Mother Country . . .' By 1973 'this group of families still appeared in the popular mind and in the work of many sociologists the most rigid upper class in Australia'. In passing, the author (no doubt an aspiring Melbourne sociologist) takes an unkind swipe at the founders of the Adelaide Club: 'Only a few of them would have been considered gentry in Great Britain.' Those few, alas, he fails to name.

Gentry or not, they founded a club that the visitor can only envy and admire. It is handy for Government House; it has the peace and gleaming surfaces of the best sort of club; the writing

152

paper is pretty. England is not far away: *Country Life*, the *Guardian* and the *Weekly Telegraph* are neatly laid out — 'Country Life is required reading,' said the Secretary — and menus may offer Stilton cheese, Welsh rarebit and pickled walnuts. The cellar is excellent: John Betjeman, invited to lunch there in the mid-1960s, was delighted by the food and the company, but disappointed and surprised (he said afterwards) to be offered only French wines; he had hoped to taste Australian, having heard that the industry had moved ahead since Evelyn Waugh's father, during the 1920s, complained at a dinner party, to his socially ambitious son's embarrassment, that Australian Emu wine made his feet itch.

In the early days it was impossible to govern South Australia effectively without the support of the powerful members of the Adelaide Club; but times have moved on. Sir Alexander Downer, writing about Menzies's genius for getting himself re-elected, said that before one election, 'In the Adelaide Club — one of the best men's clubs in the world but never a reservoir of political wisdom — the cry went up: "You will never win with Menzies."' Wise they may not always be, but the members are proud. In his journal Dutton noted an example of South Australian family pride. 'J.I.M. Stewart [an Oxford don out from the UK, who spent ten years as professor of English Literature at Adelaide University] in one of his novels called a butler Bagot. Walter Bagot wrote to him to say that no Bagot had ever been a servant; but he had once had a gardener called Stewart.'

The Weld Club

The late director of the London School of Economics, Sir Alexander Carr-Saunders, used to say decades ago that the universities he was helping to establish in British overseas territories would one day, after they had all become independent, remain the only links between the former colonies and their conquerors.

The same may well be true of the Australian clubs after Australia becomes a republic. One leading scholar of the subject is Colonel M.A. Count, secretary of the Weld Club in Perth, who described himself to me as the dean of club secretaries in Australia, having occupied his office since 1980. At my request, he ran through the roll-call of these noble and almost unchanging institutions. 'Going round the country, there is the Queensland Club. The Newcastle Club, which was formed in 1875 but only sought reciprocity with the rest of us in 1993; that's the squattocracy of New England, the old money of NSW. The Union Club in Sydney. The Australian in Sydney. The Hobart Club, the Launceston Club. The Melbourne Club, the Australian Club, Melbourne, and the Athenaeum. The Adelaide Club and the Weld. That's eleven. We meet every January in a different club to discuss matters of mutual interest; we don't compete, because we're all in the same business.'

The Weld Club was the first Australian member of the Distinguished Clubs of the World Association, which has twenty-five members: five from the UK, fifteen from North America and five from the rest of the world. The British clubs are White's, Brooks's and the Garrick, with two vacancies. The American clubs include the Knickerbocker and the Pacific Union in San Francisco. Who decides? 'They do. You have to be over a hundred years old. The secretary has to have an impressive CV. You have to be visited. In our case we were visited by a couple of committee members from Boodles and the Carlton, who stayed here and went back and reported on us to their respective secretaries. These visits are surreptitious. They test the accommodation and the feel of the place. You do not apply to join; you are asked if you would like to apply – which doesn't mean that you're going to get in.'

I could see why the visiting English scrutineers would have been favourably impressed by the Weld Club, starting with the secretary, for the colonel exuded an air of military efficiency combined with a decently restrained pride in the club he was running and an amused view of its tribal character and eccentricities. 'Every now and again we put on beef and Guinness stew,' he said. 'The manager has to ring up eight particular members and they all come rushing in.' The visiting stickybeaks would also have been favourably impressed by the club comforts. Australians, whether at the racetrack or at home, rate comfort more highly than the British; they are not stuck with cramped old buildings

154

and are not inhibited by the strange belief that the grander you are, the more uncomfortable you should be. Club bedrooms in London have only lately advanced beyond the washstand and iron bedstead era; the Weld Club regards itself as being in competition with Perth's best hotels. The assessor would also have noted with approval *Country Life* and *The Spectator*, a portrait in the front hall of the first patron of the club, after whom it is named – His Excellency Governor Weld – in his Dundreary whiskers, a shell from Gallipoli and a painting of 'The Return of Henry V' from Agincourt.

The English connection has always been strong. 'The Club was founded in 1871 after a meeting in the Perth Town Hall called by Colonel Henry Weld-Blundell, cousin to Governor Weld, and of course the Welds are the Welds of Lulworth Castle, Dorset. I'm the only one in the Club who knows the family, because I did two years on exchange with the British army as a tank–gunnery instructor at Lulworth Gunnery School. My tanks did a bit of damage to the Welds' tenants' cottages. That's when I first met the head of the family.

'Weld was the first Catholic governor of the colony, and he was reported to the Vatican by the senior Roman Catholic priest because, after dinner one night at Government House, he had asked the Anglican Bishop of Perth to say grace. Weld explained to the Vatican that Western Australia was a Protestant colony and it was only fitting that the bishop should say grace. The Vatican then made him a papal knight, which must have upset the Monsignor.

'The Welds are a romantic story,' said the Colonel. 'There was no room on the Dorset land for the man who became governor, a third child; so he went share-farming in New Zealand, where he became Premier before being appointed to Western Australia. Then he was promoted to be governor of Tasmania, followed by the Straits Settlements. After he died his wife, by now Lady Weld, who had borne ten children, went into a nunnery whose abbess was one of her daughters.'

The man who designed the Club buildings, just out from England aged twenty-six, secured as his second job the design of the Swan Brewery. Later he became second-in-command to

General Monash in the First World War, as Lieutenant-General Sir J. Talbot Hobbs, and President of the Weld Club in 1928. 'Monash described being entertained at the Club in his diary, which was published in Geoffrey Serle's wonderful biography,' the colonel went on. 'He made the comment that there were these nine or ten families represented at dinner and "the whole universe revolved around their utterance". Nothing's changed. I reprinted the extract and sent round a copy because five of the nine members on the committee were from those same families named by Monash in 1904.'

Perth's population was only 3,000 when the Club was founded. Fremantle had 5,000 and Guilford 4,000 inhabitants. The rest of the state had 4,000. There were only taverns in Perth; there was nowhere to stay. The Club had twenty single rooms. So when the members came in from the bush, they at least had a room to stay in. Until the turn of the century the overflow slept in tents on the lawn. 'No problem with these gentlemen; they spent their lives out in the Kimberleys: a tent on a grass lawn was luxury. In 1893 of course this remote little world changed with the discovery of gold at Kalgoorlie.'

All members – now numbering 720 – have been invited to join. There is an aversion to serving politicians. Sir Charles Court (born in Crawley, Sussex; Premier of Western Australia 1974–82) was elected only after he had retired. His father was an English migrant, a working man; in the 1930s he hid from the police in the gardens of the Club after they broke up a Labor Party rally, a fact that Sir Charles revealed at a Club dinner held in his honour. 'There is almost an inherited dislike of politicians in the Club; this is not a political club, not like the Carlton. All you hear, lunching, is condemnation of whoever is in government; it's like reading *The Spectator*. They've only broken the rule once, for a man who was a bachelor, a Hungarian, a migrant and a lawyer; you would think all those things would be against him, but the late Andrew Mensaros was that rare thing in Western Australia, a respected politician.

'Entry into the Club used to be refused to tradesmen. You know Anthony Hordern's, the great store in Sydney? Hordern put up the money for railways in Western Austraia, but he still

156

couldn't get honorary membership here. The state couldn't afford to finance the railways; he could, but he didn't get in these doors. He was in trade – and in Sydney, what was more.'

The colonel explained that the British links were still pretty strong. For many British, Perth was the first port of call, the jumping-off point for the growing tourist trade to the Kimberleys and the round trip to Darwin. Then there are the British business interests in Perth, particularly mining. A lot of British investment flows through the state. It is a two-way traffic. Sometimes in the Cavalry and Guards Club in London, he said, there are more Weld Club members staying there than Cavalry and Guards Club members. 'All the London clubs have now got some pretty good accommodation, except the Carlton. The Oriental does me favours; it'll take my widows; and it'll take members with quite small children.

'There's another aspect too. This has always been a very loyal state. The enlistment rate in both wars was higher here than in any other state. Even today, the regular army is composed of eleven per cent West Australians, yet we're only four per cent of the population. After leaving the regular army in 1980, I was amazed to find so many ex-prisoners of war – most of them prisoners of the Japanese, because the 8th Division taken at Singapore had only two brigades, and one was West Australian. A lot of the men captured in Crete were West Australians, too. Dr Alan King was one of them; he spent the war in Silesia and tells marvellous tales about how the Russian prisoners made excellent vodka out of potato peelings, using rainwater butts outside the huts.'

The Melbourne Club

Of the other prominent Australian clubs, the Melbourne Club is the most prominent and the most abused. Of all Australian cities, Melbourne alone is credited with an 'establishment' that exerts a powerful, unelected sway over the fortunes of the state; and the Melbourne Club is usually identified as the place where this shadowy body allegedly congregates. Alan Moorehead, born in Melbourne, was invited to a formal dinner there when he went back to his home town in 1952, having won fame as a war correspondent and author. 'Certainly no English club could keep pace with it,' he wrote to his wife in London. 'Waiters all in full livery, drinks laid out in decanters from which you help yourself, barrels of oysters and millionaires in spats and English voices. The furniture is Buckingham Palace.' The Club certainly looks like a power-centre: prominently sited and easily identified by its solid façade and big windows on Collins Street, close to Parliament; but personally I have never been able to believe the legends about its power. The Club possesses an extensive garden not visible from the street; but the members were evidently powerless to stop a hefty modern office block being erected alongside the garden and overshadowing it.

Some of the abuse has been justified, such as the charge of anti-Semitism. In 1969 Ranald Macdonald, managing director of David Syme & Co., owners of *The Age* newspaper, and some young Turks proposed Baillieu Myer for membership – Myer being a scion of the Myer store clan, a philanthropic Jewish family that had always taken seriously its obligations to the city that made it rich. But the proposal was strongly opposed, until Macdonald and his supporters got the rules changed. (The Weld Club elected its first Jewish member in 1921.)

Behind that imposing Club façade, odd things have gone on. An agreeable youngish member owned the Margaret Webber bookshop; my eyes opened wide on my first visit in 1977 when I saw for sale there not one but two copies of the complete *Oxford English Dictionary*: an impressively lavish use of shelf space. A side-room overflowed with expensive art books. Tables at the entrance displayed the latest literary biographies and critical works from the UK, with special attention to Bloomsbury. Flowers stood around in bowls. One or two comfortable chairs were occupied by browsing customers. The owner took me to lunch at the Club and talked about Virginia Woolf. One day he was arrested; and it turned out that he had been defrauding his clients at the insurance firm where he worked, in order to fund his ideal bookshop. He went to prison.

Another instance: after a smart Melbourne wedding the reception was held at the Club. A friend of mine, a visiting

English Etonian, and a Scottish school friend of his entered the Club together and, as they did so, the Scotsman exclaimed: 'I know that man! He owes me money!' The man was the new Club secretary, a retired Australian naval officer, who also owed money elsewhere. He was in addition the unnamed informant who had supplied Anthony Gray with material for a weird book published by Weidenfeld & Nicolson in the UK, which purported to demonstrate that Harold Holt, the Australian Prime Minister drowned off Portsea, had not been drowned at all but had been picked up by a Chinese submarine and spirited off to China. Holt had been, the book claimed, a spy for China. The Etonians approached a member of the Melbourne Club Committee, and the new Club secretary was instantly dismissed. He must have thought he and his debts were well out of the reach of Anglo-Australian, or rather Scottish-Australian, upper-class tentacles.

While I was in Melbourne, Sam White, the *Evening Standard*'s long-established Paris correspondent and an Australian, came to stay at the Melbourne Club by virtue of his membership of the Travellers' Club in Paris. Sam was amused to have penetrated to the heart of his old home-town's establishment, especially as he had scarcely been back to Melbourne since he had eloped to Europe before the war with the daughter of the state Premier. Heading for the Club bar on arrival, he fell into the embrace of a leading surgeon whom he had not seen since they were both clandestine members of the Communist Party. That gratified him still more: a Jewish ex-communist hobnobbing in the Club with an old comrade among unsuspecting WASP supporters of the Liberal Party. He felt, he said, as if at last he must have arrived.

However, Sam would never have made it to the red-letter day that occurs once every four years in the Club calendar. That is when ex-Oxford and -Cambridge members of the Club entertain, with a slap-up dinner and speeches, ex-Oxford and -Cambridge cricketers, reporters and commentators who are in Melbourne for the quadrennial Ashes test match. It is a symbolic occasion, lively and intimate: the Club as keeper of the Anglo-Australian flame.

8

Whingeing Poms

It must have been in the early 1960s that anyone with even half an ear cocked to Anglo-Australian relations would have become aware of disconcerting noises.

First, there was the ever-louder, grating voice of the Whingeing Pom. Next, and still more ominous, were the tongues of fury spitting out from even the most Anglophile of ministers in the 1961 Menzies government as Britain began to inch her way into Europe; this change of direction by Britain undoubtedly helped to launch the slow-moving glacier of modern republicanism. And third, there were bitter complaints about the mean-minded restrictions placed upon Australians before they were permitted to enter the UK.

The Whingeing Pom grew out of Australia's post-war migration policy. 'Populate or perish' was the watchword, inspired by the fear that an empty continent was a tempting target for heavily populated countries to the north. To begin with, after the war, the Australian government had high hopes that it would draw almost all its new population from Britain. Arthur Calwell, the Labor politician, was Australia's first immigration minister. A strong supporter of the White Australia policy, who had the gall to entitle one of his publications *Be Just and Fear Not*, Calwell said that he wanted an annual population increase of 2 per cent, of which 1 per cent would come from natural growth and 1 per cent from immigration. The government would admit refugees from the continent of Europe, but he hoped there would be ten British migrants for every foreign migrant.

The British–Australian Migration Agreement was signed in 1946. Under what came to be known as the Assisted Passage Scheme, any British citizen over the age of nineteen, being of good health and character and having been scrutinised and selected by immigration officials at Australia House in London, could take passage to their new home for ten pounds sterling.

It soon became obvious that Calwell's ideas about predominantly British migration were too rigid, and that others must be let in.

Here we need some figures. When the post-war emigration of Britons got under way, the total population of Australia was 7,579,358, slightly less than the population of London. Of this, 90 per cent had been born in Australia, almost entirely of British or Irish stock, and of those born elsewhere 8 per cent came from Britain or from a Commonwealth country. Fifteen years later the total population had increased to 12,728,500, but only 80 per cent had been born in Australia, and 42 per cent of those born outside Australia had come from Britain. (Just 4 per cent came from Asian countries. The reason for this low figure is vividly brought home by a display in the immigration museum in Adelaide; it illustrates the tests that, as a non-European, you had to pass – dictation tests, economic circumstances, and so on – before you had a hope of qualifying for entry. Enacted by the new Commonwealth Parliament in 1901, the policy lasted more or less unchanged until the 1950s.) Thus the big difference between the flow of immigrants to Australia after the Second World War and in earlier periods was the high proportion of non-British Europeans.

These are Charles Price's figures from the department of demography at the Australian National University, showing the origins of people who came to Australia between July 1947 and June 1970 with the intention of settling there:

British Isles	1,086,500	Germany	121,300
Italy	337,700	Malta	68,400
Greece	200,000	Other E. Europe	220,600
Netherlands	140,600	Others	334,100
Yugoslavia	136,800	*Total*	2,646,000

161

We never heard anything about the Whingeing Dutch or the Whingeing Greeks. But to get the low-down on the Poms, the place to go is the spacious and comfortable campus of the University of Western Australia. There is the man who, for some forty years, has kept a professional eye on the British who arrived in Australia under the Assisted Passage Scheme: Professor R.T. Appleyard, Reg to his friends.

His genial attitude to the British is perhaps surprising, since his father, as the professor puts it, 'had very emotional views about them'. Appleyard senior, as a member of the AIF (the Australian Imperial Force) had been through the horrors of the trenches in France during the First World War and had seen the carnage; 'he came back and took it out on the Brits, particularly because of the superiority of the British officers, which he detested. That attitude now is not very common in Australia. I think we've grown up a bit.' The professor said he thought that these days Australians felt even more strongly about the First World War than they used to, not because of Gallipoli, or in any anti-British sense, 'but in terms of how could people – whoever they were – have been so stupid as to allow many hundreds of thousands of people to die in order to gain such a small amount of territory'.

I had always imagined that the British and Australian governments collaborated happily over migration; and I was taken aback to learn that they did not. About a year after it was agreed that the programme would be equally funded, Britain stopped paying her share. Few people in wartime and post-war Australia had closer contacts with the UK than Richard Casey: Cambridge University, British minister in Cairo during the war and eventually a life peer and Governor-General. Apart from his questionable liking for shooting eagles from a private light aircraft, he was generally regarded as a shrewd fellow; yet he seriously prophesied after the war that 'a considerable part of the future of the British race will lie in Australia'.

That was not how the British government saw it. Before long, they realised that they had been rather too hasty in backing the migration schemes. 'Attlee and those succeeding him were pretty hard-nosed, and they soon saw that this wasn't a very bright policy for them to be following,' said Appleyard. 'When there were post-war labour shortages in Britain, with Italian workers coming into the mines, what was the logic in supporting a large shift of skilled British workers to Australia? One senior official in the Department of Labour in St James's Square often expressed to me the absurdity of Britain getting involved in a policy that was all for Australia's benefit. The Australians respected the need not to select people who at that time were desperately needed in Britain – especially coal miners and nurses. But Australia House had half a million British people on its books at one stage under the Assisted Passage Scheme, when it only required 50,000 or 60,000 a year to meet its quota, so it was in a position to select the very best applicants. Those tough-minded bureaucrats in the labour offices could see that giving the Australians *carte blanche* to pick anyone and have the British government pay for their passage made no sense.'

So the Australian government had to be very careful at the political level, the professor went on, and had to keep saying that it was only taking 'a cross-section' of the British population. 'Well, of course it wasn't getting a cross-section; it was getting a very high proportion of skilled and semi-skilled labour and a few professional people.' Australia was disappointed that Britain wasn't making more of a financial contribution, but what was Australia getting? People educated and trained in the British system; all they had to do was to pay ten pounds, and Australia would put them into an Australian system that replicated British practices. A carpenter who had done his apprenticeship in Sheffield, and who then got a job in a factory in Melbourne, needed no retraining whatsoever. You could not say the same about the Italians, for instance. In fact the Australian government became quite concerned about the skill levels of not only the Italians but of other southern European immigrants; and this persuaded it of the importance of sticking with the British programme.

The trade-union movement caused trouble over the non-British; it resisted admitting them into industries where a less than fully skilled worker could be dangerous, particularly mining or anything to do with electricity – especially if, as was often the case, the non-British worker could not speak English.

Western Australia is a good place to study British immigrants, since its British connection is particularly strong. It joined the Federation at the last possible minute; the Commonwealth of Australia Constitution Act, dated 9 July 1900, says that the colony was to be included in the Federal Commonwealth only 'if Her Majesty [Queen Victoria] is satisfied that the people of Western Australia have agreed thereto'. Every Western Australian knows that in 1933, at the height of the depression, the state would have left the Federation and reverted to some kind of special relationship with Britain had its application to secede not been vetoed by the British Parliament. Besides, there is a very large proportion of British migrants in Western Australia: 15 per cent of its citizens were born in the UK, which is double the Australian average.

The professor told me about an old lady of one hundred whom he interviewed around 1980 as part of an oral history project. 'She was born in Western Australia; her parents were early settlers here in the 1840s or 1850s. She had a long and wonderful life as a postmistress and, towards the end of the interview, I asked her what stood out in her memory as the most dramatic event; and without thinking she said, "Oh, that would be the day Queen Victoria died." I said, "Really?" and she said, "Yes, I remember it well. I was in the West Perth post office when the news came through." She said you walked down the street of West Perth and the people were looking at each other shaking their heads and saying, "What shall we do? Whatever will become of us? She's gone." And it was like – this was her analogy – it was like everyone's mother had died on the same day. That gives you an idea of the real closeness of this outlying post of empire to Britain. The people here saw not the eastern states as their main source of inspiration, but Britain.'

Professor Appleyard came to Britain in 1959–60, stayed at University House in Tavistock Square, and spent his days cornering British migrants to Australia, asking them question and getting them to talk about their circumstances and reasons for emigrating. He and his assistants interviewed 860 people, which he hopes – and assumes – was a representative sample of those emigrating under the Assisted Passage Scheme at the time. He carried out follow-up surveys of the same group in 1961, 1967 and 1975. These records stood in boxes in his study as we talked. He knows more about the history of these people than they know themselves, since most of them are by now quite vague about why they came to Australia in the first place, whereas Professor Appleyard has preserved on file their conversations of nearly forty years ago. And he has not finished with his respondents yet. He proposes to find out what happened to their children.

Now where, I asked him finally, did the Whingeing Pom come from? 'It's hard to know its origin,' he said, 'but it was certainly manifest during the 1960s. The Assisted Passage Scheme made it very easy for Brits to come to Australia and try it; to see whether it was what they wanted. After all, you only had to pay ten pounds, and if you stayed two years that was your commitment. Even if you went back within two years you only had to pay back the cost of the outward passage. So a lot of those who came out weren't really dedicated settlers; they hadn't really cut the painter. The ideal migrants had made a decision and said, "Look, I want my future and the future for my kids to be Australia; I'll come back on holiday, but I'm going." But many other people, because it was so easy for them to come out, saw it as a long holiday; and if they hadn't made that commitment, to take all the lumps as well as the benefits, then they were going to have a difficult time. These were the people who became quite critical about Australia — the Australian system, Australian laziness, Australian attitudes. And the weather. And the spiders. Oh yes, the Whingeing Pom really was a huge problem. And probably also a problem to those who really were first-class settlers, because they got tarred with the same brush.

'A surprisingly large number of British migrants became trade-union officials. It was really quite remarkable. You would turn the radio on and find that almost every time a union secretary or shop steward spoke, it would be with a British accent — that includes the Scots.' The Irish were far less prominent.

The professor talked about the flaws in the migration pro-gramme. If you did not have a relation already in Australia, you could still get an assisted passage, but you would have to stay in a

Commonwealth hostel. These tended to be old army barracks or converted warehouses: terrible places. The families would be put in there and the husbands would go away to work. 'Imagine, a thousand British migrants in a hostel and they can't find the money to get out, and so the whole thing festers and builds up. That was a genuine whinge.'

The Australian government should never have allowed the hostels to develop in the way they did. On the other hand, with a shortage of housing in the community, and a national policy of taking in migrants, what more could have been done? The British were really complaining about the unsatisfactory nature of the hostels, the lack of imagination. Yet when the authorities tried to say, 'Let's build small units!' the Australians would cry: 'God, look what they're doing for these Pommie bastards! I've been on the waiting list for years!'

The Australian government produced numerous pamphlets for prospective migrants to Australia; but most people did not absorb them. 'I once was on a migrant ship coming out here – I travelled incognito to get a feel of what it was like – all British migrants; and they had a great time: all going to the same place for the same purpose. The kids got to know each other, there were games, and so forth. So the voyage out by and large was pretty good. But what impressed me was that it was only when the ship started to get close to Australia that they would turn up at the information office the Australian immigration people had established on board and start asking basic questions. The average amount of capital taken to Australia was eight hundred quid – and that was after they'd sold everything: eight hundred pounds, average. You could get rid of a good proportion of that on the ship out. So they came out with virtually nothing. You've got a wife and four kids; you haven't got a relative to go to; you're going to land in a government hostel; and the hostel will probably swallow up sixty or seventy per cent of your earnings. That's pretty hard to take. So your wife has got to go out to work; somehow the kids have got to be looked after. You've got to get out of the hostel as quickly as possible, because you can save a higher proportion of your earnings if you're living in a privately rented shack somewhere than if you're living in a hostel, because in the hostel you're being charged "full board".

'There weren't many entrepreneurs among them. When we followed them up in 1961, 1967 and 1975 their status was still much the same. They were working-class people – skilled or semi-skilled – who came from a typical three-bedroom semi-detached terraced house, and when they got here they found a job . . . Our figures show that their increase in real income was quite high, and that was satisfying to them. Once they'd got past this initial problem of the hostel and had found accommodation: the kids went to the local school, you had a good job. There was no unemployment in Australia in the sixties. If you had a job you could keep it, and certainly change it if you wanted to. Get a block with a detached house on it and that's it. Most of them are still in those situations.

'I think that's what an Assisted Passage Scheme really creates,' the professor went on. If people hated their environment, and wanted to get out and go somewhere else, because they thought there were greater opportunities in America, Canada, Australia or Brazil – and if they were not being assisted – then they had to have extra drive to impel them to act. They took a risk, paid the passage, got there, scratched around and were always looking for opportunities, because they had come to make their fortune. 'But if you walk into Australia House and they put you on a ship for nothing . . . We had a policy of increasing the population by one per cent a year, we were prepared to pay the passage, we wanted the British – so you get those sort of people.'

What proportion went back to Britain and never returned? The professor said that that was an almost impossible question to answer. Of 860 families and some single people whom he studied, some 200 had gone back to Britain. Of those 200, some 100 had returned to Australia: so in a sense that gave a net loss of 100. But his follow-up interviews revealed that 'going back' could seldom – if ever – be seen as a decision to abandon Australia completely. People might go back, spend a summer in the UK and then return to Australia; their kids might go back, get trained and then return. 'People live in two places. That's common. So to ask how many people went back is not the appropriate question. The question should be: what sort of mobility is being displayed by these people, and for what reason?'

Elizabeth

The mausoleum of the Whingeing Pom is to be found, I believe, not in Western Australia but in South Australia, some eighteen miles north of Adelaide, in Elizabeth, a sprawling new town that attracted many of the British who emigrated under the Assisted Passage Scheme. As recently as 1996, eight of its twelve councillors were born in Britain. It was named after Queen Elizabeth; and it contains a Prince Charles Walk and a Princess Anne Boulevard.

Entry in Geoffrey Dutton's diary: 'July 1960. Robin Boyd over from Melbourne . . . took him out to Elizabeth. He thought it the essence of modern Australia. Flat, few trees, comfort, no centre.'

In 1963 the Queen visited Elizabeth wearing long gloves, a short-sleeved dress and a flowery hat, and unveiled a fountain featuring one larger-than-life-sized, bare-breasted maiden and another holding a child. The sun shone, the crowds gathered, the men in the ceremonial party wore suits, and the Union Jack waved.

Guardian, 29 February 1996:

Last year the Duchess of Kent came to Elizabeth. Everyone knew she was coming and it was billed as a royal visit. But there were no big crowds and no big plans and no excitement at all. Less than fifty people turned out to see her. She slipped in and out like a stranger and disappeared without inspecting the grand fountain, which now stands parched of water with weeds pushing their way up through the cracks in its stonework. Someone has daubed blue paint over it and then printed neatly at its foot a simple message for the monarch: 'Fuck the Queen'.

March 1997, conversation with an Adelaide student of current affairs:
MD: 'How would you describe Elizabeth?'

AS: 'It's regarded in Adelaide as a sort of neat slum. It's one of the lowest socio-economic areas, with juvenile delinquency, unemployment, massive welfare benefits; generally not one of the more salubrious parts of the city. Teachers try hard not to get appointed to those schools. You drive through it, but never actually see it because it was so well planned and beautified in the first place, with big double carriageways, bush on either side and well laid-out public areas.'

'Is it thought of as specially British?'

'No. Some people might say it was. There were all those British Holden car workers; it's certainly known that that's why it was built. But I don't think that subsequently it's seen as only British. Adelaide has a smaller ethnic population than most Australian cities, and Elizabeth is where what migrants Adelaide does have tend to go, because it's cheap.'

'I think it's the home of the Whingeing Pom.'

'What's your evidence for this, Mr Davie?'

'In the mid-sixties, when everyone in Australia had a job, the unions were particularly active and awkward, because whatever they did nobody was going to be thrown out of work; and many of the union leaders turned out to be British. Why were they different from the Aussies, who you might think had a very strong trade-union tradition? The answer is that the Australian trade-union leaders negotiated, used the courts and called strikes, whereas the British shop stewards, coming from Ford Dagenham etc., believed in causing trouble on the shop floor. And that was what was constantly happening.'

'Disruption of production.'

'Precisely. That's one important way in which the British trade-union tradition is different from the Aussie tradition.'

'A deeper bastardry!'

'More tactical than strategic. Short-termist.'

'More Marxist [i.e. more Marxist than the Australians.] Probably more consciously strategic than the Australians. And more backed up by class rhetoric. It is amazing that, even now, you'll have a lot of union spokesmen with really thick English accents from somewhere or other. Dialect.'

'The dialect of the Whingeing Pom.'

The Sandys Visit

One Saturday morning in the second week of July 1961 found me hanging about outside the Cabinet Room in the old Parliament building in Canberra. Duncan Sandys, the British Minister of Commonwealth Relations, was in town to talk to the Australian government, and *The Observer* in London had asked me to try to produce a story; being a Sunday paper, we were always a bit pushed to find anything that could be regarded as news on a Saturday. I was about the only reporter on the premises; in those days Australia had no Sunday papers, or certainly no Sunday paper that was interested in as recondite a subject as a visit from Duncan Sandys. I withdrew into the shadows as the Australian Cabinet filed in, including Menzies and the unsmiling, limping figure of Sandys.

He was someone to be reckoned with, was Sandys. He had acquired his limp in Norway during the war; he had married (though by 1961 had divorced) a daughter of Churchill; and his manner was that of a tough, offhand Etonian. (He rather disgraced himself later on, after he left politics and became, as Lord Duncan-Sandys, the chairman of the international conglomerate Lonrho and drew his large salary from the Cayman Islands, thus avoiding income tax.) After I had hung about for some time, the door of the Cabinet Room opened and the ministers started to file out. Alexander Downer was first, looking grim. Up I boldly went, identified myself and said that I knew his cousin, Sidney Downer, who reported cricket for the Adelaide *Advertiser*, could we speak? Downer gripped my arm. 'Come with me,' he said. He took me into a side-room, muttered that what he had to say was not to be attributed to him and then laid into Sandys, the British government, and everything he had just heard. What it amounted to was that the UK was proposing to sell Australia down the river by applying for membership of the European Economic Community – also known as The Six, or the Common Market – while trying to pretend that this policy would not affect her relations with the Commonwealth, including Australia. Downer left me in no doubt that: (a) none of the Australian ministers believed for a moment that Australia's interests would not be affected, despite Sandys's protests to the contrary; and (b) Australia had been taken aback by, and bitterly resented, the suddenness of the UK approach and decision.

In the Archives

It was odd to be going back, thirty-six years later, to look at the Cabinet papers dealing with that critical time in Anglo-Australian relations. Now, it appears to have been that rare historical event, a genuine and identifiable turning point: the moment when Australia was quasi-officially informed that Britain's future lay in Europe, and that her Commonwealth connections were henceforth going to play second fiddle to that overriding aim (achieved when the second British assault on the EEC citadel succeeded in 1973).

The archives are held in a low concrete building with three mysterious and incongruous shiny chimneys sticking up from one end. Whatever problems Canberra may have, parking is not one of them; nevertheless, the deserted archives car park was a forest of bossy signs, proof of make-work bureaucrats in action: 'Commonwealth Cars Only'; 'Five Minutes'; 'Motor Bicycles Only'; 'Disabled Vehicles Only'. Inside, the place was silent and almost empty: four people at pale wood desks; a glass screen to protect the staff from the readers; a state-of-the-art electric pencil sharpener.

I knew that on 31 July 1961 Macmillan, the British Prime Minister, had publicly announced his intention of applying to join the Common Market. Much was made at the time of the Commonwealth having been consulted. Strictly speaking, the claim was accurate; but the consultations about this momentous decision, so far as Australia was concerned, had only started three weeks before the Sandys visit and had taken senior Australian civil servants by surprise.

On 15 June two of these officials, K.C.O. Shand and C.G. Woodard, had a conversation at the Foreign Office in London with the Hon. Peter Ramsbotham (the Etonian son of a pre-war

171

Conservative minister, and later British ambassador to Washington, where he was known as 'Rowbum'). Ramsbotham was head of the Western Organisation and Planning Department. Sandys was due to arrive in Australia on 6 July. What was the reason, the Australians wanted to know, for the sudden 'particular urgency'? Ramsbotham explained. Four months earlier Britain had had three choices: (a) to go in at once; (b) to drop the whole idea; (c) to postpone the decision for two or three years.

Now, however, given the rate of The Six's economic development, the UK had decided that it dare not wait around. Postponement was no longer an option, and of the remaining alternatives Britain had chosen the first. With hindsight, one can see that the Foreign Office seems to have had its feet firmly in space. The UK, Rowbotham said, was thinking of a unified Europe as a halfway house towards ultimate Atlantic Union. 'Mr Sandys would be arguing as far ahead as this. We said this still rather left Australia on the shelf, because we had our relationship with Asia to think about, too.' Rowbotham agreed; he said that the Foreign Office had written some 'really long-term policy papers', endorsed by the Prime Minister, looking beyond Atlantic Union to a stage when 'key countries' would be associated with it; Australia had been 'specifically mentioned', as had Brazil and Japan.

Next day, as the documents show, it was the turn of the Commonwealth Office – again civil servants speaking to civil servants – to try to explain and justify what was afoot. Sir Henry Lintott, Deputy Under-Secretary in the department, told the Australians that the object of the Sandys visit would be 'to convince us of the need to join The Six, provided adequate safeguards can be negotiated'. Lintott – a trade expert – admitted that 'some damage' was inevitable. He explained what would happen if Britain stayed out of Europe: either Europe plus the United States would leave Britain 'out in the cold'; or Europe would become a Third Force (between the United States and the Soviet Union), either neutralist or – still worse – chauvinistic. If Britain went in, it would 'not be isolated from Western policy', and could influence Europe in the interests of Western unity.

'Lintott,' the Australians noted, 'as did Ramsbotham, sees the eventual spread of European political unity across the Atlantic into Atlantic Union . . .'

Sir Allan Brown, CBE, Deputy High Commissioner in London, wrote to E.J. Bunting, CBE, the Cabinet Secretary in the Prime Minister's Department in Canberra, saying that all this 'seemed to imply that the UK will ignore the solemnly given and frequently repeated assurance that Australia and other Commonwealth countries will be fully consulted before a decision is taken'. Brown pondered the reason for the sudden rush. 'It may be City [of London] apprehension, it may be one of those things that happen without identifiable explanation.' But it was 'more likely that it can all be traced back to the Prime Minister'.

In Canberra, on 20 June, Bunting chaired an inter-departmental meeting. Sandys's purpose, it was stated, was to secure a 'strong political asset'. Once the UK got Australia's okay, it could then represent Australia as having acquiesced in the UK action to join the EEC. But Australia should 'not be stampeded'. The Treaty of Rome, which set up the EEC in 1957, could in the long run result in the establishment of a federated Europe, with federal institutions. Even if it did not go that far, the economic provisions alone would have the effect of tying the UK into Europe and therefore away from the Commonwealth and individual Commonwealth countries. As time went on, the UK might have to modify its Commonwealth outlook enormously. The purpose of the Community would be to develop Europe as a world political force. 'Australia (and New Zealand) being where they are – out of Europe, out of the Atlantic, and out of Asia – seem to stand to lose most in terms of its own place and influence with the United Kingdom.' The memo feared that the UK might need to reduce its commitment in South-East Asia and to Australia. With Britain in Europe, the consequences for Australian trade could be disastrous.

The Australian Department of Foreign Affairs was equally alarmed. Would not the present intimacy of consultation with Australia become impaired by the UK's loyalty to its Treaty partners? Might not Australia find itself excluded from information and a share in the decisions that were vital to its interests, in the same way that it was already excluded from proceedings in

NATO? There was already a quite evident trend for the UK to become less frank in its consultations with Australia on matters affecting sterling and the Sterling Area system.

As Sandys arrived, Bunting put on paper one 'extreme' view: if the UK goes in, this will be the end of the Commonwealth, the end of the Sterling Area and the end of defence arrangements. He summed up with clarity and foresight:

> All our international agreements have been entered into on the basis of a particular relationship with the UK . . . This relationship will no longer exist. Our whole fabric of international ties and relationships will need rethinking.
>
> Against this background the UK asks us to give some sort of approval or acquiescence, or, anyway, lack of objection, to their opening negotiations. This we cannot do. What we must say, and do say, is that we deliberately withhold support.

Sandys had produced his own preliminary document. He admitted that Britain would suffer some loss of sovereignty – an argument that would still be raging forty years later. 'Our parliament at Westminster would have to give up its independent control of our commercial and agricultural policies and certain aspects of policy in the field of social welfare. To part with our sovereignty . . . very serious . . . proof of the importance . . .' But he insisted that the UK going into Europe would benefit the Commonwealth. 'We do not see that there are any good grounds for this fear – the weakening of this close relationship.'

Bunting advised Menzies on the eve of the first meeting with Sandys: 'This is our first real acquaintance with the mind of the UK.'

This is where I sloped in. Twelve Cabinet ministers were present, with Menzies in the chair, and me in the corridor. Sandys must have been told by the UK High Commisioner that the Australians were convinced that British entry would have profound repercussions on the Commonwealth in general, and Australia in particular, and that they were in a mood to cause trouble. He made no concessions, however. He wanted a blank cheque. He kept stating – rather implausibly, it must be said – that

UK membership of the EEC would not affect the Commonwealth: there was no conflict of interest. Menzies disagreed. There
was a risk, he stated, that Europe would develop into a 'tight
system' – whether the UK joined or not. If it joined, it was likely
to be caught up in that system.

These were the opening shots in what soon developed into a
full-scale row. Menzies told Sandys that the UK underestimated
the effect that a regime of common tariffs, a common agricultural
policy, and uniform labour and social conditions would have on
the political development of Europe. 'Once these arrangements
are established and experienced, Europe would be halfway along
the road to a Federation.'

Two future Prime Ministers were hostile to the whole British
project. William McMahon thought the UK would be better off
outside the EEC. 'Black Jack' McEwen, the Minister for Trade
and a devil for detail, said that Australia had not been given any
indication of how its important interests in individual countries
could be protected. Until he got it, he would have to be regarded
as an opponent of any proposal that the UK should negotiate with
the Community. The UK was Australia's principal export market.
Anxious talks continued about sugar, butter, apples and pears,
dried fruit, beef and veal, and wheat.

Before going to Australia, Sandys had visited New Zealand. In
the files is a copy of the communiqué issued after that visit. An
unknown Australian hand has written at the bottom a summing-
up note cutting through the verbiage to say that, in other words,
New Zealand would not cause a fuss if the UK went ahead.

There then took place a series of intense and ill-tempered
negotiations about the communiqué to be issued in Canberra.
Sandys had not fancied the Australian draft. A Cabinet minute of
10 July taken by Bunting says that Sandys, though stating that he
would work from the Australian draft, 'had in fact discarded the
Australian approach and reverted to an approach of his own,
resembling the form of the New Zealand communiqué'.

The Cabinet told Sandys that it was willing to remove 'any
sharpness', but was not willing to sacrifice the meaning of the
'vital parts'. The Cabinet also agreed that it might be necessary to

warn Sandys that the 'possibility of failure to agree on a communiqué might exist'.

The Cabinet decided that it could not object to Britain negotiating. However, it could not approve: first, because that would be taken to imply that Australia was willing to see the UK going into the EEC; second, because Australia was not convinced that the UK's best interests would be served by joining; third, because 'our trade position is by no means secured'; fourth, because Australia had other apprehensions, for instance about Sterling Area arrangements.

Menzies insisted to Sandys that it must be on record as the view of the Australian government that, as the Community became more politically powerful, Great Britain would become so much engaged in European affairs that her Commonwealth interests would decline.

Sandys said that that would be 'disastrous'. Menzies stated that the UK was faced with a very difficult choice between the Commonwealth and Europe. 'The answer, either way, was a momentous answer.' Sandys insisted it was not a choice. If it was, the UK could not choose Europe. Menzies said there were powerful reasons for the UK to enter the EEC, but one consequence would be a fundamental change in her relationship with the rest of the Commonwealth.

Other Cabinet members backed him up. Harold Holt, the Treasurer, said that Commonwealth relations were not just sentiment. As practical considerations abated, Commonwealth relations would become far less intimate. However powerful the UK's reasons for going into the EEC might be, Australian ministers could not see any outcome other than the weakening of the Commonwealth.

Here was the key point of the Sandys mission: he had totally failed to convince the Australians with his argument that Commonwealth interests would not be affected, and might actually be improved. Instead he had annoyed them, including Menzies, with his attempts to do so. At one point Sandys said that a draft prepared by Menzies himself – if it went out as worded – 'could create a major crisis in UK–Australian relations'. The draft, he said, amounted to a strong condemnation of UK policy in seeking negotiations. Holt commented that Sandys apparently did not appreciate the strength of feeling of the Australian ministers. At one point Menzies and Sandys thought about not issuing a communiqué at all.

No fewer than eight drafts were produced before a communiqué was finally agreed upon. It fell far short of the friendly and respectful endorsement that Sandys had originally sought. Australia went on record as taking a different view from the British about the impact on Commonwealth affairs; refrained from giving its approval to the opening of negotiations; and demanded a role in any negotiations that affected Australian interests.

Britain did not succeed in getting into Europe until 1973. But that week in 1961 was the moment when even the most passionately pro-British Australian ministers, such as Menzies and Downer, heard the old links snapping. Britain was obviously not going to take Commonwealth and Australian interests into account any more than was strictly necessary, as the imperialist and fiercely anti-Common Market press baron Lord Beaverbrook quickly pointed out in the *Daily Express*: 'Once in the Market we shall cut ourselves off from the great Dominions ... Let the people demand that our ties with the Dominions be strengthened and not cut off. We must not abandon those great nations which sent their sons to die for us.'

As usual, nobody in power took any notice of Beaverbrook and his newspapers. British friends of mine living in Australia, and I myself, felt embarrassed – and for once inclined to share some of Beaverbrook's views. Though pro-Europe, we were taken aback by the insouciance with which the British government was prepared to sell out the Commonwealth. However, it was the sound of the next snapping link that made us all feel really ashamed.

Passport Shocks

Professor Appleyard, years later, tended to confirm an uneasy feeling that my circle had had at the time of the EEC drama, which was that, as he put it – rather brutally for a mild man: 'The

British government has very little interest in British people in Australia.'

The whole relationship between the mother country and Australia had changed in his own comparatively brief academic lifetime. When he first went to London in 1959 to study British migrants, there was no suggestion when he walked through Immigration that he had to have a visa. He had the right to vote. He remembered canvassing in Mecklenburgh Square for Labour and meeting the great economic historian R.H. Tawney on the doorstep. Australians were issued in Australia with a British passport. There were no restrictions whatsoever: on health care or dental treatment: 'I was as British as you were.'

Than came the passport shock. 'It certainly had a negative impact for most Australians, who felt so close to the British, to find that they had to queue up behind all the foreigners at London Airport, whereas the European Union people squeezed in. That arrangement symbolises just where British connections are; they're not with the Commonwealth, but with the Continent.'

I had long wanted to insert a drill into the archives at the moment when immigration rules changed, to see from the contemporary documents how the British government could have been so clumsy. It was, after all, predictable that an Australian who had served, say, with the RAF in the Second World War and had held a British passport for twenty years was going to get the shock of his life when he arrived at Heathrow and was required to join the queue for foreigners. Something of the same shock was going to be felt by every one of his fellow-Australians. How had it happened? Once again, as with the Sandys visit, I felt embarrassed by what I found.

R.A. Butler presented the Commonwealth Immigrants Bill to the House of Commons on 1 November 1961. Alexander Downer was Australian Minister of Immigration. He came from one of Adelaide's main families; his father had been state Premier; he himself had been sent to Oxford, then spent three years in a Japanese prisoner-of-war camp, the notorious Changi; all in all, he was typical of the breed of well-off Australians that valued its British connections, and was slightly mocked by other Australians for a tendency towards pomposity. Sir Thomas Playford, the

record-breaking Premier of South Australia (twenty-seven continuous years in office), took great pleasure in routing a new main
road virtually past the front door of the Downer mansion outside
Adelaide. Pompous Downer might have been, but he was not
illiberal; he started to dismantle the White Australia policy. Nor
was he blind: he saw clearly what was coming with the
Commonwealth Immigrants Bill, and the deep and lasting
resentments that it would cause in Australia – and still causes
today.

Downer made a submission to Cabinet on 12 January 1962.
The primary aim of the bill, he explained, was to control the
influx of unskilled immigrants to Britain from the West Indies,
Pakistan and India. To avoid any appearance of discrimination,
however, the legislation was to apply to immigrants from all
Commonwealth countries.

The bill, he pointed out, would end the traditional policy of
free entry into the United Kingdom, which had always been taken
for granted throughout the Commonwealth. 'This seems bound
to have some political impact,' said Downer, especially as there
would be no restrictions upon the Irish. 'It will bring home also
the extent to which Australia's traditional relationship to the
United Kingdom is changing.'

He spelled out the new conditions of entry. If an Australian was
after a job, he or she would have to get a voucher from the
Ministry of Labour, which could be applied for only in London.
Australians going on holiday would have to prove that they could
support themselves.

Reading the Downer submission today, it looks very much as if
he, the minister most concerned, felt that he had been double-
crossed – or at least misled and given a sense of false security.
Australia had originally been told that, although the controls
would not discriminate on grounds of race, the bill should not
have any effect on people coming in from countries such as
Australia. Then Australia was told about the 'administrative
arrangements' that would actually apply: the earlier optimism was
not repeated; now it was decreed that all Australian travellers
would be subject to immigration control.

What had happened, it seems, was that originally the control over Australian entries was to be no more than a formality. Then a political row had broken out in London and the government had been forced to emphasise that its bill was truly non–discriminatory; and 'so the more favourable position to be enjoyed by Australia has had to be abandoned'.

Downer raised one obvious objection to the controls. As things stood, an Australian going to the UK on holiday might get all the way there and then be turned back. Could they not be given the right of entry before they left Australia, for instance by the Australian authorities? And the work permit was pure Catch-22. You could only get a work permit from the Ministry of Labour in London; but you would not be allowed into London unless you had a work permit, which could be applied for only in London. Surely people should be allowed to collect work vouchers issued by the British High Commission in Canberra?

After this sober submission, Downer added a few passionate notes that showed both his disappointment and his disgust with the British. The whole subject, he said, needed more authoritative advocacy than he could give it: he meant that Prime Minister Menzies himself should protest. The spirit of the original assurance should be adhered to by the British. Virtually all Australians should be allowed to go to Britain freely and with the minimum of bureaucratic obstacles. Then he added: 'We believe that the English may not have thought hard enough about the impact of the measure on the traditionally loyal 'old' white Dominions people; and we would think that the potential ill-effect ought to be impressed upon them at top level.' What Downer thought Australia should be looking for was a deal whereby the restrictions would appear to include Australia, but in fact would not; permission to enter would be a formality. He wanted fair-dos: restrictions on Australians entering the UK should be no greater than those upon UK nationals entering Australia – 'and that is virtually nil'.

Downer's proposed solution sounded more reasonable in Canberra than it did in London. On what conceivable grounds could Downer's 'old' white Dominions be given special treatment, without exposing the British government to charges of racial discrimination? So the British went ahead with their controls, and the Australians responded with tit-for-tat restrictions – with an extra-malevolent bureaucratic twist. The visa issued to Britons (with reluctance, it always seemed) by the Australian immigration authorities was bigger than any other country's visa – twice the size of the United States's – and, inexplicably, had to have a clean page in the applicant's passport all to itself.

Thus did thousands of British and Australians discover that their homelands had become foreign countries; and Australians felt insulted and soured, as they joined the foreigners' queue at Heathrow.

Relations between the two countries had come a long way since the Menzies speech to Chatham House twenty-seven years earlier, when he spoke of a common destiny, in the belief that Australians were simply Britons in another part of the world, and warned his audience not to treat Australians of British birth as strangers.

In 1964 Downer went to London as High Commissioner. He was knighted the next year, acquired a beautiful country house in Wiltshire, and struck up a friendship with the Labour Secretary of State for Commonwealth Relations, Arthur Bottomley, who came from a very different background.

Downer wrote later that 1964–70 represented a difficult period in Anglo-Australian relations, years of 'controversy, disappointment and strain – probably more so than at any time since Australia's foundation in 1788'. He maintained that Australia was misled by the Wilson government for the first four years of its term of office. Australia's defence strategy, such as it was, was based on the idea that it would send troops out of Australia in support of British or American policy; this 'forward defence' would encourage these two powers to accept some responsibility for defending Australia, by interposing themselves between Australia and any potentially hostile northern neighbours. In the early 1960s Australia sent troops to support the new state of Malaysia during its 'confrontation' with Indonesia – the sixth-largest country in the world, of whose intentions Australia was particularly nervous. In 1966 Harold Wilson announced his intention of making another assault on the EEC citadel. In 1967 Britain announced its intention of withdrawing altogether from east of Suez. Australia's trade was under renewed threat; and the 'forward defence' strategy was in ruins. In his memoirs Downer recorded how Australian opinion accused the Wilson government of bad faith and short-sightedness in a part of the world that was likely to be more important than Europe. Australia, he said, felt let down, abandoned and unappreciated for its voluntary efforts to assist the mother country, not only in two World Wars but in conflicts as far back as the Sudan. Coming from Sir Alexander Downer, with his London clubs and his well-connected English friends, this was a savage indictment.

In 1961, on the eve of the Sandys visit, the inter-departmental committee meeting in Canberra had predicted that, as Britain's eyes became fixed more and more on Europe, it would feel the need to reduce its commitments in South-East Asia. That is exactly what happened. The other prediction that came true, despite Duncan Sandys's assurances, was the shift in patterns of trade. By 1996 more than half of Australia's trade was with eastern Asia.

9

Australian Accent

The full implications of Britain's move towards Europe took a long time to sink into the minds of most Australians; the same was true of British minds. The breach, for ordinary Australians, was disguised during the 1960s and early 1970s by the apparent strength of the royal link. Trade with Britain might be reduced; but British migrants were still pouring in, Australia's Commonwealth status would be unaffected; and above all, the cheerful and miraculously appropriate young Elizabeth would still be Australia's Queen. Her visit to Australia in 1954 had been a true royal progress, a triumph all round. In retrospect, it can be seen as perhaps the last of the traditional, full-scale and hugely effective royal tours. Afterwards the visits came thick and fast by one member of the royal family or another – more casual, less dignified, but never a national event that excited the interest of the whole country.

For a surprising number of my middle-aged Australian friends, mostly of cynical republican tendencies, who were schoolchildren in the early 1950s, mention of that Royal Visit sparked vivid memories. 'I thought God was coming,' said one academic and political journalist as he recalled the weeks of build-up, the preparations at school for the lining of the route through his area of suburban Melbourne, the meticulous instructions about what to wear and how to behave. He also never forgot the sacrilegious thrill when the bad boy of the class ducked across the road in front of the royal cars, waving a cheery greeting. In the archives of the

Mitchell Library I came across a government pamphlet entitled *The Royal Visit and You*, produced – acccording to the Commonwealth Minister in Charge, Royal Visit, 1954 – 'to answer many of the questions being asked about dress and procedure'. Don't panic, was the underlying message; the royal couple were really just ordinary folk. 'The Queen and the Duke of Edinburgh live a simple home life with their children.' (Charles, aged six, and Anne, aged four, had been left behind for the six-month-long post-Coronation tour of the empire.) Stand up whenever they appear and wear your best clothes, the pamphlet advised, although the Queen had apparently 'expressed the wish that no one should be put to unnecessary expense'. Gloves should be worn to garden parties, but did not have to be white. Lounge suits were approved. The various engagements around the country were listed: plenty of race meetings to vary the rounds of hospital visits and receptions, as well as firework displays, log-chopping and three displays of Aboriginal dancing. For the children who lined the roads, waving Union Jacks and cheering, the brief glimpses of blurred pink faces and white-gloved hands were often disappointing. 'We'd been up since dawn and waited all day in the boiling sun, and afterwards we wondered: what for?' said one woman, still sounding resentful after forty-five years. Indeed, looking back, she thought the experience had turned her into a republican.

Over the years the very success of the 1954 tour has come to be seen, according to a young historian, Jane Connors, as a national embarrassment. There was no doubting the facts: over one million people turned out in Sydney to greet the first reigning British monarch to set foot on Australian soil. During the next eight weeks it was estimated that around six million more lined up to see the royal couple. A poll soon afterwards found that 75 per cent of the population (then nine million) claimed to have seen them at least once. But when Connors decided, four decades on, that such an event was worthy of serious analysis and explanation, she soon came to feel that she had chosen a tricky subject. 'Some people are disturbed by my desire to pay serious attention to the Royal Tour, as if it will only encourage monarchists to further excesses,' she wrote in 1993. She herself had imagined that once she probed further, she would find that beneath the apparent success lay manipulation and reservations; but she came to realise that, as she put it, 'the high degree of consensus which accompanied that particular event at that particular time in Australian history is its central and therefore most interesting feature'. No one dared to criticise the Queen; no politician or journalist questioned the expense, the ceremony, the disruption of it all. The press was unanimously loyal; as a tough woman journalist, Valerie Lawson, has put it, the 1954 tour was perhaps 'the last time the media *en masse* set aside its natural cynicism to wallow in superlatives and purple prose'. One women's magazine held a 'What would you say to the Queen?' competition, with prizes for the most sincere and carefully chosen greetings.

Connors unearthed some good stories. In Mt Gambier, eleven sub-committees met every month for a year; the Royal Visit there lasted just under two hours. One headmistress pretended to be the Queen for months on end, so that her pupils would feel familiar with Her Majesty as she flashed past. Connors's own family was not unaffected: 'My Auntie Mona bought a corgi.' She found very little criticism or resistance in her own circle, although her mother did disclose that an uncle had once remarked in private that 'with all the fuss you'd think the woman peed lavender water'. She concluded that in the early 1950s the British monarchy, both as an institution and as embodied in a popular young woman, was simply not seen as an appropriate target for criticism or attack; it was outside politics and hence unconnected with social problems. Thus the phenomenon of Australia's mass support for the monarchy in 1954 became an unfashionable – even a worrying – topic for later historians.

'"Royal studies" has been the sole province of conservative biographers until recently,' Connors writes:

and difficult questions of theory or practice have been passed over . . . In Australia, where an examination of the monarchist past is necessarily overshadowed by the hope of a republican future, disdain is still running high . . . many of the people I have spoken to who still remember the tour fondly are aware of general scorn, tingeing their

185

recollections with guilt. This attitude will not induce willingness for change.

The 1954 Royal Visit may still present historians with problems; it is certainly still also a fund of anecdotes. One of my favourites tells how the Queen visited Stanthorpe in south Queensland, which used to grow apples until the UK went into the Common Market. The local Member of Parliament was Sir Arthur Fadden, KCMG ('Artie', son of an Irish immigrant policeman and Prime Minister for forty days in 1941). He owned a famous rose garden. As Sir Arthur showed her round, the Queen said, 'Oh, what lovely blooms! Do tell me: what's the secret?'

'Horse manure, ma'am, horse manure,' said Sir Arthur. Behind them, within earshot, strolled the Duke of Edinburgh and Lady Fadden – Ilma, who had married Sir Arthur in 1914. She leaned confidentially towards the Duke. 'You know,' she said, 'it's taken me forty years to get him to say manure.'

For once, complete reliance may be placed on the veracity of a royal anecdote. The impeccable source was the late C.F.C. Macaskie, CMG, former Chief Justice and acting governor of North Borneo, who had retired to Stanthorpe; he too was present in the rose garden, overheard the exchanges, which he treasured for the rest of his life, and relayed them to the journalist Peter Cole-Adams, his stepson, who has kindly waived his copyright and repeated them, verbatim, to me.

Another incident from that tour has stayed in my mind, reported to me – but unsourced – during an idle moment at the Melbourne Cricket Ground in 1958 by John Woodcock, *The Times*'s cricket correspondent. When in Queensland, the Queen's attention had been attracted to a huge portrait of herself that filled a roadside billboard. In front of it stood the hairy perpetrator in a clean white singlet. Her Majesty politely expressed admiration, and asked him about his artistic technique. 'I did it with a spray-gun,' he said.

For reasons hard to explain, these stories seem to be quintessentially Australian: something to do with the idiom, perhaps; and the way they lower the tone. For their full effect they need of course to be recounted with an Australian accent – something I never attempt.

Broad Australian

This business of the accent has long been an awkward fact, a hindrance even – absurd though that may seem – in the Anglo-Australian relationship. Professor G.A. Wilkes has written that, in pronunciation, 'Australian English exhibits differences from Southern British English, just as' – he adds rather defensively – 'the English spoken in Scotland or Ireland diverges from Received Pronunciation.' These differences, he goes on, are least marked in Cultivated Australian, perhaps used by 10 per cent of the population (the professor was writing in 1979), and most marked in Broad Australian, used by perhaps 35 per cent. Between these extremes, he wrote, lies General Australian, used by the majority of 55 per cent. He did not say how these statistics were arrived at. Nor did he estimate what proportion of Australians would be game to assert – say, to a bar full of Broad Australians – that their own accent had been classified by the professor as that of a Cultivated Australian.

The history of the accent reflects the history of the two countries. In colonial mid-Victorian days the English did not mind being directly offensive on the subject.

When Prince Alfred, Duke of Edinburgh, visited Melbourne in 1867, Marcus Clarke, who wrote about the event in *The Australasian*, did not share the lofty attitudes of some of his fellow-countrymen. He wrote:

> It seems that the infamous manner in which the sons of colonists pronounce the English language has struck the delicate ear of Mr Eliot Yorke, the Prince's equerry. Mr Yorke, in thanking a Mr T.P. Hill for a copy of the *Oratorical Trainer* presented to the Prince, remarks: 'The book is an excellent one, and worthy of so necessary an object as that of exciting a love for English literature, and teaching youth the proper pronunciation of their own tongue: the latter, I fear, is much neglected in this colony.' Mr Yorke's fears are,

187

doubtless, in some degree justified, and the unpleasant method of pronunciation must have jarred terribly in his sensitive nerves.

Clarke went on to mock the equerry for his faulty grammar, as demonstrated in another public statement; Mr Yorke must have made these blunders 'while under the influence of the mental prostration produced by this constant irritation' of the Australian accent.

A certain kind of Australian has always been self-conscious about accents. When Menzies noted in his 1930s' journal that, looking at the English competition, he could see why Melbourne girls found it easy to attract desirable English suitors, the odds were that these girls were not only pretty and possessed smaller feet than their English rivals, but had deliberately (under maternal supervision, as like as not) altered their native tones. 'Modified Australian,' says Professor Wilkes, is what some phoneticians have politely called the conscious effort to imitate British English, 'occasionally with grotesque results'; this effort is colloquially described, he says, as 'putting on jam'. This is not a phrase I have ever heard. In Wilkes's *Dictionary of Australian Colloquialisms* the latest citation for this phrase comes from Dal Stiven's *Jimmy Brockett*, published in 1951: 'Sadie put on a bit of jam when she talked, but not too much.' The *Dictionary* was published in 1978, so perhaps the expression was already obsolete. At all events, the social nervousness that impelled Australians to imitate British English seems to have been declining well before 1951. In 1944 the (Sydney) *Daily Telegraph* noted: 'The great Australian accent, and the greater Australian adjective, are two of the best advertisements Australia has in other parts of the world.' It was true: the adjective was 'bloody'; and a few words – 'My bloody oath!', say – were enough to identify the nationality of the speaker almost anywhere. Canadians enjoyed no such advertisement; in 1944 Canadian soldiers were commonly taken for Americans, to their intense irritation: fighting talk.

It appears that the Australian accent was acquiring respect in the UK, being a characteristic of a reliable fighting ally, at about the time that Australians were coming to terms with Britain's inability to defend them. It may sound like an exaggeration, but I think

Chester Wilmot had a lot to do with it. His name has faded now, but in his heyday, which was towards the end of the Second World War and the beginning of the peace – he was killed in the Comet air disaster of 1954 – his voice was familiar to millions in the UK as a BBC war correspondent. After D-Day, at an anxious time when virtually every wireless set in the UK was tuned nightly to BBC news bulletins, Wilmot was one of the handful of reporters whose voices listeners came to recognise and on whom they learned to rely. His story should be better known. Born in Melbourne, he was a forceful debater with the university debating society before he got a job as a reporter on the Melbourne *Herald*. He then became a cricket reporter with the Australian Broadcasting Commission; during the war, they sent him to cover the Japanese assault in South-East Asia, where he also acted as a stringer for the BBC. In the islands, his candid reporting of the shortcomings of the Australian high command caused his superiors to withdraw him from the Front.

The BBC wondered what had happened to him; and when they learned that he had been virtually silenced by the ABC, asked him to come to London. He turned up next in the North African desert, where his air of an extremely calm, experienced staff officer and his 'very clear brain' impressed his old friend from Melbourne, the most famous of all the newspaper war correspondents, Alan Moorehead of the *Daily Express*. But it was Wilmot's reporting of the battle for Europe that made his name: he got off to a good start when on D-Day he kept up a seamless running commentary on his recording machine, while the troop-carrying glider to which he had been assigned crash-landed in France. His courage, of course, he shared with his BBC colleagues. What he had, however, and they did not, were his voice and accent. Once, in the Nixon years, I asked Arthur Schlesinger junior to explain Henry Kissinger's dominance of the American foreign-policy establishment. He said that Kissinger's voice had a lot to do with it; when he spoke, his deep, slow, gravelly, accented voice not only virtually compelled others to listen, but seemed to give his pronouncements special authority – whether deserved or not. Wilmot was much the same. On the air, his deep tones and Australian (Cultivated) accent seemed especially reassuring. After

189

the war he wrote a huge bestseller, *The Struggle for Europe*; Moorehead found it rather dry, but it sold: the first book to offer a general picture of events that had been seen by the ordinary person only in fits and starts.

Subsequently Wilmot joined *The Observer*, where I was working, as defence correspondent. The first time I saw him he was sitting quietly in an editorial conference smoking a pipe, wearing a sports jacket, a calm, bulky man; the editor asked him something, and Wilmot, removing the pipe, said he would have a word with 'Alex' about it. We silently gasped. 'Alex' in those days referred to only one person: Field Marshal Lord Alexander, Churchill's Minister of Defence. Was Wilmot shooting a line, or was he really on 'Alex' terms with the Field Marshal? Well, he was. Thereafter I became familiar with Wilmot's voice and accent; he used to turn out for *The Observer*'s so-called cricket team as it travelled around to obscure grounds in south London; he fielded in the slips and never stopped talking. One day, when he gave me a lift, I spied a pamphlet on chicken-farming in his car's front pocket. He explained that he did not know how long his success would last. Soon afterwards he was dead.

Moorehead himself was briefly in a public position in London in the 1950s, as a senior public-relations officer at the Ministry of Defence, where his ally Field Marshal Lord Montgomery was chief of the Imperial General Staff. I was sent to see Moorehead once; 'he's like a jockey,' my editor said, having earlier hired him to report on the partition of India. So he was, a small and determined jockey in a bureaucrat's black coat and striped trousers: most unsuitable garb. The disguise could not hide either Moorehead's restless boredom with the job or his Australianness. Nobody could have taken either of this pair, Wilmot or Moorehead, at that period for anything other than an unreconstructed Australian, complete with the accent, Cultivated or not; and neither of them was for one moment a man whom the British – not excluding Alex and Monty – could patronise, given their runs on the board.

Menzies was influential in this context, too. He fell from power in 1941. He returned in triumph in 1949; and historians agree that one of the weapons that kept him in uninterrupted power until

1966, winning seven elections in a row, was his oratory. His methods were carefully contrived, distrusting emotion, 'and aimed at a cold, and as I hoped, logical exposition'. In the House, he jotted down only headings for his speeches, so that he was ready to adjust to the mood of his audience. For radio or television, he wrote out every word and noted the exact time when each passage should be reached. Television, one contemporary wrote, 'enabled him to project himself like a rich grandfather into homes throughout the country, making the most of his delightfully modulated and persuasive voice and of his superb acting ability and timing'.

Professor Colin Hughes has written that quite possibly the best assessment of Menzies came from Dr J.F. Cairns, the Labor politician, who believed that Menzies was not especially interested in the exercise of power, and that he derived most satisfaction from behaving like an actor in front of an audience. That was the way Menzies made his impact in Britain, as gradually throughout his long tenure of office he came to be seen, to behave and above all to sound like the Commonwealth's senior statesman.

To some Australians he was a lackey of London; but the fact was that the main thrust of his foreign policy – Australia by this time being undeniably independent – was to find a substitute for the old pre-war imperial connection and to inveigle the United States into filling the gap in South-East Asia left by Britain. Menzies negotiated the 1951 Anzus Treaty with the United States, which was resented by Winston Churchill; he supported the efforts of his Minister for External Affairs, R.G. Casey, to improve relations with the Asian countries (decades before the Keating government behaved as if it had invented this policy); and he sent Australian troops to Vietnam in support of the United States when Britain did not. Australians may have had their doubts about where his loyalties lay, but to the British he was never taken as an ersatz Englishman, because when he appeared before them he sounded Australian – as Australian as Chester Wilmot, who at one time was better known than Menzies was.

Of course, some circles still thought the accent 'common', with its cockney vowel sounds. Middle-class parents who talked mockingly about Orstreyelia and emphasised the second syllable of

Melbourne, and whose children went off to the Antipodes, were anxious lest their grandchildren came back, as they invariably did, with 'accents'. But the sting had gone out of the subject. It operated in a different way. Now it could be used and exploited to advantage, especially by politicians and actors. Before the war, plays in Australia invariably and automatically featured actors imitating British accents. In 1954 the Elizabethan Theatre Trust was set up in an attempt to develop the Australian theatre, and especially to stop the drift to England of talented Australian actors such as Peter Finch, Leo McKern and Keith Michell. To get jobs they had to adopt English voices: Michell could not have played Henry VIII with an Australian accent, nor McKern Rumpole.

Then something happened to the actors who stayed behind. This was the discovery, in a country that seemed to be without playwrights, of a first-rate play: Ray Lawler's *Summer of the Seventeenth Doll*. John Pringle, the Anglo–Scotsman who edited the *Sydney Morning Herald*, has recalled how the paper's drama critic, Lindsey Browne, immediately recognised the quality of the play (first produced by an Englishman, John Sumner, at the Melbourne University Little Union Theatre of which Lawler was director) when it was put on in Sydney at the Trust's own theatre with a full professional cast in January 1956. Pringle saw for himself the excitement and emotion aroused in Australian audiences when they heard, for the first time in their lives, Australian characters on the stage speaking the idiom of the streets. So great at the time was the prejudice against such a thing that Hugh Hunt, the Trust's first executive director and a former director of the Old Vic, repeatedly had to urge the cast not to modify their accents but to give them full rein. Browne, the *SMH* critic, compared the experience with that felt by the Irish when they first heard the plays of J.M. Synge or Sean O'Casey at the Abbey Theatre, or by Americans at the first plays of Eugene O'Neill. When the play was put on in London, it enjoyed a healthy commercial success; and the vernacular and the accents (which seemed to me to have been exaggerated, not modified, for the benefit of West End audiences) were a crucial part of the interest that it aroused. Since then no Australian performer has been ashamed of an Aussie accent. The great revolution on radio and television occurred, Dr Cameron Hazlehurst has surmised, with the decline of the written script in favour of ad-libbing; when every syllable was written down, the broadcasters had time to practise, which meant that they adjusted their accents; without a script, they naturally spoke in their normal voices.

The person who probably did most to persuade the British during the 1950s that Australia was not a cultural desert was Joan Sutherland; opera singers in action do not have accents, but offstage Sutherland seemed to take pleasure in surprising or disconcerting her British interviewers with her fruity Australian vowels. After *The Doll*, others took the hint; and since then there has scarcely been a moment when the British entertainment scene has been free from somebody or other using the accent as a weapon in making a career. Rolf Harris could scarcely have warbled 'Tie Me Kangaroo Down' in any other accent, which was as much a part of his act as his winsome smile and his beard. Accent has also been an integral part of the Barry Humphries-Bazza MacKenzie-Dame Edna phenomenon. Other performers, operating on the increasingly lengthy frontier where culture meets show business, have found it equally useful and profitable: Clive James, for one; Germaine Greer, for another. James's mockery of the habits and customs of foreigners in his high-rating television shows would scarcely have been tolerable – indeed, would have been thought insufferably patronising – if delivered in the Received Pronunciation of a member of the old imperial power. In Germaine Greer's case, her Australian accent (more Broad than Cultivated) has given her a licence to behave in her public appearances like a shrew, the violent eccentricity of her opinions matching a harsh and strident tone that has the effect of making her opponents or targets seem by comparison cosseted and effete. Not that these victims have complained. Reviewing *The Whole Woman* (1999) in the *Times Literary Supplement*, the editor of the *TLS*, Ferdinand Mount, wrote:

> Despite her best efforts, Professor Greer has always been held in some affection by those whose certainties she purported to undermine. In my experience, middle-aged tycoons are particularly responsive to her charms, much in the same way that Masters of Foxhounds often have

a penchant for the ballet. For a British audience, being Australian helps in this respect. We find it difficult to take umbrage at the foulest language if hurled at us in a North Queensland accent, let alone shrilled in Germaine's pleasant Melburnian mezzo.

These examples illustrate the way that Australian national self-confidence has grown up alongside Australian feelings of separateness from, or indifference to, the British connection. A recent book on *Esmond Rothermere and the Daily Mail* states that one of the newspaper's editors during the Second World War, an 'exceptionally able' Australian called Stanley Horniblow, talked 'like many Australians' – according to one contemporary – 'with the most extraordinary upper-class accent. It was almost as though he was doing a role in a film in Hollywood, playing the part of an English aristocrat.' Horniblow took his accent back to Australia, where he may have had a hard time if he retained it. That 'many Australians' similarly adopted upper-class accents, I doubt; the author of the book about the *Daily Mail* is an American. Certainly the wave of Australian journalists who followed Wilmot and Moorehead to Fleet Street brought their accents with them and kept them. Not surprisingly since, as Phillip Knightley (born in 1929 and a 1954 arrival) has said, for his generation of Australians 'the typical Englishman was short, cloth-capped, pasty-faced and whingeing' – not someone to be imitated. Knightley thought he had arrived too late. The first group of Australians-on-the-make, as he calls them, had hit the beaches years earlier – Peter Finch, Shirley Abicair, Dick Bentley, Bill Kerr, Keith Michell, Leo McKern, Joan Sutherland, June Bronhill, Sidney Nolan, Arthur Boyd, Jack Brabham, Frank Ifield, Rolf Harris. 'By the time I arrived the novelty the Australians had held for the English had worn off.'

Since then a whole new generation has grown up in Britain to whom most of these once-celebrated characters are unknown, and for whom Australians are just part of the landscape, as a flood of young, competent, good-looking, reliable au pairs, child-minders and odd-job-takers – nurses, removal men, waiters and waitresses, barmaids and bartenders – has flowed through. Their accents these days are an advertisement, an addition to their CVs. In recent

194

years the only Australian I have caught disguising his accent was a young waiter at the Café Pelican, a bistro in London's St Martin's Lane, who was attempting to pass himself off as a Frenchman. Unlike Churchill, the average Briton is more likely to think of this enterprising breed as connections of the wholesome innocents from *Neighbours* than as 'bad stock'. This is not to deny that the continuing wish in some English quarters to patronise Australians takes the form of sneering at the Australian accent. It provides evidence of 'Australian crudity'. In these dwindling quarters, accented Australian English still seems, as it did to the Duke of Edinburgh's equerry in 1867, like 'bad English'.

But the battle for 'standard English' is lost, and the forces of Received Pronunciation, cheerily known to phoneticians as RP., are on the run. I date the turning point in the battle to 1981, when a fifth column infiltrated the main section of the battlefield (the airwaves), ran up a white flag and declared the battle scarcely worth fighting. Two years earlier a well-known BBC newsreader, Alvar Lidell, had claimed that the news was no longer read in an undistorted manner. At that, the director of BBC Radio asked three people to monitor the service and report back. One of them was Dr Robert Burchfield, chief editor of the *Oxford English Dictionary*, who in 1981 published a booklet entitled *The Spoken Word, a BBC Guide*. From page one, it was plain that the Lidell supporters were not going to get much support from Dr Burchfield. 'Most of those,' he wrote magisterially, 'who express concern about the state of the English language at the present time seem to be unaware that more grievous or more fundamental changes to the language have occurred at various periods since it was first recorded in written form in the eighth century.' Examples of such fundamental changes, he went on, included 'the great vowel shift at the beginning of the fifteenth century . . .'

The booklet was divided into three sections, giving advice to broadcasters on pronunciation, vocabulary and grammar. But the advice on pronunciation could scarcely have been less prescriptive. 'It can no longer be assumed,' Burchfield wrote, '(as Alvar Lidell did) that all broadcasters should speak RP (i.e. Received Pronunciation).' 'Adjustments' to his recommendations should be made 'as the need arises', and he quoted in a footnote evidently with sympathy a programme organiser from Radio Carlisle, who had complained that 'if we pronounced everything the way suggested here our Northern listeners would feel we're a bunch of poofters'. Dr Burchfield handed the anything-goes, anti-Lidell troops a further weapon when he said, introducing his section on pronunciation, that 'the form of speech recommended is that of a person born and brought up in one of the Home Counties, educated at one of the established southern universities, and not yet so set in his ways that all linguistic change is regarded as unacceptable'. Who would want to take their standards of pronunciation from, and be classifed with, that privileged and restricted group?

How many broadcasters in 1981 actually read *The Spoken Word* cannot be known; but Dr Burchfield's recommendation about 'adjustments' was certainly followed, consciously or not, with the result that a decade or so later the airwaves – both of the BBC and of commercial television and radio – had abandoned any attempt to recommend any sort of pronunciatiom, Received or otherwise. Possessing what used to be regarded by RP speakers as a 'common' accent became, as time went by, a positive advantage throughout the BBC, apart from on television news bulletins and in a few corners of Radio Four – the (roughly) middle-class, middle-brow talk channel – where variants of RP survived intermittently.

Seventeen years after *The Spoken Word* was published, a Home Counties, southern university-educated woman, whose pronunciation exactly fitted the Burchfield template, was advised that her BBC travel programme idea, though otherwise a starter, was being spiked because her accent was too plummy. By then Australian accents, usually of the Educated variety, had become commonplace on British radio. Brian Hayes, from Perth, Western Australia, achieved metropolitan prominence as the star curmudgeonly anchorman of the commercial London Broadcasting Company (briefly owned by a former Melbourne stockbroker), before he successfully switched to the BBC. There was a more striking sign of the acceptability of the Australian accent in 1998, when the BBC's universally admired racing commentator, Peter O'Sullevan, OBE, finally retired at the age of eighty. In the 1950s newly arrived Australians who went racing in the UK could scarcely believe their ears when they first heard the humming and hawing and the vagueness of British racing commentators, both on the course and on television and radio (nor could they believe the squalid conditions that British racegoers put up with). O'Sullevan commentated on the first television Grand National in 1960 and on his last in 1997. He became as good as the best Australians, a national figure instantly recognisable by his fluent public-school tones: 'the voice of racing'. He was succeeded by an Australian, J.A. McGrath, who sounded like someone on the Tannoy at Flemington. Everybody missed O'Sullevan, but nobody objected to – or possibly even noticed – the Australianness of McGrath. When Matthew Parris, a former MP turned *Times* columnist, wrote in the spring of 1998 that one reason why Rupert Murdoch (his employer) was 'hated' in the UK was because of his (Australian) accent, he was wide of the mark; Murdoch's accent had nothing whatsoever to do with the matter.

In Australia, as the links between Australia and the UK snapped, people seemed to become more – rather than less – sensitive to what were perceived as English tones. Malcolm Fraser was born in 1930, went as a Rhodes Scholar to Oxford and was made an Honorary Fellow of Magdalen in 1982, a year before he was succeeded as Prime Minister by Bob Hawke. Hawke was six months older than Fraser, went as a Rhodes Scholar to Oxford and was made an Honorary Fellow of University College in 1984. Fraser was an obscure figure at Oxford; Hawke was better known, through his cricket and his record-breaking beer drinking. But in politics Fraser was regarded askance by the left, not only because he came from the Western District of Victoria, home of upmarket graziers, but because he was considered to have a suspiciously English accent. Hawke's UK connections were just as strong, or as weak, as Fraser's; but he had the sense to adopt the same system as Lyndon Johnson. Johnson was a Texan, but campaigning in the south – especially when he was pushing through his civil-rights bill – he sounded as if he was bone and braid in Alabama. Hawke, with his dinkum Aussie giddays, sounded as if he had never been near England, let alone Oxford. Alexander Downer junior had the same trouble as Fraser, though perhaps with more reason, since he had been educated in England and had an English wife. When he was removed from his brief leadership of the Liberal Party, following a number of embarrassing gaffes, one of the private reasons given was that, quite apart from his tenuous grasp of party policy, he sounded too English – not that an Englishman would have agreed, either in his case or in Fraser's. The Australian writer Kathy Lette has claimed that if the English are shocked by Australians' use of language when they go to Australia, then Australians 'get just as much of a shock coming to England. The English don't speak English. They say, "Oh, you're Australian. So refreshing," when what they mean is, "Rack off, you loud-mouthed colonial."' (I detect either exaggeration or paranoia. The English might well think Ms Lette loud-mouthed, but several generations have elapsed since an English person thought of an Australian as a colonial.)

Nevertheless, misunderstandings have continued to arise. When Paul and Annita Keating visited the Queen at Balmoral in 1993, a lady-in-waiting asked Annita Keating about her interests. One of them, she understood Mrs Keating to say, was fishing. Oh, said the lady-in-waiting, there was plenty of wonderful fishing near Balmoral. Mrs Keating looked bewildered: she had said fashion. The courtiers, on this occasion, were as confused as Mrs Keating, though trying as always to please, ready to do anything to keep the show on the road. They had thought it appropriate, with Australians coming as guests, to treat Balmoral as a weekender and to lay on a barbecue, with the Duke in charge of the meat and the Queen mixing a salad. From Keating's demeanour, when he saw what was afoot, the courtiers realised that they had made a serious error; he might well have preferred a sit-down banquet. For some of the misunderstanding he could blame not Buckingham Palace but his Labor predecessor, Gough Whitlam. Whitlam was the first Australian Prime Minister to distance himself from Buckingham Palace; he replaced 'God Save the Queen' with 'Advance Australia Fair', and abolished imperial honours – or partly abolished them, since the Premier of Queensland declined to accept the Federal Government's decision and in 1984 awarded himself a KCMG; he was henceforward known, at least in Queensland, as Sir Johannes Bjelke-Petersen. (His courtly manners matched his title: he used to serve even reporters whom he knew to be hostile to him with afternoon tea off a silver tray.)

Whitlam's dismissal in 1975 by the Queen's representative as Governor-General, Sir John Kerr, an event that split Australia with acrimony, gave a push to the republican movement, although the Queen had had nothing to do with Sir John's action. Some of the Australians made angriest by the dismissal seemed reluctant to acccept this proof that Australia was no longer a colony. But London was slow to learn the lessons of this psychological upheaval; Labor supporters felt robbed and looked for a scapegoat. The Palace bureaucrats were particularly slow to take the hint. With the proliferation of the royal family, too many of its younger members made visits to Australia, expecting a royal welcome. Captain Mark Phillips in particular was thought to be busy furthering his show–jumping interests. Loyal servants of the Crown in Canberra felt that Australia was being exploited, and passed the word to London to slow down the procession. London heard and acted; but not before Malcolm Fraser, for one, had started to wonder about the benefits to Australia of the royal connection.

Prince Charles's troubles with tapes began in Australia. An alleged princely telephone conversation appeared in a Sydney publication, causing immoderate excitement, while I was at *The Age* in Melbourne. This event, in 1980, presented me with an awkward editorial decision, or at least I thought it did. On the face of it, the conversation looked genuine; it was already out in the open and, if genuine, our readers ought to be told about it. But suppose it was exposed as a fake? Well, then no harm would have been done. We wrote a story reporting that the following alleged conversation, which might or might not be genuine, had been published in Sydney. For the first and only time while I was in charge, my boss, Ranald Macdonald, complained about something I had done; in fact he went through the roof. His English wife was the daughter of a courtier, which may have influenced his reaction; she was equally angry. His argument was that no newspaper, least of all *The Age*, should publish transcripts of private telephone conversations – royal or not – even if they had been published before, unless (a) they were known beyond doubt to be genuine, and (b) it was indisputable that publication was in the public interest. Neither condition was fulfilled in this case. I thought at the time that I was right; now I wonder. At all events, thereafter the publication of taped royal telephone calls got out of hand, to nobody's credit and serving no interest, beyond that of newspapers' circulation figures. Charles and Diana made one successful Australian visit together, when Diana showed for the first time her extraordinary capacity for getting on with people in trouble, comforting victims of a bush fire. Some misguided person proposed Charles for Governor-General in 1988: a last throw. When he visited Australia in 1994 he met Aborigines, but there were no Government House receptions for the ladies in gloves. The triumphant progress of the Queen in 1954 might still be remembered happily by some, but there had been a revolution in sentiment during the subsequent forty years; and those innocent flag-waving days were well and truly over.

10
Nurse's Hand

When I was a full-time resident of Australia, it was my habit in idle moments to make lists of the human activities in which contemporary Australia scored a pure alpha, from immunology to women's squash. In numerous fields they had someone who was a world-beater. So I was always surprised by their habit of turning to the UK for a solution to their problems, when the answer often lay on their own doorstep. Of this strange tick I was a beneficiary. Nor was I the first to benefit from an eccentric proprietorial belief that an Englishman was better equipped to edit an Australian newspaper than an Australian. Angus Maude (later Baron Maude of Stratford-upon-Avon) had been editor of the *Sydney Morning Herald* between 1958 and 1961. He always seemed to me an odd choice, for although he had been a financial journalist before the war, first briefly on *The Times* and then on the *Daily Mail* (he spent most of the war in a prisoner-of-war camp), after the war he had not returned to journalism, although he co-authored a journalistic book about the English middle classes; instead, he had become a one-nation Conservative MP. He looked gloomy, but may have been more cheerful than he appeared.

John Douglas Pringle, an Anglo-Scot, was a proper journalist – *Manchester Guardian, Times, Observer* – and the best leader-writer of his time, with a Ciceronian gift of clear exposition; he had been editor of the *Sydney Morning Herald* twice: from 1952 to 1957, and again from 1965 to 1970. On his first day as editor in 1952 he went out to the desk and made enquiries about what was going on the front page; he was then told, to his surprise, that the news pages had nothing to do with him; he was editor only of the editorial pages. Next time round he changed the conditions of his employment. Only once did he have a serious disagreement with his proprietor, Sir Warwick Fairfax, which was when Pringle proposed to print a secular leader on Easter Saturday. Sir Warwick was horrified: the *SMH* always had a religious leader for Easter. I believe their relationship never fully recovered.

My own case was rather different from that of Pringle and Maude, since I was not hired as editor. Besides, *The Age* (unlike the *SMH* pre-Pringle) had already entered the twentieth century, thanks to its manic editor Graham Perkin. I used to see him in London when he came over for annual meetings of some kind at Reuters, carefully timed to coincide with test matches at Lord's, which we attended together; he used to stay in one of the flashier hotels on Park Lane, staying up too late, drinking until his eyes popped out of his head and telling endless tales about the good time he was having at *The Age*, persecuting politicians. He worked himself to death. That was the prime cause of my translation to Melbourne as an assistant editor, because I think that before he died he must have mentioned my name to the management. His death was followed by other disasters among the senior journos. They ran out of hacks and came knocking on my door.

The difference between *The Age* and any British newspaper hit me in the eye even before I got into the relatively new *Age* building. A car for my exclusive use had been delivered to the Hilton Hotel, where I was temporarily staying. I drove it into the *Age* garage. There must have been forty or fifty cars in it, all white, except for a row of swish, variously coloured Mercedes, which I later learned were the perks of the editor and senior management. Nobody was counting the pennies in this establishment. It must have been rolling in the stuff (as it was, largely thanks to the avalanche of small ads that poured in for the Saturday paper). Any reporter or photographer who needed transport simply walked down to the garage, spoke to one of the friendly coves in charge and drove off. All the cars were kept in a good state of repair, filled up with petrol and cleaned by the garage staff. I think of that garage still.

When I reached the big, open-plan, air-conditioned news-room, I felt instinctively that something else was unfamiliar about this newspaper, although I could not at first put my finger on the cause. Then it dawned on me: everyone in the room – men and women alike, heads down at their desks – seemed to be aged twenty, and all the men wore ties. They looked more like insurance clerks than journalists. Many of the men, and all the 'executives' (as the heads of department were called) wore suits. When I realised that I was supposed to set an example to these young tyros and removed my tie, I felt quite subversive. Was Australia producing and training a race of journalists who were conformists? After a year the then editor decided that he wanted to move upstairs and join the management and I was appointed as his successor. On I went, doing my best, until one day one of my minders – I had two, Peter Cole-Adams and Peter Smark, both of whom had worked in London and other foreign posts – said that he had some advice for me. I was English, he said, and an Englishman of a certain type; and my way of doing business was confusing some of my subordinates. When I said, 'I wonder if we should . . .' do something or other, they went away and muttered among themselves and usually concluded that my musings must be an order, couched in English-speak; whereas I often meant, my minder now realised, merely to start a discussion. Could I be more direct?

One huge difference I did discover. At least at *The Age*, the editor was king. On any British newspaper at that time the editor was hedged about with constraints, one of the most serious being that he (there were no shes) found it almost impossible to get rid of the dead wood; obviously incompetent members of staff had to be offered another job of equal standing to the one in which they had proved incompetent, and they could turn the new offer down, if so minded. There was none of that at *The Age*. People could be moved around and fired at will. Another surprise was the rigidly hierarchical, and to me amazingly un-Australian, nature of the organisation. All executives were paid on a quite different scale from the writers. This meant that any writer, however talented, who wanted a serious jump in salary aspired to join the ranks of the executives. Thus half the best writers on the paper never wrote a word. A further curiosity was that the sub-editors, for reasons I never fully fathomed, were mostly far better paid than the best reporters. These arrangements tended to mean that all the reporters were virtual beginners, because in order to better themselves they had to stop being reporters. There were no old sweats covering city or state politics, who had been at the job for years and knew where the bones were buried.

In the UK, and in the United States, many of the political reporters had been at Westminster or in Washington for longer, and knew more, than the politicians they covered. In Canberra there were some old sweats – too many, too cut off from the normal life of the nation, I concluded – but there were very few in the state capitals because they were not properly paid. Years after I ceased to be a full-time resident of Australia, the entire nation was taken aback by the Howard landslide of 1996. The Canberra bureaux had become so immersed in Canberra politics, and so in thrall to the operations of Keating, that they failed to notice that in the world beyond Canberra the voters were less than fascinated by the policies that preoccupied the Prime Minister: Asia, the republic, Aboriginal rights. It is much easier for a British political commentator or reporter to keep in touch with ordinary opinion, because Westminster lies in the middle of the capital city; the Canberra press-gallery problem is harder to solve, but its members (and their editors) might remember the example of the veteran *New York Times* Washington bureau chief, James Reston, who made it a rule at least once a year to head off into the sticks to see what was worrying the ordinary voters. This was not an example, however, that I managed to persuade *The Age* bureau to copy, despite my theoretically unlimited power.

Apart from ignorance, an English editor at large among Australian politicians has no special difficulties to contend with. I recall being surprised and faintly annoyed, interviewing Mr Hawke at Kirribilli House in Sydney, when his lurking press officer stepped forward, as the interview began, and placed a tape recorder on the table between us. Perhaps he picked up this trick from Tony Benn, the English Labour politician, who thought it helped to keep his interlocutors honest. During the interview Mr Hawke reached behind his chair for a box and took out a cigar,

which he lit; he did not offer me one, but I did not take this as an
anti-British gesture.

Semi-social encounters with Malcolm Fraser were more testing
for the stranger. Invited to dine with the Prime Minister in
Canberra, with six or seven other journalists (all male), I found
myself in an ante-room standing in a semi-circle with the others,
waiting for our host. An aide apologised for the delay; chatter was
subdued. We fell silent when Fraser finally appeared and stood at
the ante-room doorway; he said nothing, and nor did we. I
cannot recall who broke the long silence, but it was not Fraser.
Dinner was rather grand, with Fraser at one end of a long table,
flowers and immaculate napery, butler and footmen. Come the
pudding there came a test for an Englishman: ice cream embedded
with little black additions, like currants. I popped in a mouthful
and became aware that the little black additions were certainly not
currants: too crisp; toasted currant skin, perhaps. Unconcerned, I
extruded my tongue, removed the object and put it on the edge of
my plate. The same thing happened with my next mouthful, and
the next. I then became aware that the little mound on the side of
my plate consisted of, with no possible doubt, dead insects. I
glanced round the table. The Prime Minister spoke of exports. His
guests listened with simulated interest. The ice cream was
disappearing from all plates. Was I the only person to have scored
the insects? I ate up as best I could. When the meal was over and
the Prime Minister led the others out of the dining room, I hung
back for a moment and drew the butler aside. The delicious ice
cream, I said, seemed rather unusual? Ah yes, sir, he said, a special
receipe of Mrs Fraser's: honey ants; a rare delicacy very popular, I
believe, with the Aborigines. *The Age* later ran a feature giving
recipes used by famous people; we asked Mrs Fraser for her ant
recipe, which she generously supplied.

Otherwise, I do not remember being socially challenged; the
subs, I think, remained sceptical about imported English ideas and
resented my list of banned words – for instance, 'identities', as in
'well-known sporting identities'. It was my pride that was dented,
not my colleagues', when the paper picked up and reprinted
pieces from the British newspapers whose syndication services it
bought; after all, no British newspaper ever reprinted pieces from

Australian papers. But I was never conscious of being resented as a Pommie interloper, and I cannot even remember being called a Pom, at least to my face. In fact the only time I have ever been so referred to was at a Unesco conference in Budapest when Gough Whitlam, then Australian ambassador to Unesco, introduced me to a colleague by saying my name and adding, 'He's not a bad cove for a Pom', although since we were barely acquainted he had no idea whether I was a good cove or a bad.

My wife and I made one Anglo-Australian cultural blunder soon after we arrived. We thought the banks of the Yarra would be improved by swathes of daffodils, like the Backs in Cambridge. I persuaded her to write a letter to *The Age* and say so. It provoked a storm of abuse: we don't want your nasty foreign flowers here, thank you very much, said the critics. Later on we joined the native plant lobby; the more we learned to love the delicate little flowers on Australian shrubs in the Botanical Gardens, the more we loathed the massed rhododendrons in the Dandenongs. We never owned up; 'praise the environment' had been the painter Jeffrey Smart's advice and, having learned our lesson with the daffodils, we stuck to it.

Headmasters

Imported English headmasters had a longer history than imported editors. One of them, it could be argued, had a greater influence on Australia than any other Englishman of the century. An article in *Australian Historical Studies* in 1972 was entitled 'Schooling For Ruling: The Social Composition of Admissions to Geelong Grammar School, 1930–1939'. The title made the attitude of the writer pretty clear. The main body of the piece scarcely needed research: the social composition was upper crust. Four fathers described themselves as 'gentlemen' on their son's admission forms. But the piece contained some interesting items nevertheless. It claimed that the reason the school hired James Ralph Darling in 1930 as its fifth headmaster was the result of a deliberate effort to Anglicise itself. Indeed, the article made the shocking revelation that 'the Council wanted to make the school more

English in tone but had just failed in the battle to expunge the irksome "Grammar" from the name'.

Darling was young for the job, at thirty, although he had just been old enough to serve with the Royal Artillery in France and Germany at the end of the First World War. He had been educated at Repton and Oriel College, Oxford, and had spent the five years before coming·to Australia as a master at Charterhouse public school in Surrey. One day, Dr Darling (the 'doctor' was justified merely by honorary degrees) will attract a serious biography that will not simply deal with his life but will try to establish, through a laborious follow-up of the careers of individuals (many of whom of course are still alive), the influence that he exerted on generations of Geelong Grammar boys. He was at Geelong for thirty-two years, and he can scarcely have been less influential than Arnold of Rugby in England as a disseminator of ideas. Darling was a Christian who believed in public service: a late-Victorian perhaps; and the gospel he preached was that the privileged boys who had the good fortune to be sent to Geelong Grammar should acquire self-discipline and develop a sense of social responsibility. The population of Australia in 1930 was six and a half million. Darling thought his brightest boys, to equip themselves for useful lives in their infant country, needed to get out and acquire the best university education available, which he thought was to be found at Oxford or Cambridge; he therefore encouraged them to go overseas instead of taking their first degree at Melbourne University. His prime importance in the pre-war period, the article says, was to persuade Geelong Grammar boys to go into the public service, and especially into External Affairs.

By the time I met Darling he was Sir James and in his late seventies, living with his wife in Toorak, a tall man smoking his pipe, but otherwise without a lot to do. We met through a lifelong English friend of his, and acquaintance of mine, Sir Mark Turner, a banker-businessman who was chairman of the giant mining combine RTZ. (It always surprised me to think that yet a third knight, Sir Roderick Carnegie, chairman and chief execu- tive of the mining company CRA at the time [1977], and a big wheel on the Melbourne scene, had been a pupil of Sir James and was an employee of Sir Mark.) RTZ had acquired Sefton, a property in Mount Macedon formerly owned by the Baillieus; it must have been a walk-in, walk-out deal of the kind common in Australia and unknown in the UK; family books and billiard cues were still in place. Here Sir Mark stayed, always entertaining Sir James and Lady Darling on his visits. My wife and I were sometimes invited too. I remember Sir Mark and Sir James having a serious discussion about the application of Christian ethics to business (a stained-glass window commemorates Sir Mark in a church in Highgate; he lived in the house of the former deist Coleridge). I also remember Sir Mark complaining drily about the hospitality system in Japan, whereby the grander the visitor, the older the geisha assigned to him for entertainment. Sir James always seemed calm, until playing croquet I struck him twice sharply on the ankle.

How Geelong ever appointed Darling in the first place was a mystery; in the UK he had been a Labour Party supporter and had helped to put in the Labour government in 1924. Forty years later his influence on a former pupil Ranald Macdonald, *The Age*'s managing director, caused Macdonald to back Graham Perkin in his support for an Australian Labor government in 1972. When the writer of *The Age*'s regular anonymous 'Saturday Reflection' – a sort of brief weekly sermon – died, we invited Sir James to take over; having established with the editor's secretary that he would be supplied with the paper to write it on, he performed this task until his death, applying a moral code to topical themes: a weekly irritation to some, a weekly uplift to others. He was revered in the way that the great public-school headmasters used to be thought of in Britain generations ago; an example of the way that Australia is, or was, old-fashioned. His wife told me that in retirement Sir James refused to receive one former Geelong pupil, Rupert Murdoch. He had come to believe that Murdoch had exploited him at school, by seeking from him introductions to influential people, while never intending to use these contacts except for his own purposes – having ignored, in other words, the Darling doctrine about privileged boys (and few were more privileged than Rupert) having a social obligation to others. A decade later I read William Shawcross's biography of Murdoch, in which Shawcross found Murdoch to be 'contemptuous' of Darling and quoted him as saying that, as a boy at Geelong, 'I thought he was a bit of a poseur and still do'.

Darling was succeeded at Geelong by another Englishman, Tommy Garnett (headmaster 1961–73), a member of the celebrated Garnett clan; when David Garnett's novel *Lady into Fox* was turned into a successful musical, Tommy Garnett – having by now retired to the bush, where he had developed a second career as a brilliant and scholarly gardener – inherited some of the royalties. But Australia was littered with English headmasters. A housemaster at Haileybury, where I went, suddenly disappeared to be headmaster of King's School, Parramatta. When we rented a house in South Yarra in 1978, the house opposite turned out to be occupied by the headmaster of Melbourne Grammar: another Englishman. Why did Australian school governors not invariably appoint Australians? Geoffrey Dutton remembered a conversation with Patrick White and his friend Manoly Lascaris when they were staying with him after the death of Charles Fisher, a son of the Archbishop of Canterbury, Geoffrey Fisher; Charles Fisher had just been appointed headmaster of Geelong Grammar. Manoly expressed his hope, in the strongest terms, that the governors would appoint another Englishman: Geelong was in the business of producing Australia's ruling class, and only an Englishman knew how the trick was done. Manoly, as the descendant of Byzantine emperors, might be presumed to overrate imperial superiority; but White, Dutton thought, seemed to be inclined to agree with him.

In other fields, too, while I was in Australia the English were in demand, especially in the arts. The main theatre company in Melbourne, the Melbourne Theatre Company, was run by an Englishman, John Sumner; he imported from London for two seasons an experienced freelance director, Frank Hauser, who had worked at Glyndebourne, Sadler's Wells, the Old Vic and in the West End, and who soon learned that an important part of the job was to tell Australian actors that they were by no means less talented than their English counterparts. Anne Woolliams – dancer, choreographer and internationally renowned ballet teacher – was born in Kent, and spent ten years with John Cranko's famous Stuttgart Ballet Company, first as ballet mistress and then as co-founder of his school, holding the company together after Cranko's death in 1973. While in Germany she wrote a delightful classic about teaching ballet, *Ballettsaal*, later published in Australia under the title *Ballet Studio*. This was a compendium of precise technical advice on every aspect of dancing, including the way to darn ballet shoes on the points, using concentric circles of blanket stitch, combined with the occasional *bon mot*: 'to sustain a jump is momentarily to become immortal,' she wrote. Invited to join the Australian Ballet in 1976 as artistic director, Woolliams later became Australia's first Dean of Dance, at the Victorian College of the Arts, intent on making Melbourne the teaching centre of Australian dance. The Victoria State Opera had meanwhile persuaded the seventh Earl of Harewood, managing director of the English National Opera and the only member of the royal family holding down a job, to become its president; he was useful to the VSO not only for his comprehensive knowledge of opera (he had edited and revised Kobbé's *Complete Opera Book*), but because he could lift up the receiver and talk to any musician or singer in the world on the VSO's behalf; he was attracted to the job not only because he had married (as his second wife) a locally born pianist, the sister of the horn soloist Barry Tuckwell, but because he could time their visits from England to her home town to coincide with test matches.

The National Gallery of Victoria was founded in 1861 by an Irishman (the lawyer Sir Redmond Barry, who sentenced Ned Kelly to death), but came to depend on the English. Bernard Hall, aged thirty-three when he arrived in Melbourne in 1891, remained director for forty years. He was described as a 'great director' by another Englishman, Eric Westbrook, who became director in 1956. Dr Ursula Hoff was assistant director by the time she retired after thirty years' service to the Gallery in 1973; she then became a trustee and published (in London) the standard guide to the collection. The Gallery's most unexpected English link, however, is with Robert (Robbie) Ross, Oscar Wilde's friend and literary executor whose ashes were placed in Wilde's tomb in the Père Lachaise cemetery in Paris. Ross, as London adviser to the Gallery's Felton Bequest, acquired for the Gallery one of its glories, thirty-six watercolours from William Blake's series of illustrations to Dante's *Divine Comedy* – one of which, *Antaeus*, adorns the cover of Dr Hoff's guide. And in Sydney, throughout the 1980s and 1990s, Edmund Capon from England was director of the Gallery of New South Wales.

Less often, now, do plum Australian jobs go to the British. And plenty of Australian talent, of course, has flowed the other way, not always by invitation. One humbling example – humbling because British people rarely do the reverse – is of the head of Reuters, Glen Renfrew, who arrived in London with no job, walked down Fleet Street literally knocking on every door and was rejected until he reached Reuters where he secured an interview. Renfrew told them that he would do any work they cared to give him without wages for a given period; they could then decide whether to sack him or hire him. They hired him, he became managing director, then the firm went public and Renfrew became a multimillionaire. Another example of the reverse tide is the former headmaster of Geelong Grammar, John Lewis, who was head-hunted to be headmaster of Eton. (I asked a small Etonian what he was like: 'Oh,' said the boy, 'we don't think much of him. You see, he's a foreigner.')

As Carr-Saunders foresaw, the most tenacious connections to survive the end of empire have been with the universities. Oxford and Cambridge have attracted and exported talent all over the world. Long after the days when aspiring Australian families had ceased to send their children to school in England, young Australians continued to regard a stint at Oxford or Cambridge as a passport to a high-flying career back home. Of Australians who had been at Oxford alone, I encountered two Prime Ministers, one Liberal (Fraser) and one Labor (Hawke); two newspaper proprietors (James Fairfax and Rupert Murdoch); one Governor-General (Sir Zelman Cowen); one editor (Creighton Burns); five historians (W.K. Hancock, Manning Clark, Geoffrey Serle, Stuart Macintyre, Cameron Hazlehurst); one head of the Treasury (John Stone, wearing the tie of Oxford's leading sporting club, Vincents); one state senator (James Guest); one philosopher (Peter Singer, the inventor of animal rights); and two businessmen: the lawyer with an ice-cold brain, Richard Searby (Murdoch's old schoolfriend and his chairman and right-hand man at News Corp., until he was discarded by Murdoch), and Sir Roderick Carnegie (chairman and managing director of Conzinc Riotinto). I will conceal the name of another Oxford graduate who lamented his three years there because the experience had caused him to feel permanently at odds with his own country.

Australians and Their History

Behind Anglo-Australian relations stands all Australian history. When I arrived in Australia to work, I knew that one of my first tasks must be to scale the great mountain being piled up by Professor C.M.H. Clark. He had just got to Volume IV of *A History of Australia*; I acquired the four volumes, pulled on my climbing boots and set forth. I had not got very far on the lower slopes before I became uneasy. My copy of Volume I is disfigured throughout by the subbing marks I made then; and even now almost all of them seem to be fully justified. The prose was turgid, repetitious and in places opaque. Nor did this much-praised work seem to me to be the work of an historian at all: at no point did Clark attempt to identify the underlying movements or causes of the story that he had to tell. He seemed more like a prophet. Of the massive and pervasive influence that Marx, the father of modern economic history and of modern sociology, had exerted on the other historians of the Western world I could detect no trace. The proposition, advanced after Clark's death, accompanied by personal vilification, that he had been a covert Marxist or fellow-traveller, can only have been entertained by people who had not opened his book. While affecting to be writing history on the grand scale, Clark in practice seemed to have reduced the colossal mass of material he had mastered largely to a stream of (admittedly often fascinating) anecdotal history, to which he had given significance and drama by the use of exaggerated, or at least elevated, rhetoric.

I did not broadcast these views. In the circles in which I moved, Clark's volumes, in their dignified red dust-covers, were to be sighted on almost everyone's shelves. Manning Clark himself was spoken of with deep respect, although strange tales circulated of his private eccentricities. But as time went by I did venture to question people in these circles about whether they had, like me, perhaps found the master's prose a shade difficult to read. Yes, it turned out, they had; and not many people, I gathered, had read all the volumes right through. Even so, it was universally agreed that Clark had performed a wonderful feat – not exactly of history-writing, but of national identity-forming. That anyone could find so much to write about Australian history, so many volumes, seemed to be regarded as proof that Australia was a more interesting place than they had hitherto been led to suppose, and that Lawson or Deakin (besides a parade of hithero unlauded characters rescued by Clark from obscurity) were quite as considerable figures – and, in the cases of Lawson and Deakin, quite as tragic – as those of any other country. Readers learned too – those who had read almost any part of the opus – that the Almighty had played a larger role in the Australian past than they had realised; and so, accordingly, had good and evil. By executing his vast narrative Clark, I came to feel, had liberated the educated classes. But what exactly had he liberated them from?

Mingling with younger historians nearly twenty years later, I began to get some idea of the answer. David Day dismissed my idea that *A History* was not a history at all, but he conceded that it was a Christmas pudding of a book that needed editing and failed to give the reader a sense of the big picture. Nevertheless, he added, Manning Clark could take most of the credit for saying that there was a great story in Australian history. Before Clark, historians had tended to see Australian history as merely an episode in British history. That was the clue, obvious enough in its way, that I had been looking for. The book had told Australians that it was time they came out from the shadow of the mother country: that they had grown up and, in the metaphor that Professor Appleyard found useful, could safely cut the umbilical cord without leaving themselves bereft of a past. 'Men make their own history more wisely when they know what that history has been about,' Clark had written. Now they knew – or would know, if they read his book.

At Melbourne University, the Ernest Scott Professor of History and Dean of Arts, Stuart Macintyre, took a more critical view of the Clark legacy. He said that people looking back at the way history was understood thought that 'empire history' – as taught at Melbourne, for instance – was the opposite of 'Australian history', which it was not. It was undoubtedly Australian history, but it looked at Australia both regionally and imperially, so that students learned about New Zealand alongside Australia, about the British empire in the Pacific and about the other great European empires.

'The new subject called Australian history which Manning is credited with first having taught undergraduates, and which then spread through the school and university curricula, is something rather different. It insists that Australia is to be understood in purely geographical term – that is, Australian history is what happens inside Australia.

'To many people this was an exciting and liberating way of understanding their country. Australia was no longer a derivative version of something somewhere else that Australia had to replicate or imitate in order to fulfil its national destiny. Instead, it could be understood as a place apart: hence that emphasis on the discovery of certain forms of literature and art which suggested there was genuine and original creativity in this country.

'My view is that that's become a rather tired and tyrannical orthodoxy. My view of Australian history is that it has to be understood comparatively. I've always had that view; it seemed to me that the notion that you could study and understand Australian history as self-sufficient was crazy.'

I told Macintyre that I was always surprised by the lack of attention paid in Australia to Canada, and the parallels and differences between the way the two societies had developed.

'And New Zealand!' Macintyre exclaimed. Most New Zealand history departments taught Australian history, he said, but not one in Australia taught New Zealand history. This was rather odd: because if you wanted a control group, with rather similar demographic stock and a slightly different environment, so that you could try and understand the reasons for the similarities and differences between the two societies, there it was. That comparative element was very strong in the older way of studying history, but it had been abandoned in the second half of the twentieth century.

'I have to teach a class of second- and third-year students on the history of Australian citizenship: "From Subject to Citizen". I'm going to have to explain to them the process whereby the colonies became self-governing. If I say Statute of Westminster, even those who've studied Australian history at school will just look at me as if I've gone bonkers. The things that connect Australia and Britain are the very things that scholars and popular interest have turned away from.'

The proportion of young people at senior level who studied history had declined dramatically, to less than 10 per cent, he estimated. In the last years of the Keating government Macintyre was asked to conduct an inquiry into citizenship and education with the Director-General of Education of New South Wales. They made a number of recommendations; but at the time Macintyre restrained himself from 'pushing' history because he felt, with his special interest, that this might have seemed improper. They did say that the teaching of citizenship must contain an element of history, but more and more he wished that he had made that point much more stongly.

'Unless Australians have some understanding of historical processes, how can anyone understand the issues behind the republican proposal? How can anyone participate sensibly in the discussion without some knowledge of constitutional history? All across the English-speaking world, history is under strain. History used to be thought of as a way we would understand ourselves. But it has been displaced in the twentieth century by economics and by subsequent disciplines. To some degree it's been marginalised. None of the universities created in the 1980s have history departments. They have historians, but they're likely to be teaching in something called media studies, or Australian studies, or women's studies. The discipline of history is not taught in these places. I suppose that half, or even more, of the undergraduates who come to Australian universities cannot choose to do a degree in history.

'The generation of people to whom Paul Keating spoke, and to whom he appealed with his calculated anti-imperial gestures, was perhaps the last generation to have any real knowledge − and a partial one at that − of the history that connected Australia and

Britain. It seems to me to be a problem: we've now reached a point – as a result of a number of factors, not least the educational curriculum – where there is no historical understanding of that relationship at all.'

So for most Australians, what would that relationship be? 'For most Australians who go back to Britain it would be the discovery that Australia doesn't matter very much. For some, it would be based on their origins; it's now a matter of pride to have had convict ancestors, not so much as village Hampdens but as in recent historiography, when the convict is seen as more skilled, more enterprising and more spirited than the person who stayed behind. Paradoxically war, I suppose, would be another one, wouldn't it? That cuts both ways; it binds certain Australians to the UK, but also contains the notion that the Australians were, if you like, the white Gurkhas of the British empire who never had their services fully recognised.'

Two Soils

I left Macintyre wondering what Professor Sir Keith Hancock would have had to say on these topics, particularly about Manning Clark. Ten years earlier I had interviewed Hancock, just after a party in Canberra at which the Vice-Chancellor of the Australian National University (an Englishman) had described him as Australia's greatest historian. The party was for Hancock's eightieth birthday, in 1978, and I thought the Vice-Chancellor might have gone further, without dissent, and described him as among the half-dozen most distinguished living Australians, even though to most Australians the name 'Hancock' signified either an iron-ore tycoon or a dead comedian.

For thirty years W. K. Hancock had been a revered figure in my intellectual pantheon. He was someone who had divided his life between Australia and Britain without, it seemed to me, feeling the need to be obviously Australian and without being swallowed up by the British 'establishment'; this despite his fellowship of All Souls College, Oxford (he had become a Fellow exactly fifty-five years before I interviewed him, he told me), his

216

job in the Cabinet Offices in London during the Second World War (where he had worked on the official history of the war while it was in progress, like Thucydides) and his membership of the Athenaeum. In 1976, after twenty years back in Australia, he still found himself 'in love with two soils'. Besides Oxford and Birmingham, he had held professorships in Adelaide and Canberra; he helped to bring Canberra's university into existence and, in 1978, still worked there ten years after his theoretical retirement.

Hancock was no armchair pundit. R.H. Tawney advised historians to get their boots on; I had even seen Tawney's own boots, while interviewing him in 1958: 'workmanlike' might describe them. Taking Tawney's advice to heart, Hancock had tramped over Tuscany in the 1920s, to explain how Mazzini had turned into Mussolini; had reconnoitred the bush in Uganda during the 1950s, as a political adviser to the governor; and had walked the South African veldt in the 1960s while researching his massive biography of Smuts.

When I saw him, Hancock was wearing not boots but orange shoes. He also wore a green tweed suit: a small man, with a high forehead, white hair and a long equine face, which would have gone well above a dog collar (his father was an archdeacon). He greeted me with the word 'Hiya'. His voice was neither British nor Australian, but somewhere in between.

He once said that an historian needed what he called 'span'. His own intellectual interests had certainly had that quality. In Adelaide as a young man Hancock had written a stimulating short history of Australia (convicting Australia of being content with a 'middling standard' in manners, morals, knowledge and the arts). He had written a three-volume survey of Commonwealth affairs and, after he returned to Australia in the mid–1950s after twenty-three years of voluntary exile, a marvellous book entitled *Discovering Monaro*.

This was the shift of gears that interested me. What had happened inside the mind of an historian of his distinction when he came back? In one of his lectures Hancock had noted that the historian Henri Pirenne, arriving in Stockholm for the first time, went to see the new town hall rather than the monuments of an earlier period. 'I'm not an antiquarian,' he told his companion, Marc Bloch, 'but an historian – and therefore I love life.' Hancock had gone to see the Snowy Mountains hydro-electric project. He was excited. The construction authority, although aesthetically crude, was ecologically sophisticated. Then he visited Melbourne, noted its ruined skyline and his mood changed. 'Have you been to the Western Suburbs?' he asked me. 'A spiritual and cultural desert.' The Moonee Ponds Creek, where he used to swim as a boy, was now a drain. He decided that, having spent so long on non-Australian themes, he must write a book for Australians. The question that he asked himself (believing, like R.G. Collingwood, the Oxford historian and philosopher, that an historian should proceed not by studying 'slabs' of history but by asking questions) was: how, for good or ill, have Australians used the land on which they live? In framing this historical question, Hancock was also asking what present-day Australians were doing to the land; and therefore what they were doing to themselves.

After four years' work, with much use of boots, Hancock produced (aged seventy-four) his Monaro book, whose full title was *Discovering Monaro, a study of man's impact on his environment*. It is an immensely detailed history of a small community – 600 generations of Aborigines and six generations of whites – that nevertheless illuminates great tracts of Australian life and, in the end, becomes a blueprint for Australia's future. I asked him about its effect, but he did not reply directly. Instead, he lamented the 'chasm' in Australia between 'thinkers' and 'doers'. In London, he said, he knew the heads of every major government department, a few bishops, some bankers. 'But I don't know anybody in Canberra's Whitehall.' He never met a banker. 'I'm worried about how to break down the apartheid.'

I could see that he had in mind here, not only his Monaro book, but the celebrated Battle of Black Mountain, in which he and others tried to stop the allegedly civilised Whitlam government from building a monstrous telecommunications tower on the summit of the most precious of Canberra's encircling hills. It was characteristic of that battle that the bureaucrats and politicians paid not the slightest attention to the expert and rational arguments of Hancock and his 'thinker' colleagues.

218

Nevertheless, Hancock could not be accused of falling into despair. He struck me, on the contrary, as an historical optimist. Here he seemed to be different from Clark, who scatters the word 'tragic' freely throughout his opus. The Tuscans, said Hancock, with whose economy over twenty centuries he had made himself familiar, had first wrecked their environment, then restored it to be the best managed and most beautiful in Italy – although he was understating the horrors they had perpetrated, for instance, in the outskirts of Florence. The people of Monaro had, by their grazing practices, damaged their water resources, but then saved them. 'All these problems can be tackled.'

In 1950 Hancock, then director of the Institute of Commonwealth Studies at the University of London (to which the Sir Robert Menzies Centre for Australian Studies is now attached), delivered the first Sidney and Beatrice Webb lecture. He concluded by saying, 'The historian is neither a prophet nor a priest. Let us hope he has a religion or a philosophy for ruling his own life; history alone will not guide him through its perplexities, nor qualify him as a guide to others. The historian is not a man who knows all the answers, but one who knows how to search for some of them. If his search is fruitful, the frontiers of truth here and there will advance a little. A little – the word has to be used, since the Sahara of our ignorance is so vast; but it may be an encouraging, an exhilarating word. In human history, English local government is only a little thing; but how important in the record of our national self-knowledge and self-mastery is *English Local Government*, by Sidney and Beatrice Webb.'

Manning Clark taught history at Blundell's School at the beginning of the Second World War. John Jones, later Professor of Poetry at Oxford, remembered Clark telling the history sixth to put away Trevelyan and take up Pirenne – to lift their eyes beyond England and learn about Europe. In 1930 Hancock was the first person to draw attention to, and to deplore, the damage done by Europeans to their Australian environment, as Professor Geoffrey Bolton has pointed out; *Discovering Monaro* was in a direct line of descent from what he had written in *Australia*, when he was thirty-two. Put away Clark and take up Hancock might be a precept to be considered by all Australians concerned with 'self-knowledge and self-mastery': forget Clark's wild laments about the fight of good, honest Aussies against British philistinism and its imported representatives; and, adopting instead Hancock's superficially narrower but actually wider view of the past, make war on a more tangible and destructive British import, the rabbit.

11

Letting Go

During the latest phase of Anglo–Australian relations, a strange dynamic has been at work. On the surface, it has been dominated by Australia's nervous advance, as in a prolonged game of grandmother's footsteps, towards a republic. Australians often assume that these moves must annoy or even anger the British, who, it is imagined, are bound to resent such a rude and final assertion of independence by the colonials. On the contrary: while in Australia the UK has become a bit of a target, and historic grudges such as Gallipoli and Singapore have been disinterred and polished up as a necessary accompaniment to republican sentiment, in the UK Australia has become more and more fashionable.

I find this trend irritating. In the good old days – when Hoad and Rosewall, followed some way behind by Menzies, were the only names known to the average Briton – British membership of the Australian fan club was small and select: a handful of people who refused to be misled either by the wave of drunken Australian dentists who poured into London during the 1950s to rip off the National Health Service, or by the post-war ten–pound British migrants who returned home complaining that they had been robbed.

Australia from the earliest days of the Commonwealth was not generally considered a popular destination, even for Governor-Generals. A cousin of mine went briefly to Canberra for the World Bank and came back quoting the French ambassador, similarly exiled, who had delivered a harsh Gallic verdict: '*pas de protocole, pas de restaurants, pas de maîtresses*'. Literary people and intellectuals who went there, from Mrs Sidney Webb in the 1890s ('rather gross materialism') to Angela Thirkell in the 1920s ('an entire continent peopled by the Lower Orders'), looked down on Australia and did not hide their views. Nor did the refugees from Menzies's Australia who arrived in Britain in the 1960s – Richard Neville, Clive James, Germaine Greer, Barry Humphries, Sidney Nolan – give their country a good press. They used to say they were in Britain not only to advance their own careers on a wider stage, but because they could not stand the stuffiness, provincialism and hostility to talent that were characteristic of the bulk of their fellow-citizens. My wife sat next to Clive James at a dinner in 1977. 'I'm going to Australia for a year,' she said. 'Oh, bad luck,' said he. Australian plays that reached the London stage tended to be written by playwrights who had appointed themselves the scourges and consciences of the nation, as noted by one of the best of them, Alan Seymour. David Williamson's *Don's Party*, for instance, confirmed the worst suspicions of British theatre-goers, as his once idealistic bourgeois characters slid into compromise, savagery and beer.

All that has dramatically changed. In the old days not many members of the chattering classes – the people who not only talk but write and broadcast, the so-called opinion-formers – actually went to Australia. It was too far away, and too expensive to reach. Besides, what would one do when one got there? Now 'everyone' seems to have been, or to be planning to go: and they go, in contrast with the old days, with high expectations. How many of these travellers have paid their own fares is another matter. The rise of the freebie has something to do with it: the music and literary festivals that invite overseas stars, the paid tours of vineyards for the platoons of wine writers and buyers, the vast expansion of travel supplements in magazines and newspapers ('I flew courtesy of Qantas . . .'). Still, they like it when they get there, as my private anthology of quotes demonstrates.

Linda Christmas thinks the change started in the mid-1980s. In 1982 she was on the staff of the slightly left-of-centre *Guardian* newspaper, whose reporters are supposed to be unconventional and adventurous. The travel section was offered a free trip to Australia; nobody wanted to go. Christmas, in a mood to go anywhere, volunteered, in the same spirit that she would have volunteered, she has said, to go to Vietnam. She expected to find Great Britain beyond the seas, and did not; but what was it that she had found? She consulted the literature, and found it unenlightening. So she decided to write a book about it herself. When she resigned from the paper, giving her reasons, her colleagues reacted, she says, 'as if I was joining the Foreign Legion'; her editor, Peter Preston, called her in, leaned across his desk with an expression of grave concern, and asked whether everything was all right. He thought she must be in some kind of crisis, to want to go to Australia.

Christmas ascribes the change to new patterns of travel. She now teaches at City University in London. It has become quite fashionable, she says, for students to spend their 'gap year' in Australia. The Bicentenary and the attendant television publicity helped: 'people thought, "Worth an eight-part series, is it?"' Christmas likes 'the openness, the directness, the access – the way you can pick up a phone and talk as a journalist to anyone in the country. My informality and directness can get me into trouble here; there, people seem to warm to me.'

Hugh Johnson, who is probably the most successful wine writer in Britain, seriously contends that wine has caused the new fashion. He first went to Australia in the early 1970s, expecting it to be rather like the rural parts of the United States, which he knew well. First, he could not believe the size of the place, flying in from Hong Kong and spending hours aloft over what was still the same country; then, 'what struck me most of all was the incredible lack of inhibition. You were so quickly not just on first-name terms but trading insults. Such fun!'

The reputation of Australia's wine in the early 1970s was 'generally very low. But there were signs of it waking up.' He still remembers exactly what he saw on his first drive through the Hunter Valley and northern Victoria. 'I was so excited by the wines of several vineyards that I shipped some back – privately, not from commercial motives – and put on a wine tasting in the tasting room at Christie's. I wrote a little outline, and invited people along: come and taste what I've found! I think that was the first time that the famous Grange Hermitage was ever shipped. We were all absolutely knocked sideways.' He is now a director of an Australian winery.

Johnson is confident of the importance of wine in changing British perceptions of Australia. 'Each year for the last couple of years, two million cases of quality Australian wines have been shipped to this country. Australian wines are on every smart dinner table. Britain is no longer in the looking-down business. Wine is a terrific cultural ambassador. That chap, what's his name, Sir Les Patterson, is almost forgotten.'

He is upset by the divisive rows about the Queen, but notes that every Australian wine offer still advises customers how to send wines to 'friends in the UK'.

The much-hated (and also, it must be said, much-defended) knockabout journalist Auberon Waugh has been to Australia four or five times, always 'in wine'. In print, Waugh bats on his personality: wrong-headed, reactionary, pro-smoking, deliberately contrary. Some would maintain that his most serious writing has appeared in his wine column in the *Spectator*.

Waugh, rather surprisingly – given his neurotic obsession with class, and his public pose as a beleaguered defender of the English upper-middle class against the lager-lout proletariat – is wholly in favour not only of Australian wines (which he often commends), but of Australia itself, although 'deeply suspicious of Murdoch'. When he first went to Australia, he was expecting 'them' to be 'straight up'; but 'I didn't expect them to be quite so charming with it. Here when you say someone is frank, you mean they are bloody rude. But there the frankness comes naturally. It's particularly attractive of course in women.'

Waugh adds, 'And they send those brilliant nannies, the best in the world; they don't argue, they're just friendly and good at the work. We have one or two Australians at the Academy Club [a small literary club in London that Waugh started] and if you ask them to do something they don't think it's lower class to do it; they just think it's a job that has to be done.'

The fan club likes the landscape: a change from the past, when visitors usually complained about its monotony. Waugh 'loves all those gum trees and the beaches with huge whale turds'.

Lord Gowrie, a senior functionary with Sotheby's, the auction-eers, is that rare bird, a Conservative intellectual who has served in the Cabinet; he is also the grandson of the former Governor-General of Australia.

'It was bit different for me because I was brought up by my grandparents, and my childhood was dominated by Australians coming in and out. That produced the natural reaction. It would be logical for someone in their twenties to visit the country and people to whom he owed so much, but in the prejudiced way of the young, I didn't. Instead I was drawn to the United States. I thought of Australia as a curious mixture of Mars, another planet, and Bournemouth. Like everybody, I sloughed off my misconceptions, in my case influenced by the very remarkable generation of intellectuals who came here, and who were clever, unpseudish and salty. Barry Humphries didn't become a friend until later, but I remember the first time I saw Edna. I found her Proustian and horrific rather than funny – not unlike some of the people who used to hang around my grandparents.

'By the time I went to Australia I was quite old and a company chairman. We arrived dazed from Japan in the early morning, and the Sotheby's representative in Sydney had the brilliant idea of taking us straight to the fish market. Sydney is one of the most beautiful places in the world, and the slightly Middlesex architecture is neither here nor there. Sydney was amazingly civilised and amazingly cheap.'

Gowrie cannot forget the flight that he and his wife made across the heart of Australia, as guests on a private aircraft. The pilot flew very high when the landscape below was boring, and suddenly dived when it was interesting. 'It was indeed like another planet, a different light, a different atmosphere, the whole continent like different gradations of mother-of-pearl.' He went to Broome, which he found exotic. He saw mountains that he was told had been on the map for only seven years. He was shown a sea crocodile born in captivity which, he was also told, if released into the sea would live for 200 years and grow to the length of a cricket pitch. He was taken to a beach eighty miles long, with white sand – 'like a rum ad' – where he was advised not to bathe because of the crocodiles.

'If forced to live in one place, and one couldn't move, Australia would be the place to choose: an easygoing Mediterranean civilisation, like California before the cities grew, primal and different, with great attractions for an eye-oriented bloke like me.'

Sir David Attenborough, the distinguished conservationist and maker of television series about the wonders of the universe, goes off like a rocket as soon as you mention Australia. 'I'm a total convert. Partly because of my Australian grandchildren, and partly because of the nature of my avocation. It's a fantastic place. I adore Australia: some of the best food in the world, the best wines, loveliest scenery, and lots and lots of space: what more do you want?' But what about the attitude of Australians towards their space and the cavalier way they have treated it? 'I'll tell you something. They have the best camping and the best bush gear anywhere – and it's Australian-made. That must mean there's a very good market and that the young are going out and doing it. I've got no hang-ups about that. My favourite bit? Northern Queensland. What a place! The rain forest and the reef. And the history. You can still see the blazes on the trees cut by the Jardine brothers when they went to Cape York in the 1870s. Fabulous! The geology is wonderful, too; lava tubes thirty feet high!'

The novelist Jane Gardam still feels the 'curious pull' of Australia after fifteen years. She speaks of the sense of power of the land itself; the fierce landscape; the reversal of colour, as in a photographic negative: dark was light, trees had light trunks and dark leaves, the lack of green; the brilliant birds. 'I knew from babyhood about the extraordinary animals; yet everything was weird; the koalas, the kangaroos. I hadn't been prepared for the savage light. I felt very lonely. I made friends I have kept, whom I write to and who visit me here; at the same time I felt extraordinarily separate. Yet I adored it. I was so mystified, really. *I* know I must go back.'

The artist Glen Baxter, went to Australia as the guest of the Adelaide Festival, was amazed that the city was so much like Texas. 'The signs were hilarious: a Thai restaurant called "Thai me kangaroo down, sport". It was not at all as I'd imagined it. The key moment for me was a sign saying that Adelaide was twinned with Austin, Texas. The look of the place was Texan: little shops and façades with nothing behind them; the straight, wide streets with the lights seemingly always at green. Pedestrians would wait patiently for the lights to change, but I would go marching off, feeling really naughty, as if a sinister force, a death-ray, might punish me. It's a bit like the England of thirty years ago that's more or less disappeared: you see these queues for buses standing exactly three feet back from the kerb, and old women being allowed to get on first, instead of being elbowed aside by someone with a Sony Walkman. I felt I ought to start littering; it's got this unreal quality.

'I found the people charming. My only trouble was when Keating spoke at a book launch and I made an ironic remark about his outrageous attitude to the Queen. I'm on Keating's side! This bloke burst in with a twenty-minute lecture, completely missing the point.

'I went to that big national gallery in Canberra. There were only three people in it. In a car park that would take 8,000 cars there were two Volvos; it was like an American science-fiction movie. Canberra is very spooky; everything is ersatz. You know the fountain in the water? That pond is full of toxic water. I thought that was a nice touch.'

Baxter did not care for Canberra. 'When I left, I told a taxi man the flight, and he said, "But the plane doesn't leave for three hours," and I said, "I want to make sure I don't miss it." '

Some surprising people like Australia, and none more surprising than Sir Peregrine Worsthorne, one of Britain's best-known Men of Opinion and conservative philosophers, who for thirty years has been defending the English class system, mocking the left and deploring the way things are going. Egalitarian and casual Australia, one might assume, would be the last place to appeal to him.

He expected, 'like everyone else of my generation' – he was born in 1923 – 'that it would be rough and ready, a lot of Pom-bashing, awful food. But I was pleasantly surprised. Sydney was an eye-opener: lots of jolly people, delicious meals. The only person I disliked was Malcolm Fraser. I liked Hawke. Frankly, the person very much up my street was that Scandinavian Premier of Queensland, the right-winger who got into trouble [here Worsthorne laughed], Bjelke Petersen. A marvellous girl who was head of the PR side of the Australian film industry took me to lunch at that lovely restaurant on Sydney Harbour: it was like Blackpool in a heatwave: and rather endearingly old-fashioned, like an English seaside resort in the 1930s.

'I remember James Fairfax serving coffee from a Georgian coffee pot – very different from most Fleet Street press barons. I found Australia not so much part of the modern world as agreeably nostalgic, rooted in a world that's largely disappeared: heart-warmingly unprogressive. My impression is that my generation, if we'd gone out before the war, would have found it absolutely outlandish. We've changed by comparison; we've abandoned the things that most tourists would have said were characteristic of England – orderly queues, people standing up to give women a seat – and Australia has held on to them rather longer. Our manners are so much worse, and theirs are relatively civilised.'

The theatre director Frank Hauser, who has often worked with the Melbourne Theatre Company, has said, 'I like the cities, which are handsome, and I like the people in them, and I find people there more stimulating than people here – partly because I'm idle here and I'm bound to be doing something there, or I wouldn't be there. I like the fact that they're doing things for the first or second time, and not the fiftieth, as here. I enjoy the blatant pursuit of self-interest by most Australian politicians; like the United States in 1910. It's disgraceful – and worst when taken as a sign of virility – but it's public. Here, it's covered up much more. I don't like their race relations; as bad as they are here, but with less excuse, though I wouldn't argue if you said that the British way of life is more hypocritical.

'When I was first there, some twenty years ago, they had a huge identity crisis, a hangover from the sixties when everyone was having identity crises. They were saying, "We don't want to be British, we want to be American"; but the Americans didn't want them. They were fighting the fact that they are an Asian offshore island. It was a great trauma. They had their own Catch-22: "If you leave, you're a traitor; if you go and come back, you're a failure; if you don't go, you were never any good in the first place." That's much less true now. Actors and actresses are well paid on TV, and they don't rely on a big break in London's West End. I used to spend my time defending Australia against Australians. Their own critics were so destructive. But when I defended Australian standards, they thought I was patronising them.'

Dr David Butler of Nuffield College, Oxford, Britain's leading psephologist, warns against any assumption that Britain even now takes much interest in Australia – or at least in Australian politics. In some ways things are worse than they used to be, since these days no British national newspaper has a full-time Australian correspondent. Butler belongs to an informal club in Oxford that meets once a term, purely to exchange information about what's going on in Australian public affairs. 'Still, there is a shift. The slightly patronising attitude to Australia has changed. Australia itself has changed. It's a much more sophisticated country than it was twenty-five years ago. It's decidedly more on the map. But one mustn't press the point too far; there is still deep ignorance in Britain about Australia, and there are very few English people with whom one can have a serious conversation about Australia. On the other hand, there is less surprise now that one is an Australophile.'

Finally, a prominent businessman who refuses to be named says, 'It's true that mutual attitudes have changed. Australians have got a lot less chippy. You don't get the impression that they feel inferior to you, and you don't feel superior to them. We've both grown up.

'Also, we're not so in love with the United States. Australia has much of the best of the United States: niceness, space, middle-class life with barbecues, and so on. Our feelings are quite complicated. We're not so sure about being Americanised, which is a famously bad thing to be, but we're not scared of being Australianised. So Australia is pretty attractive as an America substitute. We get in Australia certain kinds of things we like in England, without the disconcerting or irritating accompaniments: the appalling anxiety you get in England about status, the caution, the nervousness

229

about what others will think, the refusal to experiment.

'Speaking as a businessman, mind you, the country's an absolute shambles.'

Separation Anxiety

The 1990s' republican revival came out of nowhere taking the politicians – as well as everyone else – by surprise. Looking back now, when a republic does seem at last to be inevitable (despite the results of the 1999 referendum), the most striking historical fact is Australian reluctance, at every stage, to cut the links with Britain, despite a national reputation for independence of spirit. Separation anxiety affected even the boldest. Henry Parkes, a republican in the middle of the nineteenth century, became a fervent supporter of Queen Victoria – 'the Protectress of the Free'. He told delegates to the National Australasian Convention of 1891, of which he was President, 'We seek to remain side by side with that dear old England that we all love so well.' Simultaneously the young Henry Lawson was yearning for the day when Australians ceased to grovel to the English; but, at the end of his life, he was an empire man. After the mysterious transformation of the British empire into the Commonwealth of Nations, the Labor Prime Minister, Joseph Chifley, and his Minister of External Affairs, Herbert Evatt, played a prominent part at the Prime Ministers' conference of 1949 in London; this allowed a form of republican government within the Commonwealth, but they regretted that India had become a republic; 'The Australian Government,' they affirmed, 'believed the personal relationship of the sovereign to the Commonwealth to be of supreme importance.'

Australia was subject to colonial restraints until the Second World War. The Statute of Westminster was passed by the British Parliament in 1931. But, as Professor Colin Howard has written, 'national torpor towards the liberalising steps embodied in the Statute is well revealed by the failure of successive governments to adopt it until 1942'; and then only under the pressure of legal complications arising out of the Second World War, and not from a desire to assert their separate nationhood and 'equal status', as defined in the Statute. Thus until 1942 the British Parliament retained the right to enact for Australia such laws as it saw fit. Only in 1986 were these restraints formally swept away by the Australia Act; until then, for instance, the sovereign continued to appoint state governors on the advice of the British – not the state – government. It was only in three cautious stages that appeals to the Privy Council were abolished, as if the entire legal system might be put at risk by one clean cut – although it could also be argued that the true cause of such gradualism was the reluctance of lawyers to give up the opportunity of free trips to London.

Two events of the late 1980s give us a fix on the state of the republican movement – that is to say, its immobility. One is a lecture delivered in 1987 to the Australian Studies Centre in London entitled 'The Crown and Australia' by D.J. Markwell, a Fellow of Merton College, Oxford. The other is the inquiry into constitutional reform at around the same time chaired by Sir Zelman Cowen.

Markwell surveyed in scholarly fashion what he called the Australianisation of the Crown. He then asked: what are the chances of Australia becoming a republic? A republic, he said, was very low down on Australia's political agenda. The polls fairly consistently showed strong majorities – around 60 per cent – in favour of retaining the monarchy. He next quoted the well-known republican Professor George Winterton as saying, in his book *Monarchy to Republic*, published in 1986, that 'an Australian republic is inevitable'. Many people, Markwell stated, would probably agree with Winterton. It was widely argued that the tide of events would lead inexorably to a republic; that there had been a gradual shift of public opinion in favour of a republic; that the 1975 constitutional crisis had encouraged the shift, as had non-British immigration; and that republican sentiment was strongest among the young and would therefore grow over time.

But then Markwell used Winterton's own survey of over twenty opinion polls against him. The clearest message of these polls, Markwell noted, was that 'there has been very little decline in support for the monarchy or growth in republican sentiment' in the past two decades.

Between 1966 and 1986 the republican vote had risen by a mere 2 per cent – from 28 to 30 per cent. 'Where in such minor shifts an "inevitable" republic is to be found I do not know.' Both Professor Winterton and Labor's Senator Gareth Evans had acknowledged, in Winterton's words of 1986, 'the absence of any appreciable growth in republican sentiment during the last decade'. So much for the alleged impact of the 1975 crisis, said Markwell. Clearly it converted some Australians to republicanism – Whitlam being the most important – but its greater effect seemed to have been to activate existing republicans and to 'give acute emotional intensity to some advocates of a republic'.

Max Walsh, the political commentator, had already taken a similar view in his book *Poor Little Rich Country*, published in 1979. He observed that the emotional outpourings caused by the Whitlam dismissal had briefly created a surge of republican sentiment, but the issue had failed to take any serious hold on the electorate. 'Rather it appeared that the Whitlam dismissal served to depoliticise the intellectuals, and they retreated from the political spotlight shaken by the performance of the Whitlam government and deprived of any unifying cause.'

At about the same time that Markwell was delivering his lecture in London – which he wound up by concluding that a republic might well come one day, but that that day was probably far off and that it could not be assumed to be inevitable – Sir Zelman was chairing his inquiry into the constitution. The extraordinary point here, he told me, was that although three proclaimed republicans sat on his committee (Professor Winterton himself, Donald Horne and David Solomon), the committee unanimously agreed that there was no point in even raising the question of a republic in their report, because it was a political non-starter.

A year or two later, in 1991, Professor Cheryl Saunders of the faculty of law at Melbourne University was one of those involved in the Constitutional Centenary Conference that led to the establishment of the Constitutional Centenary Foundation. With the centenary of the Constitution coming up in ten years' time, the Foundation's aim was to involve the people in any revision of the Constitution, just as they had been involved in the run-up to 1901. 'If anyone had said,' Professor Saunders told me in 1997, 'that a republic would be the big issue of the decade I would have laughed.'

The Sudden Rush

How did it happen? On the public record, it all began with the passage of a republican motion proposed by a senator of Anglo-German background at the Labor Party conference of June 1991. But it did not become a serious political issue until Keating raised the subject in the course of 1992. It was driven by Keating, his speechwriter and close adviser, Don Watson, and Mark Ryan, Keating's twenty-eight-year-old media adviser, who later became chief executive of the Australian republican movement. There will be many accounts of how it gathered steam. What seems certain is that the decision to include republicanism in Keating's policy speech of 1993 was not finally taken until the last minute. Dr Blewett, then Labor's Health Minister and later Australian High Commissioner in London, assured me that the republican question was never discussed in Cabinet. Professor Saunders told me she was telephoned by Keating's office just before he made his policy speech. 'It was all very hush-hush; the Prime Minister was going to make a statement about the republic in his speech and would like to say that the Constitutional Centenary Foundation would be asked to advise on the options for a republican model, and was that all right? I said, "Well, I'm not the person to ask. I'm not the chairman; Sir Ninian is [Sir Ninian Stephen, QC, the former Governor-General], and I'm not the Board and this would need to be considered by the Board. But given the apolitical role of the Foundation, I don't think it would be appropriate." The announcement was still made, without reference to us, but they distrusted the Foundation for evermore.'

I happened to cover that election for *The Observer* of London, and saw Don Watson the day of the Keating speech. Watson, an unflashy man, was housed rather apologetically in the flash Sydney hotel that was serving as Labor's base for the election launch, working in a large room scattered with files and newspapers.

He told me that he had written into the first draft of Keating's speech, off his own bat, a bit about the republic – although Keating would have expected him to do so and soon he consulted others. Watson thought the Labor Party badly needed a cause to give it, and Australia, a sense of direction. The final version, I gathered, had only been agreed after some backtracking and nervousness on the part of Keating and his advisers, at pretty much the last moment.

At all events, it was that section of the speech, delivered in Bankstown, the modest Sydney suburb that Keating comes from, that got the biggest round of applause. It was now government policy, the Prime Minister read out in the drab platform style so different from his slash–and–burn parliamentary style, 'only to have an Australian, chosen by Australians, as Australia's head of state'.

Watson told me more about the way republicanism became the Labor government's official policy a few years later, after Labor's defeat in 1996. His own republicanism had been set on fire again on hearing Hawke – Hawkie, he called him – when he was Prime Minister say that a republic did not matter, and that he was not going to do anything about it. This struck Watson as typically Australian: letting things rumble on, instead of trying to change them. And Hawke was so popular that he could have done it, Watson was convinced.

The debate picked up momentum under Keating, first, because he was a republican; second, because he and several of his advisers, including some of his foreign-policy people, thought it was a rational and useful adjunct to the effort to move closer to Asia; third, because it suited Labor to widen the debate with the then leader of the Liberal Party, the narrow and ideological Dr Hewson; fourth, because the end of a century of Federation was looming and a republican effort was only going to succeed if the government drove it. 'Keating did believe,' said Watson, 'that governments had a responsibility to do things which ought to be done. What he did took courage and judgement. No one else would have had to wear the derision and loathing if the thing had blown up in Labor's face. I can think of no other Australian PM who would have been prepared to risk it.' The referendum of November 1999 was Keating's legacy.

Courageous Keating may have been in the event, but preannouncement wheel-wobble certainly occurred. Watson had consulted two senior Keating advisers, Mark Ryan and Don Russell, and Senator Bob McMullen in Brisbane about his first draft. It was agreed that the speech would announce Labor's intentions about a republic. Then, in the early hours of the morning of the speech, Watson and Ryan realised that Keating and his campaign advisers might back off. Might not the republic be a distraction from the government's core election strategy, which was to focus on Hewson's proposal for a sales tax, the dreaded GST? Might not the press and the Opposition make republicanism the issue, with unpredictable results? Some people in the Australian Labor Party's Head Office shared these doubts. The speech was being checked and finalised at 4 am by a little group consisting of Keating, Russell, Ryan and Watson. Watson and Ryan were thinking: we've got a promise off them and now they're backing off!

What changed their mind? Well, Watson and Ryan had said, if you don't mention it, you'll be called too scared to mention it. It will look as if republicanism really *was* a diversion from the economy. And you'll be left with a record on the issue no better than Hawke's. That was the last shot in the locker. The Prime Minister picked up his fountain pen and wrote the actual line announcing the republic himself.

The *Sydney Morning Herald* headlined the speech 'Pork-Barrel Republic', but, as it happened, the republic played almost no part in the election. Keating's opponent, Dr Hewson, responded to the announcement by saying that it was merely designed to distract attention from Labor's dismal economic performance; besides, a number of Liberals were republicans themselves.

Only the British press wrote about the republic, because they could find nothing else that might excite a British readership. I remember being in despair when *The Observer* reached Sydney a few days after the vote; someone had cobbled together a few lively paragraphs for page one implying that the campaign had been fought on the republican issue, while my piece filed earlier and printed inside reported that the republic had scarcely been mentioned.

Nevertheless, few people expected Keating to win that election;

when he did so, the republican idea seemed part of the win. He had not taken the idea to Cabinet before the election, as Blewett said; and he had no reason to do so afterwards. It thus seems perfectly possible that Don Watson can single-handedly take the credit for pushing the republic right up the political agenda. The intellectuals – depoliticised, in Max Walsh's words, by the collapse of the Whitlam dream – emerged again blinking into the political spotlight, united by a new cause. The most unlikely people found themselves on stage. Thomas Keneally, the sweet-natured Booker prize-winner, became – at the urging of 'Nifty' Wran, the controversial former Labor Premier of New South Wales – the first chairman of the Australian Republican Movement. The novelist's grandfather, Old Mick, had embarrassed young Tom (Keneally shortened his first name, presumably as a republican gesture) by refusing to stand up when they played 'God Save the King' in the Vogue Theatre in Homebush; and Keneally himself had refused a CBE, so his credentials were sound. His only difficulty, which he probably shared with others of his circle, was that although he strongly approved of Keating's newly proclaimed republicanism, he had equally strongly disapproved of his Thatcherite policies as Treasurer; the explanation for this performance, Keneally surmised, was that Keating must have been the captive of the 'colonial and derivative subservience' of his Treasury civil servants – a defence that Keating would not have found flattering. Keneally wrote a book about republicanism, *Memoirs from a Young Republic*, and its argument surprised me. He said that becoming a republic would benefit Australia not only culturally and morally but economically, since the economic disasters of the Keating years had arisen from 'the whole culture of dependence and small thought of which the attachment to the Monarchy is the living symbol'. Summing up, he wrote, 'The Republic is part of the mechanism of our deliverance.' This romanticism, investing a symbol with mystical aura and power, struck me as an approach more often associated with simple-minded monarchists than with republicans.

I did not consider Keneally's book much of a contribution to the debate; indeed, the debate itself was desperately slow to catch fire. The cause was not helped nationally by its identification with

Keating and the right-wing of the NSW Labor Party, and by the way that it seemed to be captured and promoted by the lawyer-banker Malcolm Turnbull.

I came across Turnbull in 1986, during the famous *Spycatcher* case, and recall being astonished that the British government was being shaken and embarrassed, and ultimately humiliated, by a lawyer who was only thirty-two years old. His dealings with Sir Robert Armstrong, then Secretary of the Cabinet, became a classic episode in modern Anglo-Australian relations. Sir Robert was dragged off to Sydney to substantiate in court the British government's view that publication of the *Spycatcher* book would damage British security. Turnbull was his legal opponent. While I was in Sydney, Sir William Rees-Mogg, former editor of *The Times*, opined publicly that the case demonstrated Australian chippiness about the British Establishment as personified by Sir Robert, who found himself trapped in Sydney under absurd and humiliating circumstances.

Sir William was making a typically British error – or, more precisely, an error typical of a certain sort of Briton. It was of course true that Australians resented being patronised by the British. Turnbull had been to London before the case opened, in an attempt to do a deal with the Treasury solicitor, Mr John Bailey. The negotiation failed. As Turnbull was leaving, Mr Bailey patted him on the back – this was the Turnbull story – and said, 'Well, young man, we'll see what you're like on your feet in court, won't we?' This is the sort of remark an Australian is likely to remember – although Turnbull told me he was neither Anglophile nor Anglophobe (I marked him down as a Turnbullophile, which subsequent events did nothing to change).

It was also true that the case illustrated a culture clash. Shortly before I met him, Turnbull had been dining, in leisurewear, with a boisterous party that included some British reporters when who should walk in but Sir Robert, wearing a suit and escorted by the local British Consul-General, with whom he was staying. 'Come and join us, Sir Bob!' Turnbull called out. An Australian would have replied with a brief expletive and walked on; but Sir Robert's crippling English politeness impelled him to go over to the Turnbull table and subject himself and the Consul-General to introductions all round, before he could invent an excuse to disengage. He was followed by cheeful taunts from Turnbull.

The point that Sir William failed to grasp is that Sydney has an Establishment of its own. Its most prominent members are not at all like Sir William or Sir Robert (Lord Rees-Mogg and Lord Armstrong as they became), but they were and are richer and not necessarily less intelligent. Turnbull's annual income was probably ten times that of Sir William, and his brain seemed to work faster, at least in court. He was a typical member of the Sydney power Establishment, whose motto could be said to be: 'Go for your life, and up yours for the rent.'

Turnbull was well placed to become the engine of the Sydney republican push. His ancestors arrived in Australia in 1802 as free settlers. His father owned pubs and left him a lot of money. His mother was a great-niece of George Lansbury, the Labour politician, pacifist and founding father and later owner-editor of Britain's left-wing *Daily Herald*, which eventually metamorphosed into Rupert Murdoch's soaraway tabloid, the *Sun*. She left home when Turnbull was eleven and became a professor and dean of graduate studies at Rutgers University in the United States.

Turnbull read law at Sydney University. He was then picked up by the Packer organisation to write a law column for its *Bulletin*, aptly called 'The Officious Bystander'. Next he went to Oxford (Brasenose College) as a Rhodes Scholar, with a glittering list of sponsors that included Neville Wran, then the NSW Premier. At Oxford he married, in the Anglican church of Cumnor, Lucy Hughes, from one of Sydney's leading families. The rector, as Turnbull tells the tale, did not at first see why he should marry a non-practising Presbyterian (Turnbull) to a non-practising Roman Catholic (Hughes), but Turnbull explained to him that it was his duty, as the agent of the state Church, to do what he could to prevent fornication outside marriage in his parish. Turnbull won the case. While in England he spent some months in London working for the *Sunday Times*, which evidently taught him something about handling journalists. During the *Spycatcher* case I was struck by the way he became a semi-hero to left-wing British reporters as he did battle with the representatives of the Thatcher government; they were unaware of his close connections with

Kerry Packer, whose politics always seemed to be much the same as those of Genghis Khan before the spin-doctors of Mongolia proved him to have been a democrat.

When Turnbull returned to Sydney after Oxford, he worked with his wife's father, Tom Hughes, one of Australia's leading QC's, and a former Liberal Attorney-General. Then he became Packer's in-house counsel. His brother-in-law was Robert Hughes, the *Time* magazine art critic who wrote the bestseller about the convict era, *The Fatal Shore*, and dedicated it to Turnbull's son, Alexander Bligh Turnbull, 'a seventh-generation Australian'. After Packer, Turnbull formed a bank with Whitlam's son; the bank was paid ten million dollars by Fairfax newspapers for its part in trying to sell Fairfax assets, including *The Age*, to Robert Maxwell, the British newspaper tycoon crook. Another newspaper tycoon, Conrad Black, was highly critical of the aggressive and greedy part Turnbull played during the battle for control of Fairfax, which Black won.

Turnbull found favour with Keating, however, and to a degree with Watson. To get the show moving, they needed a plan. To get a plan, they needed some sort of commission of inquiry. The announcement that Turnbull was to chair this commission was not greeted with enthusiasm, but the government wanted a document rapidly, and Turnbull was a first-rate advocate and someone of barely controlled energy and ambition; and it was Turnbull who wrote the subsequent report virtually single-handed, 'while the academics and lawyers were fiddling about', as Watson put it. If and when one day a new republican Constitution is drawn up, Turnbull will be able to take the credit for having played a key role, which he will regard as nothing less than his due: Australia's James Madison.

The report was followed in 1998 by a Constitutional Convention, which surprised the cynics by being good-tempered. It set the stage for the removal of the sovereign. It also proposed that Aborigines should be recognised as the original custodians of the country. Australians were due to vote on a new constitutional preamble when it was included as a second question during the referendum on whether Australia should become a republic.

Neither step proved easy. How would the new head of state be chosen? Keating told colleagues that if it was proposed to elect the head of state by popular vote, he would cease to be a republican. His successor, John Howard, a stubborn monarchist, agreed with him about popular election. It would destroy the political system. The government even made a mess of a proposed new 169-word preamble to the Constitution; it was rejected by Aboriginal groups and the Labor opposition, attacked by feminists for its reference to mateship, and pilloried by others for its windy illiteracy, not to say gibberish.

Sitting in a café in Melbourne, out of office, Don Watson wondered glumly whether Australia was a country at all. 'We have bursts of passionate nationalism, or national disgruntlement, and then you lapse back into thinking: well, it's not a country, it's a way of life. That's what the people want. It's sort of ungovernable.' The Keating government had been trying to impose a type of north European social democracy on what was still in many ways a frontier society. Federation made it hard to move the country in any direction.

I did not fully share these black thoughts. The country might be hard to govern, but it was undeniably changing. Its Englishness had been hugely diluted in the past twenty years, which would please the group that had always been passionately anti-English. In 1951, when the ship bearing the poet Peter Porter to Britain arrived at Tilbury, he went on deck, glanced around and returned to his cabin: he had known what to expect. But, he told BBC listeners in 1999, the same would not be true of young people today. Very different, I thought, from Menzies's emotional reaction to his first sight of home in 1935. Sitting in a pub near Circular Quay on another occasion with Watson — Henry Lawson's old pub, he said — we commented on the number of young mixed couples we saw, Australian and Asian, black and white. Why wouldn't young male Australian eyes be focused on Asia and its beautiful women, when their parents' world-view was filled by Europe?

Spiritual independence cannot be rushed. It happens over time, at its own speed. Not long ago I asked rather loftily on Australian radio: does a republic really matter? Had Australia not got far more urgent things to worry about? Friends, including the instigator of this book, Di Gribble, were very cross. Yes, it does matter, they said. It matters greatly. I failed to understand the power of the symbolism, and the way that clinging on to the apron strings belittled them and made them feel like children. The only way to deal with separation anxiety was to separate – however tortuous and painful the process might be – and face up to the consequences.

Bruce Grant, the writer and former diplomat, wrote a decade or so ago that the emptiness of the official role of the royal family was already obvious. He went on to wonder whether their usefulness in bridge-building and public relations might even be enhanced, from both a British and Australian standpoint, if no formal links existed. If their reception in the United States and Europe, and in Commonwealth countries where the Queen is not head of state, was any guide, then republican Australia might become more fascinated than ever by the royal family saga. Australians fit the republican mould, Grant wrote.

So they do. The history of Anglo-Australian relations is long and murky, suddenly illuminated by flashpoints along the way, as I have tried to show. At last in the 1990s everyone saw a republic approaching, step by step, and in 1999 after a century of talk the moment of truth arrived, driven by Keating and in his wake other republicans. But the republicans blew it. The reason had nothing to do with the mother country, or indeed with Anglo-Australian attitudes. David Malouf pointed out after the referendum failed that a true republic has to do with real figures, not symbolic ones, and is founded not on a people's loyalty to a figurehead but on the sense of obligation of its members to one another. The No vote, he wrote, and his theory rang true, was 'a cry from the heart from those who did not feel like full participants in the new Australia'. The gulf, one might add, turned out to be between the prosperous, self-confident Australians, neatly personified by Malcolm Turnbull, and the numerous, more anxious Australians who were in no mood for a change that seemed irrelevant to them. The vote against a republic was thus not so much a matter of keeping hold of nurse's hand, as it was to do with the fear of finding something worse: a moment of hesitation. Polls showed that the majority of Australians had already decided to let go of

241

nurse (the sovereign); but they were dissuaded from doing so formally, in the voting booth, for fear of the sort of 'republic' they were offered. It was a classic case of political separation anxiety.

Into the 21st Century

Talk of a republic finally stirred up British officialdom. Foreign Secretary Douglas Hurd decided that British–Australian relations needed a brush-up. Prime Minister Major wrote to Keating on 6 April 1995 saying that, although the close family and historical ties between the countries were well known, what was less understood was that Britain was the second-largest investor in Australia (around A$100 billion), and Australia the third-largest in the UK. 'We both have dynamic and innovative societies,' he added. A PR job was needed (although he did not use those words). So Britain planned to mount a series of events in 1997 called 'New Images: Britain and Australia into the 21st Century', to 'challenge old stereotypes' and prepare the two countries for the next millennium – or, as the acting UK High Commissioner put it, for 'their third century of partnership'. Keating wrote back promising his 'whole-hearted support'. Signs of dynamism that followed were the ejection of both Major and Keating from power. The project went ahead, nevertheless.

As I read the literature, one point interested me. In October 1996 Major reiterated to Howard that Australia was the third-largest investor in Britain. By June 1997, five months after the '*newImages*' year started (*newImages* was the label given it for some reason by Saatchi & Saatchi, the advertising agents), it was stated in a brochure produced by the British Council, which was responsible for organising the events, to be the fifth-largest investor. This dramatic decline puzzled me, until I noticed a piece by Philip Morrice, described as Britain's Director-General of Trade and Investment Promotion in Australia, that included Rupert Murdoch's News Corporation among Australia's significant investors in the UK. His piece was dated December 1996. He must have learned belatedly, I thought, probably by seamail, that Murdoch (an American) did not so much invest capital in the UK as extract it. The profits of his UK operations, especially the *Sun* newspaper, helped to support his other companies; and he paid on his UK earnings only a fraction of the UK tax paid by comparable organisations. Mr Morrice redoing his sums, I surmised, putting Murdoch in the debit instead of the credit column, would account for the drop.

The year 1997 had been chosen to celebrate the fiftieth anniversary of the British Council, which raised the question of what the British Council had been doing for fifty years, if there was still need for a special effort to repair and promote Anglo-Australian relations.

It looked as if many of the 150 events in both countries − touring stage shows and exhibitions, the Johnnie Walker Golf Classic sponsored by United Distillers − had simply agreed to have the *newImages* label attached to them. However, some of the events had the true ring of the British Council about them. Children from remote Aboriginal community schools were to be linked with schoolchildren in Wales to exchange stories from books they had produced in their own languages. 'We have so much to learn from one another,' Professor Lloyd Dawe from Sydney University was quoted as saying. The example chosen by the British Council to illustrate the professor's point was that *The Little Frog* − or, in an Aboriginal language book, *Bardbarrarrangana-manda* − becomes *Y broga fach* in Welsh. Bilingual teachers were to be exchanged − assuming, presumably, that any could be found.

The Australian Foreign Minister, Alexander Downer, launched *newImages* in Britain at a party serving kangaroo and emu canapés. Asked on the BBC what the point of it all was, he said that one aim was to counter stereotypes; Australians might say, for instance, 'as dry as a Pommie's bathtowel'. Not that he himself, he quickly added (though perhaps not quite quickly enough), would ever say any such thing.

That was the last I heard of *newImages*, until a couple of years later. The project was supposed to impart a new impetus to the relationship that would carry on into the next century. Saatchi & Saatchi, the advertising agency whose creative team had helped with promotion and designed the annoying logo and a patronis-ing, would-be comical cattle dog/bulldog symbol, had undertaken to assist in measuring its impact when the project was over. The British Council promised to issue a report within six months of the year's end – that is, mid-1998. When telephoned in 1999 and asked about the promised assessment, a British Council spokeswoman said that she would hunt around and, if she found anything, would pop it in the post. If she popped it in, it never popped out. I wanted to know how many Welsh-speaking schoolchildren now knew the Aboriginal word for little frog.

Acknowledgements

I am grateful to the National Library of Australia for permission to quote from the papers of Lord Novar (MS 696), Lord Gowrie (MS 2852) and the diaries of Geoffrey Dutton. For permission to publish extracts from these diaries I am additionally grateful to Robin Lucas, the copyright holder of the works of the late Geoffrey Dutton and the literary executor for his estate. My thanks are due also to the present Earl of Gowrie for permission to quote from the papers of his grandfather. I also consulted Gowrie (Hore-Ruthven) papers held by the State Library of South Australia.

Quotations from the letters of Lord Beauchamp and G.O. Allen are from original manuscripts held in the Mitchell Library, State Library of New South Wales.

Over the years I have acquired more debts – personal and intellectual, not financial – than I can ever hope to repay, particularly to those mentioned in the text on whose experiences and ideas, no doubt in a distorted form, this book is largely based. Others to whom I am no less indebted and grateful include – moving across the continent from west to east – in Western Australia, John Brunner and Professor Geoffrey Bolton; in South Australia, Kerry (née Wakefield) and Senator Nick Minchin, and Lady Downer; in Victoria, my former boss, Ranald Macdonald and his wife Patricia, and all (or almost all) of my former colleagues, not only on the editorial but also on the managerial staff of *The Age* (with special reference to Bill Bland, Creighton Burns, Brigid and Peter Cole-Adams, Michelle Grattan, the late Robert Haupt, Lis Sterel and Peter Smark, John Stevens, John Spooner, Greg Taylor, Jackie and John Tidey, and the person modestly entitled editor's secretary who in fact kept the whole show on the road, Lorna Earl), as well as Sir Zelman Cowen, Rachel Faggetter, Helen Garner, Tommy Garnett, Joan Grant, Diana Gribble, Sarah and James Guest, Lyn Williams and her family and Professor David Yencken; in New South Wales, Roz and Peter Davie, Murray Bail, Virginia Duigan and Bruce Beresford, Jennifer Byrne and Andrew Dainton, Judy and Michael Gleeson-White and David Marr; in Tasmania, Rose Talbot; and in Queensland, Mary and Professor Don Gallagher and Professor Cameron Hazlehurst.

In the U.K., Simon Davie helped me with research, and I was also encouraged by Gillon Aitken, Carmen Callil and Professor Brian Matthews, then head of the Sir Robert Menzies Centre for Australian Studies at the University of London.

Without the collaboration of my wife Anne Chisholm the book would not have been started and, without her and Susannah Clapp, certainly not finished.

Index

246

Index

Index

PIMLICO

457

ANGLO-AUSTRALIAN ATTITUDES

Michael Davie worked on the *Observer* for many years and is a former editor of *The Age,* Melbourne. He has been Journalist of the Year, and is the author of books about California, Lyndon B. Johnson and the *Titanic*; he also edited *The Diaries of Evelyn Waugh*. His most recent book, written with his wife, Anne Chisholm, is a biography of the first Lord Beaverbrook. He lives in London.